THE EVERYTHING® LAW OF ATTRACTION BOOK

Dear Reader,

For as long as I can remember, my life has had cycles of decrease and increase. Growing up, I recall conversations with my parents, who were farmers, about poor crops and lack of money. Later, after I had married, money seemingly came easier. We began to save. But when my husband passed away, I watched our savings dwindle and began to worry just as my parents had done. Determined not to let negative thinking rule my life as it had theirs, I began reading books about different spiritual traditions and their approaches to the concept of a universal Law of Attraction.

My intention and vision to create my life anew began with optimism and gratitude for what I already had. The results were dramatic. In no time, I sold our California home and purchased a house on a lake near Miami. I eventually met a new romantic partner and began work on two exciting business ventures. The life I am still creating is characterized more these days by increase rather than decrease and peace rather than worry.

I encourage you to learn about the Law of Attraction and put it to work in your life. Be fearless, engage in transformational thinking, and dare to dream in cinematic large-screen format. It's never too late to create the life you desire.

Meera Lester

Welcome to the EVERYTHING Series!

These handy, accessible books give you all you need to tackle a difficult project, gain a new hobby, comprehend a fascinating topic, prepare for an exam, or even brush up on something you learned back in school but have since forgotten.

You can choose to read an *Everything®* book from cover to cover or just pick out the information you want from our four useful boxes: e-questions, e-facts, e-alerts, and e-ssentials.

We give you everything you need to know on the subject, but throw in a lot of fun stuff along the way, too.

We now have more than 400 *Everything®* books in print, spanning such wide-ranging categories as weddings, pregnancy, cooking, music instruction, foreign language, crafts, pets, New Age, and so much more. When you're done reading them all, you can finally say you know *Everything®*!

QUESTIONS?
Answers to
common questions

FACTS
Important snippets
of information

QUOTE
Words of wisdom
from experts
in the field

ESSENTIALS
Quick
handy tips

PUBLISHER Karen Cooper

DIRECTOR OF ACQUISITIONS AND INNOVATION Paula Munier

MANAGING EDITOR, EVERYTHING SERIES Lisa Laing

COPY CHIEF Casey Ebert

ACQUISITIONS EDITOR Brielle Matson

DEVELOPMENT EDITOR Elizabeth Kassab

EDITORIAL ASSISTANT Hillary Thompson

Visit the entire Everything® series at *www.everything.com*

THE
EVERYTHING®
LAW OF ATTRACTION BOOK

Harness the power of
positive thinking and transform your life

Meera Lester

Avon, Massachusetts

*This book is dedicated to the Holy One who is called by
myriad names in various religious and cultural traditions
and whose unseen power works through the universal
spiritual laws and those of nature to transform human lives.*

An Everything® Series Book.
Everything® and everything.com® are registered trademarks of F+W Publications, Inc.

Published by Adams Media, an F+W Publications Company
57 Littlefield Street, Avon, MA 02322 U.S.A.
www.adamsmedia.com

ISBN 10: 1-59869-775-7
ISBN 13: 978-1-59869-775-9

Printed in the United States of America.

J   I   H   G   F   E   D   C   B   A

Library of Congress Cataloging-in-Publication Data
is available from the publisher.

This publication is designed to provide accurate and authoritative information with regard to the subject matter covered. It is sold with the understanding that the publisher is not engaged in rendering legal, accounting, or other professional advice. If legal advice or other expert assistance is required, the services of a competent professional person should be sought.

—From a *Declaration of Principles* jointly adopted by a Committee of the American Bar Association and a Committee of Publishers and Associations

Many of the designations used by manufacturers and sellers to distinguish their products are claimed as trademarks. Where those designations appear in this book and Adams Media was aware of a trademark claim, the designations have been printed with initial capital letters.

*This book is available at quantity discounts for bulk purchases.
For information, please call 1-800-289-0963.*

Contents

Acknowledgments

I wish to thank Brielle Matson for bringing this project to me and for all her suggestions and insights to make the book as useful and informative as possible. I also want to thank everyone who was involved in this project at Adams. Finally, I owe special thanks to Paula Munier for her steadfast friendship and continuing support of my work.

The Top Ten Ways the Law of Attraction Can Change Your Life

1. You can begin to attract financial prosperity.

2. You can draw into your life the perfect romantic partner.

3. You can gain greater control over your mind and emotions.

4. You learn how to not attract the things you don't want.

5. You can become vibrantly healthy and have greater vitality.

6. You can attract beneficial relationships with emotionally healthy people.

7. You can help your career into take off.

8. You can manifest powerful spiritual results.

9. You can help others have better lives by teaching them about the law.

10. You can get solutions to seemingly intractable problems.

Introduction

▶ THIS BOOK PROVIDES DIFFERENT lenses through which to view the Law of Attraction. This concept of harmonious alignment allows you to draw the things you desire into your life. You may seek spiritual advancement and want to learn how the law is understood within various spiritual traditions. Perhaps you are more interested in achieving robust health or longevity. Maybe you desire to attract some of the finer things in life such as a sleek car, a lovely piece of jewelry, or a new set of china. You may hope to attract the perfect romantic partner, a well-paying job, a path to a new career, or happiness and peace of mind.

Those are perfectly reasonable and attainable goals. But even if they weren't, it doesn't matter. Whatever you most desire and think about most often is sure to manifest. You can have whatever you want. The universal Law of Attraction is always working to produce the experiences, relationships, and things you think about most. If you are worried about breaking a bone, you will likely draw it in and it will happen. Fear attracts more of the thing you fear. Here's another example: Your worry about an inability to meet your financial obligations results in bringing you more of the same. You are already drawing into your life both positive and negative experiences through the power of your thoughts.

But take heart. The good news is that the reverse is also true. When you desire to manifest money, your desire yoked with feelings of excited anticipation can bring you financial prosperity. You can shift your thoughts to bring more positive and happy experiences, and through transformational thinking, you can radically change your life. And it doesn't stop there. When you team up harmoniously with the Law of Attraction and with other like-minded people, you can work together to bring about change in the world. You and everyone who is deliberately working with the Law of Attraction become co-creators with the Divine through the power of your heart and mind.

You may already be familiar with the concept of the law. The popular books and CDs about the Law of Attraction by Esther and Jerry Hicks and Michael Losier, among others, as well as the mega-hit *The Secret*, by Rhonda Byrne, have catapulted the ages-old principles of that universal spiritual law into greater public awareness.

There are certain basic steps to working with the law, but the approaches to those steps are necessarily as varied and unique as the person using them. You'll need to cultivate trust in the process, a feeling that you are worthy to receive the things you desire, openness to receive, an attitude of gratitude, and an understanding of how to magnetize your desire with feeling and emotion.

These steps are not difficult steps to master. With the insights and worksheets provided in this book, you will soon be engaged in the transformational thinking that brings about exciting and positive life changes. How much or how little you want to shift the paradigm of your life and relationships depends upon you.

Some who believe in the philosophy of karma might wonder if they can abate their karma in any way. Those who teach how to deliberately work with the Law of Attraction and other universal spiritual laws say that little can be done to undo past thoughts and actions, but they assert that there is enormous power in every moment of every day to change your patterns of thinking and, thus, the potential future karmic ramifications of your thoughts, words, and deeds.

Use this book to become informed, inspired, and confident as you begin to work with the Law of Attraction. Dare to join the dance of transformation. Like the Hindu god Shiva Nataraja, who dances the universe into creation and destruction, you can change your destiny by destroying patterns of negative thought and replacing them with positive thinking and feeling. Shiva's dance destroys ignorance and awakens the latent divine force of kundalini, the sacred energy that conveys mortal consciousness to a state of enlightenment. Through your powerful intentions and alignment with the Law of Attraction, perhaps you, too, will awaken from the dark slumber of unintentionally attracting what you don't want. This is the first step in drawing what you do want into your life.

CHAPTER 1

Basic Principles of the Law of Attraction

Modern spiritual seekers have called the Law of Attraction a recently discovered ancient secret teaching. Indeed, the law is ancient in its origins. Whether or not it was ever lost or purposefully kept secret is arguable. What is true is that through the centuries, various spiritual teachers, philosophers, and others have mentioned or discussed the Law of Attraction, although they used various other names in their teachings and writings. Today, renewed interest in the subject has catapulted the ages-old concept into mainstream popular culture while simultaneously placing it under a lens of scrutiny.

What the Law Is and Isn't

You've heard old adages such as "like attracts like," "birds of a feather flock together," "as above, so below," "what you send out comes back multiplied many times over," and "ask and ye shall receive." Consider these, and you have an idea of what the Law of Attraction is. Simply put, the Law of Attraction asserts that a person's thoughts attract objects, people, and situations and circumstances, both positive and negative, into his life.

Attraction Can Bring What You Do or Don't Want

Proponents of the Law of Attraction say that the law brings you whatever you think about most. Thoughts can become emotionally charged. When you desire something—say, a new outfit—you feel emotion each time your mind thinks about having that new dress, jacket, shoes, and handbag. You are filled with excitement at the possibility of having your desire fulfilled. You believe you can have it. You deserve it. It is coming. You consider ways to speed up getting that outfit. You might even develop a plan of action for getting the money to go shopping at the mall. Consider the following example, a true story.

Evidence of the Law of Attraction

During a recent move from Illinois to Missouri, a single mother inadvertently left behind her favorite cast-iron skillet. Each day she thought of that old skillet in which she could cook anything, even a cake. She obsessed about getting another one and even asked for it in her prayers. Throughout the day, she thought about how much she would enjoy cooking again once she got her new skillet. She knew that a cast-iron skillet was not too expensive, but her financial resources were limited and she would have to budget carefully. Whenever she thought about having the skillet, she felt happy and joyful. At the end of the month, however, after she had paid all her bills, there was not enough money left over to make her purchase. Undaunted, the mother reaffirmed her goal to save a little whenever and however she could in order to get her skillet.

A few months after her move, the young mother met an elderly gentleman carrying a box of discarded kitchen items from a nearby apartment to the dumpster. On top of the box was a cast-iron skillet. The woman inquired of the man whether he was throwing it away. When he told her he was, she asked if she could have it. He gave it to her. Overcome with gratitude, the young mother thanked the man again and again. Her fixation on having the skillet brought it to her, and she did not have to purchase it.

Proponents of the Law of Attraction assert that the law brings you what you desire when you (1) are clear about what you want; (2) energize your desire for the item with thoughts, emotion, visual imagery, and a strong conviction that it is coming to you; and (3) feel and express gratitude for what you already have and that which you desire, even if it has not yet come into your experience.

The Law of Attraction is not wishful thinking, daydreaming, or a momentary flight of fancy. If the young mother had simply wished for the skillet, it is unlikely that the skillet would have shown up in her life. A wish is not a strong enough intention. The law is always working to give people the very things they most desire.

Where the Law Came From

According to some who have studied it, the universal great Law of Attraction has been with us since the beginning of time, perhaps even at the moment of creation and the beginning of thought. Others say it is impossible to pinpoint exactly when the concept entered human consciousness.

In the beginning God created the heaven and the earth. And the earth was without form and void: and darkness was upon the face of the deep. And the Spirit of God moved upon the face of the waters. And God said, Let there be light: and there was light. And God saw the light, that it was good: and God divided the light from the darkness.—Genesis 1:1–3

In the Beginning

Some people say that the entire universe and our world were first conceived in the mind of our Creator and then were manifested through the creative energies of the universe out of the realms of infinite potential and substance. Further, they suggest that God created humans as sentient beings with minds that could also imagine and create. New Age spiritual seekers refer to the Creator as Divine Mind, the Universe, the Source, and many other names. For those with a more traditional viewpoint, the Creator is God. Genesis, the first book of the Bible, sets forth the creation story, which begins in the mind of God. With His intention and declaration, heaven and earth and everything therein were formed.

The Creator has been called by myriad names, including God, Divine Mind, Divine Intelligence, Elohim, Holy One, Yahweh, Powers That Be, Abba, Divine Father, Divine Mother, Universe, Source, Allah, Friend, Maker, Primordial Consciousness, Everlasting Lord, Supreme Being, Alpha and the Omega, Ishvara, and the Beloved.

Ancient Possibilities

Some self-help experts say the Law of Attraction possibly dates as far back as 6,000 to 7,000 years ago, where it found expression in the mystical traditions and beliefs of the ancients. Magicians of long ago certainly observed and wrote about affinities between things before the advent of science. Translations of ancient texts suggest that our spiritual ancestors thought a lot about the heaven and earth and pondered the relationships between things. *The Emerald Tablet of Hermes*, whose date of origin is uncertain, contains verses by Hermes, purportedly an Egyptian sage. His verses assert that all things in the world are interconnected and that thoughts impact things. The tablet contains the verse that has been translated to become the well-known adage "as above, so below."

Wattles and Peale

Others say the Law of Attraction concept is decidedly more modern and is possibly just an updated version of the teachings of the late Wallace D. Wattles (1860–1911) and Dr. Norman Vincent Peale (1898–1993). Wattles, who was born into poverty and became wealthy, wrote about the science of getting rich. Peale became famous for his ideas about the power of positive thinking. Both men emphasized the role of conscious and intensely focused thought in achieving the desired goal. Both men believed in a higher power at work in human lives. Wattles referred to it as "formless" intelligence and substance.

FACT

Norman Vincent Peale, author of *The Power of Positive Thinking*, a popular self-help guide first published in 1952, advocated that people trust that God's higher power was always with them. He observed that when they affirmed, visualized, and believed that God's power was at work in their lives, they energized their belief, actualized that power, and achieved astonishing results.

Peale, a clergyman, spoke and wrote of the power and presence of God. Today many people believe that divine consciousness permeates the universe and that when they align themselves in harmony with that consciousness, they become co-creators of their destinies with the Divine. Individuals can tap into the realm of infinite potential and substance. Through their thoughts, they draw into their lives all circumstances, situations, relationships, experiences, and things. The process is continuous and unending.

Fundamentals of the Law

The Law of Attraction works in response to thoughts that have become energized. What if you deliberately focused your attention on something that you wanted to call forth in your life, something you deeply desired to manifest? Would the Law of Attraction bring it to you? The answer is yes. Always.

Be Aware of Your Thoughts

It matters not if you seek wealth, great relationships, spiritual insights, good health, a large house, a new power saw, or a cast-iron skillet. But it is important to understand that your thoughts can also attract things you do not want. Whatever you fear most and think about often or obsessively can also manifest.

For example, you may love hiking around the Mojave Desert, but your greatest fear is that someday you'll encounter a rattlesnake that you didn't see until you were right upon it. You've thought about how terrified you would be when the snake strikes at your leg or foot. Repetitive thoughts that are charged with fear can set up the experience unless you let go of it. It is better to banish such dark thoughts. Don't give up hiking in the desert. Instead, be measured, thoughtful, studied, and prudent about undertaking such a hike. Know what precautions to take in order to have a safe hike. Replace your fearful thoughts with a sure-fire belief in a higher power working through you and with you and at all times ensuring your safety.

Let Go of the Negatives, Focus on the Positives

A thorough understanding of the fundamentals of the Law of Attraction allows us to quickly achieve our goals, get more of what we want, and avoid attracting what we do not want. With deliberate and focused application of the principles of the Law of Attraction, we can all achieve our full human potential and work together toward creating a more harmonious and just world.

Who Can Use the Law

Anyone can work with the Law of Attraction to deliberately make choices about what she wants and doesn't want in her life. She can use the law to help her work out her dreams, desires, and ambitions. So, too, she can repel the things she does not want. Worries about debt, for example, can bring more debt. But when thoughts of poverty are replaced by images of abundance, the Law of Attraction springs into action to replace lack with abundance.

Know That Anything Is Possible

At first it may seem impossible that a person could shrink his debt, acquire wealth, and grow that wealth as much as his mind could imagine. But the Law of Attraction makes anything possible. There are myriad resources to teach individuals how to get rich. Often such books offer advice about how to assess your indebtedness, develop a financial plan, imagine putting every step of the plan in place, visualize what's going to happen, and actualize the events. In this way, the person accelerates the working of the Law of Attraction. Anyone can use the Law of Attraction to change his financial status or anything else he desires. You can have the kind of life you choose. It just takes a little imagination.

QUESTION?

What is the role of imagination in attracting the objects I desire?
Whether it is dreaming or awake, the mind thinks in images and symbols. Proponents of the Law of Attraction say that when we can clearly imagine having what we most want, the Law of Attraction takes over and gives it to us.

Some experts on the Law of Attraction have pointed out that as soon as someone begins focusing on the thing he really wants, the universe gets busy arranging or rearranging the necessary elements and circumstances to make manifestation of that thing possible. The process can be accelerated with a little planning. A debt-free life, new friends, a loving life partner, plenty of money, a new car, or a dream job—whatever the person desires will manifest. When someone decides to accelerate the process and works out a plan to allow for that manifestation, myriad opportunities begin to present themselves. A person working with the Law of Attraction need only change his mindset and be aware that the opportunities for manifestation of his desire will become more commonplace. It is as if the universe is working with you, putting wind in the sail of your dream ship to take you anywhere you want to go and give you the experiences, relationships, money, wealth, and things you most desire.

The Law Is Unbiased

The Law of Attraction does not judge the value or worth of your thoughts. It cares not whether they are harmful or well intentioned, nor does it value whether your thoughts arise from a particular belief system. You may eschew religion and be an atheist or agnostic or you may be deeply religious. Knowledge and practice of a spiritual tradition (or lack of belief) doesn't concern the working of the law. What matters is how you feel about what you are thinking.

Gratitude plays a role because of how it makes you feel. For example, when you are grateful for having something, you feel good and the thoughts of possession and the positive feelings of possession bring more of the same. The law always responds to what you focus on in your thoughts and the emotion you generate in response to those thoughts; feeling strengthens the attracting power of thought.

At the beginning of this chapter, you read about the young mother who wanted a cast-iron skillet. If she had felt an abiding desperation that she was doomed to always be poor and never have the basic necessities, her fears would have manifested that lack. Her thoughts of poverty would have brought more lack in her life rather than the skillet she desired.

Biblical Figures

Consider the biblical figure of Job, a successful man with a large household that included his ten children, wife, and servants. Well-respected by his neighbors, Job owned many acres of land and herds of sheep, donkeys, and camels numbering in the thousands. Then one day, the good things in Job's life began to go away. A wind blew down the house and killed his children. Thieves took away his herds. Even his health failed him. Boils appeared upon his body and erupted into weeping sores that he cleaned in the shade of a tree with a piece of broken pottery. With his possessions, relationships, and health gone, Job cried out, "The thing which I greatly feared is come upon me, and that which I was afraid of is come unto me." (Job 3:25) God gave Job a mind, perhaps the most powerful creative tool in the universe, but Job quite possibly did not understand that his positive thoughts had brought him good fortune and his fear and dread had taken them away.

Many Christians believe that Job's suffering was a lesson about the importance of having unwavering faith in God. Job never cursed God or wavered in his allegiance, no matter how much was taken from him. God rewarded Job for being faithful by restoring his riches and giving him more children.

Solomon, the wise son of ancient Israel's King David, surely understood what Job did not, for he wrote: "For as he thinketh in his heart, so is he. . . ." (Proverbs 23:7) In the New Testament, the Apostle Paul exhorted the Christians at Ephesus to do good, "Knowing that whatever good thing any man doeth, the same shall he receive. . . ." (Ephesians 6:8) Thinking good thoughts instead of dark or evil ones is a way of doing good. When you silently bless others, that is a good thing and good is attracted back into your life. You've no doubt heard the phrase "What goes around comes around." It comes back to magnetic attraction. When you pray and do good deeds—acts of kindness such as putting money in a stranger's expired parking meter—your thoughts and actions bear the fruit of goodness. Consider for a moment what kinds of thoughts and feelings, mental images, words, and deeds you are sending out. What is in your life that you don't like? What would you change? What do you desire?

Deliberate Intention Takes Focus

Think of how something looks under a magnifying glass or a microscope. The subject being studied comes into crisp focus and is magnified many times. This is what you do when you work with the Law of Attraction. With deliberate intention, your thoughts necessarily become not only highly focused but more concentrated and energized. You must have the intent of receiving what you wish for and not waver in your belief that the manifestation is already in the works. Dream what may have been impossible for you before you knew about the Law of Attraction. Now you understand that anything you desire will be possible to achieve or obtain. The Law of Attraction is continually responding to whatever you are thinking and feeling.

The Law of Attraction is unbiased. Whatever you think about is manifested. Careless thinking about negative events can just as easily draw similar negative experiences into your life. Most likely you'll protest and declare that you would never want those things to happen; you would never have deliberately drawn them to you. But when you begin to correlate your thinking with events that have happened or that are occurring in your life, you will begin to see how your thoughts influence your life experiences. If you think you are doing everything correctly to manifest your desires but they haven't come to you as yet, perhaps you need to clear some clutter and make a space for it—in other words, create a vacuum.

FACT

The most powerful tool you have for creating is your brain, or more precisely, a particular area of your brain. According to Science Daily, the brain's "default network" enables you to do introspective tasks. Because of this you can construct a self-narrative of your life story—crucial for imagining your life story—and mentalize or analyze another's mental state so you can appropriately adjust your own—important for developing relationships.

The Law Works When There Is a Vacuum

If someone wants to manifest something in his work or life experience, he may first have to create the space for it. In other words, he must tear down, remove, and otherwise clean and clear a space to make it ready to receive the object or create the right climate for getting a new job, raise in pay, loving companion, or group of friends. The ancient Chinese tradition of feng shui emphasizes the clearing of space and the art of placement to attract the things you desire in your life. Clutter impedes or blocks energy flow. When you are trying to bring something good into your life, you certainly don't want to block its arrival. You can use the principles of feng shui to enhance your intentional work with the Law of Attraction, especially if you are seeking harmony, peace, and prosperity in all areas of your life. One of the major maxims of feng shui states "Less is more."

Seeing Blockages

A woman whose freelance writing career seemed stalled decided to consult a feng shui expert who clearly understood the Law of Attraction. A cursory examination of the writer's home office revealed multiple problems with the space. Her plants were dying. Dust-covered books filled bookcases, some in precarious stacks that threatened to topple off if they were bumped. The partially open drawers of the file cabinet revealed the need for a vigorous pruning of outdated files. Multiple calendars, a photocopied page of editing marks, and other pieces of paper with notes that had been tacked above the desk overpowered the framed art on the walls. The room was cluttered and unwelcoming. The writer complained of lack of money and writing jobs. Her life, she said, like her office, seemed to be spiraling out of control. She wanted to attract better assignments for more money.

The consultant first asked the writer to clarify what she wanted. She also asked the writer to be clear about what she didn't want in her business life. Then she had the writer clear and clean the space. She suggested to the writer that she throw out the dead plants and box up some of the books for storage. The rest fit in neat rows on the shelves. She recommended bringing in a thriving money plant, a beautiful orchid, and a small desktop fountain to shift the energies in the office.

The writer was encouraged to become more organized. Her organization efforts meant she became more productive and had more time to pursue new project ideas. The newly cleaned and well-organized space inspired the writer to be more creative. She began to spend a few minutes each day visualizing the kinds of projects she wanted and the amount of money she desired for each. When new writing assignments started flowing in, the writer saw for herself why creating a vacuum for the work she desired had been necessary.

When you open the space in your life to manifest something, the substance of the universe will fill it, according to Catherine Ponder, author of

The Dynamic Laws of Prosperity. Test the Law of Attraction for yourself. If you are experiencing lack when you seek abundance, look first to your thoughts. Are they positive? Have you unwittingly created any blockages? If so, remove them. Create a vacuum for what you want. Riches, expensive jewelry, a new house, a hot car, a super-healthy body, a new boyfriend, spiritual insights, weight loss, or even a business of your own—you can have whatever you want. That's the promise of the law when you work deliberately with it.

CHAPTER 2

Using the Law of Attraction

To deliberately utilize the Law of Attraction, it's important to understand how the mind works and then train it as your tool. If you have practiced meditation, you've experienced the mind's restless nature. Thoughts keep jumping around because of word associations, direct linkage, or internal and external stimuli. Learn to train your mind to stay on topic. Contemplate all things related to the object or circumstance that you seek to manifest. Wrap your thoughts around your desire, sharpen your focus, and feel expectant to draw the desired object to you.

The Building Block of the Universe

Many practitioners of the Law of Attraction have noted that the interrelationship between thoughts and things is dependent on the psychic energy generated by creative thought. Such energized thought sets up the attraction. Just as the mind can use the power of creative and positive thought to attract things, such as healing in the body, it can also attract objects and situations it desires through thought energy.

Psychic energy was a concept first developed by a German named Ernst von Brücke, whose ideas influenced Dr. Sigmund Freud and later Freud's student, the noted psychologist Carl Jung. Their work and writings put forth the idea that humans emanated a mental or psychic energy that could be detected and that was utilized in certain psychological activities.

Atoms are the building blocks of matter, while energy has been called the workhorse of creation. From grade-school science, you may have learned that the energy of the universe can change from one form to another, seem to disappear, move about, or remain available as potential energy. You probably also learned about the two main categories of energy: kinetic, or energy in motion; and potential, or energy stored or in position to be released. Both energy types have relevance to the Law of Attraction. The following is a sampling of some of the different types of kinetic energy:

- Electrical energy is produced when tiny atoms move about, producing electrical charges. In nature, a thunderstorm produces lightning. In a dryer, static electricity in, say, a nylon jacket causes other garments to cling to it.
- Magnetic energy encompasses the earth as a magnetic field due to the planet's rotation and a mostly liquid metallic core at the earth's center. In your everyday life, you can find magnetic energy in, for example, kitchen magnets, stereo speakers, and compasses.

- Motion energy is characterized by moving molecules. The wind is an example of motion energy.
- Radiant energy is electromagnetic energy that moves in waves, such as radio waves, X-rays, light, and solar rays.
- Sound energy is produced when air is forced over or through a substance to create longitudinal waves. One example is the vibration of air molecules through a reed.
- Thermal or heat energy is produced when molecules move about within a substance. Hydropower, one type of thermal energy, is created by water from a river that runs through a dam's turbine to an electric generator in order to produce electricity.

Energy is what enables the work of the entire universe to get done, whether the work is fueling the tasks of creation or simply digesting food or thinking thoughts. When you eat a meal, your body receives energy from the food it has digested. It stores excess calories to be accessed later. Energy of one type can change or be converted into a different type. For example, electric energy becomes magnetic when it is run through an electromagnet. But what kind of energy is associated with our thoughts? That's a difficult question to answer, although some insight can be gained by shifting our lens from empirical science to esoteric and metaphysical ideas found in Eastern philosophy.

Thoughts Are Things

Some people believe that our lives express our interior worlds, or what we think about. You have undoubtedly heard the saying that "thoughts are things." In fact, in Hinduism, nothing exists apart from the Divine because it permeates all things.

Although it is invisible to the naked eye, energy may be perceived and felt. It's been said that you can't fool kids or dogs because they have a natural ability to sense whether someone's energy and intention toward them are good or bad. Kids and dogs may be able to detect more readily than others the feelings or mood someone is generating by thought. Certain psychics, mediums, and empathic people possess a heightened sensitivity to the electromagnetic energy that is retained in objects, haunted houses, sacred places, crime scenes, and the like. Psychic energy lives on in those objects and places.

Even as doctors work in integrative medicine, using both Western and Eastern medical knowledge, and high-performance sports experts counsel their athletes about an intrinsic mind/body connection, scientific research continues on the subject of thoughts as energy.

In *Shri Ramcharitramanas*, northern India's popular version of the story of Lord Rama, Goswami Tulsidas wrote that Ramadasa (literally, the servant of Lord Rama) prayed to Lord Rama while he was imprisoned, "When all is your form, how can I be apart from you?"

While some skeptics doubt that consciousness and human thought has any measurable energy, others, including spiritual seekers, scientists, practitioners of Eastern religions, and philosophers, disagree. Indeed, some people believe human consciousness itself may be energy.

Shakti

In India, modern spiritual seekers make pilgrimages to the sacred places associated with holy people of the past because the shakti (divine energy or holy psychic energy) of those beings remains in the places where those saints prayed, meditated, and became enlightened. Many modern spiritual seekers further believe that the energy stored in the sacred places has a beneficial effect on their spiritual efforts to attain enlightenment. Contact with the shakti of enlightened beings, although those saints no longer live in human form, could awaken the Kundalini Shakti. This is the innate and essential divine energy that leads human consciousness to union with God (or Absolute divine consciousness) as the energy makes its ascent from the base of the spine to the energy center located on top of the head. The modern seekers' thought, magnetized by their spiritual desire for enlightenment, could manifest their desire, making their thought become the thing they most ardently seek and desire.

Prana

Pranic energy represents a kind of bridge between thoughts becoming or manifesting as things. In ancient Hindu writings, the body's vital airs or energies were referred to as prana. Pranic energy permeates all things, including the human mind (and, thus, thought), according to the Hindu sacred scriptures known as the Upanishads. Those sacred writings associated prana, which means "breath" in Sanskrit, with vitality and expressed the idea that a person's prana survives throughout eternity or until a being's soul reincarnates. Prana, often mistakenly thought of as breath, is more correctly understood as a life-sustaining force. Prana underlies and sustains the universe, according to Hindu belief. Prana, therefore, is found in thoughts and also material objects. The pranic energy of one human, for example, directed toward another person or object can trigger a response, reaction, or change. Even an energized or magnetized thought can instantly or eventually become the thing that the psychic energy of the creative mind conceives, giving rise to the New Age idea that "thoughts are things."

The University of Arizona's Center for Consciousness Studies is one of a number of educational centers, associations, and organizations currently studying various aspects of human consciousness. For more information, see the website *www.consciousness.arizona.edu/mission.htm*.

Chi

The Chinese use the word *chi* (pronounced *chee*) to mean the natural, supernatural, and spiritual energy of the physical universe and the human body and mind. An imbalance of chi in a person's body or life brings disharmony and disease upon him. Practitioners of acupuncture, chi gong, and other disciplines embrace the concept of chi as a subtle force underlying and permeating all things (like prana). They say restoring the balance of the flow of the chi is what restores balance, health, and harmony. When balance is restored, the things a person desires become manifest through his thought energy.

Subtle Energies and Healing

Aura healing, chakra healing, reiki (pronounced RAY kee), quantum touch, and no-touch healing are all examples of alternative medicine/belief systems that suggest that the vital energy of the body, whether it is called prana, chi, ki, or life force, can be manipulated. Skeptics classify such healings as faith-healing and say that if it works at all it is because of the thoughts of the patient, or the placebo effect—that is, the patient believes something is being done to help her feel better, she hopes she will feel better, and subsequently she does. Some might say that the placebo effect causes changes in the patient's neurochemistry that might, in part, explain the healing she received.

Polarity of Thought Energy

Thought, as most Law of Attraction experts point out, is associated with two elements: content (what the thought is about) and energy (of varying intensity, from weak to strong). Your thought energy has a polarity, too. The energy flows either inward or outward. If it is stationary, then it lacks any momentum to carry your intention inward or outward. Intention, or your desire for something, requires energy and polarity to manifest that desire. If you need healing from a chronic illness or seek spiritual unfolding, you will focus your thought energy or polarity inward, whereas if you desire a new house or car, you'll focus the polarity outward. Another way to think of it is that when the energy is polarized outward, you become engaged in some action—you create or do something. When the polarity is turned inward, you acquire or become the recipient of something.

If you have the desire and intention to launch a business, write a screenplay, build a bridge, invent a better mousetrap, or establish a women's collective in a Third-World country, your thoughts have an outward polarity. The thing you hope to manifest is not so much for you as it is an outward expression of something you wish to do or accomplish. Other examples of outward polarity might include creating a beautiful concrete statue and covering it with mosaics for your local community park, establishing an oral history program that links children with senior citizens in your town, or starting a new nonprofit venture. Think of these manifestations as your gift to the universe.

FACT

Randolph Stone, an Austrian immigrant, combined his lifelong interest in spiritualism and medicine when he formulated the concept that polarized fields of attraction and repulsion exist in all of nature, including the human body. He subsequently developed a holistic treatment for many maladies and called it Polarity Therapy.

Some Law of Attraction teachers have explained the outward and inward polarities of thought energy as follows: Outward polarity requires an action of giving something to the universe; inward polarity requires a receptive state in which you receive something from the universe. Understanding the concept is vital to putting the Law of Attraction to work in a deliberate way in your life.

FACT

Our thoughts can lift us to joyful heights or cause us to sink in the depths of despair. When we think positively, we bring or attract positive situations and people. But when we focus on the negative aspects of our life, we attract more negativity. Our thoughts are often charged with positive or negative emotion and are rarely neutral.

Positive or Negative Attraction

Inherent in the Law of Attraction is the power to attract and repel. Just as batteries have poles that are positive and negative and function to attract and repel, your thoughts also have that power. Have you ever met people who were so self-focused that they seemed to derive pleasure from dwelling on all the things that were going wrong in their lives? They couldn't seem to quit talking about their woes. And you would listen and agree that things seemed pretty bad for them.

Perhaps you wondered what was wrong with that person that his life had enough problems to last several lifetimes. Have you ever heard the expression "stinkin' thinkin'"? His outer life may simply be a reflection of his interior world. Knowingly or unwittingly, that person is attracting more of what he is thinking about most. And most likely, he is dwelling on everything that could go wrong or get worse.

If you want more goodness in your life, be good and be grateful. Feel joy and peace and happiness. Spread it out into the universe as your gift to others. Keep your mind clean from clutter, worry, and fear. Don't give mental energy to negative thinking. Just let it go. Focus on the positive to draw more of that into your life.

Conscious and Unconscious Manifesting

Like attracts like. That sums up how the Law of Attraction works. It is not possible for the law to be biased. If you are a happy, upbeat person with a smile for everyone, expect to find friends and good experiences wherever you go. Your thoughts bring those experiences into your life. On the other hand, if you have a negative attitude, a sour expression, and complaints about everything (including each ache and pain in your body), do not be surprised if people avoid you and disease, disaster, and disappointment seem to lurk around every corner.

Expecting the Worst

From time to time, you may have had a gut feeling about something you wanted to manifest but you reasoned or rationalized yourself into not having it. Ignore your inner guidance and you risk putting yourself in peril. You may discover the hard way that you didn't really want what you thought you wanted. For example, a young man from Omaha who had very little money and badly needed a car bought one against his better judgment. At a used car lot, he spotted a hot-looking muscle car. Intuitively, the man knew the car would need a high level of maintenance and buying it didn't make much sense when he simply needed a good commuter car, but he discounted his gut feeling and bought it anyway.

The salesman told him that since the car was a high-performance car, the man should be especially attentive whenever he was driving. He admonished the young man to listen for any strange sounds coming from the car that could signal that something might be wrong with it. The young man listened intently to the purr of the engine, the slap of the wipers, the sound of the heater, the whine of the gears. Mentally and emotionally convinced that an engine problem was going to appear, he listened expectantly for a problem whenever he drove the car.

Norman Vincent Peale counseled in *The Power of Positive Thinking* that the obstacles in a person's life couldn't be removed if she believed they couldn't. It's only when an individual clears her mind and redirects her thoughts onto a positive course that her life issues and obstacles can finally be resolved and removed. To not correct one's thoughts is to invite negative life circumstances and disappointment.

Shortly after the young man had purchased the car, he heard a knocking. He discovered the problem—a damaged hose that he easily replaced. Soon, he detected a squeaking and replaced the brake shoes. Not long after that, he heard a grinding noise and worried that there was trouble in the transmission. Repair costs began to mount.

The young man complained about the car to everyone. He warned family and friends that he had been suckered into buying that car and that they should be careful not to do as he had. He remembered that the car salesman had been a smooth talker and had convinced him the car was a great deal. The young man blamed forces beyond his control, but he never considered that his own thoughts might be the culprit . . . or that he was giving more energy to negative thinking by constantly talking about the problem.

No Corrective Action Taken

Was the young man simply a victim of bad luck? Maybe. But a more likely explanation is that the ever-working Law of Attraction was simply responding to the man's concern that something was going to go wrong with his car. Obsessively listening for a problem energized his concern, and the negative result he most feared finally manifested.

Beginning Basics

An understanding of the fundamentals of the Law of Attraction is the foundation upon which to build your house of dreams. To get started with the work of bringing into your life experience the various circumstances and things that you desire, read and practice the following list of steps. Each is simple and easy to do whenever you have a quiet moment during the day.

The Six Basic Steps of Manifesting

1. Clear the clutter, confusion, and negativity from your mind. Try deep breathing, meditation, or quiet reflection to release any doubt, conflicting ideas, or disbelief. Be calmly but intensely focused on the thing you desire to manifest.
2. Set forth the intention to manifest something. Make a mental declaration of your intent. No fuzzy thinking and weak, wishy-washy dreaming allowed. Be bold and let your mind wrap around the possibility that the thing you most want is already allocated to you by the abundant universe. Perhaps what is coming is even bigger, better, and more beautiful than your desire. Allow for that in your life.
3. Be expectant. Be ready to receive. Believe you deserve it, and it is already yours.
4. Visualize yourself having it. Feel the emotion associated with getting what you desired. Resist the temptation to question or concern yourself with how the universe rearranges itself to allow your desire to manifest. In other words, don't worry about or question the "how" aspect of manifestation. This is where you suspend disbelief.

5. Feel and express gratitude for the blessings you already have, the gifts of the universe that the higher power makes available to you, and the power that makes each manifestation possible.
6. Repeat these steps often each day.

You can ramp up the energy of your thought, turning it into a high-energy idea or concept, just as you can build muscle in your body. It just takes practice and frequent repetition. There are many other things you can do as well to intensify the energy about your intention. You can read more about those subjects in Chapters 8 and 9, but a brief discussion of the use of symbols follows.

The Indian yogi Paramahansa Yogananda once asked a holy man if it were possible to find one's way to God. The holy man replied that just the simple act of thinking about such a high-minded notion changed a person. Moreover, if one held on to that thought and nurtured it, he would eventually attain his desire. His point seemed clear: Desire and intention to satisfy the desire through manifestation must be strong.

QUESTION?

What happens if I skip a day or two of focused thinking about my intention to manifest my desire?
Your desire is still there. Over time the thought energy around your intention may weaken, but if the desire is still strong, the object, situation, or relationship can still come into your life experience; it simply may take longer to manifest.

Intensify Desire and Intention Through Symbolism

In Jungian psychology, symbolism has always served as an important and powerful tool, especially in the healing process. Patients are often encouraged to focus on symbols that embody special meaning for them. These symbols may appear in patients' dreams or in their mindless scribbles and doodles. Those symbols deemed most potent may become departure points or pathways inward into the psyche.

Use a specific symbol that holds cultural or spiritual meaning for you. Use the symbol throughout the day and also at bedtime as a reminder to meditate or visualize having the thing you most desire. Place the image on a refrigerator, bathroom mirror, or bedside table where it can be easily seen.

Use a Symbol to Represent Transcendental Consciousness

Symbols have the power to alter consciousness. For example, perhaps you desire to use a symbol to represent a metaphysical truth or a transcendent state of mind. Consider the Hindu symbol for Om as a point of reflection. It is believed to be the sound of the cosmic vibration of the universe. The yin/yang symbol that represents the opposite principles of masculine and feminine in Chinese philosophy means harmony, balance, and universal fellowship. A dragon or bear image suggests strength and fortitude.

There are literally thousands of symbols, from ancient to modern. Some may have obscure meanings while others are universally understood. While certain symbols may be associated with myths and cultural traditions, others hold special meaning only for certain groups. The following list contains a few common symbols with their popular meanings:

- **Bat:** darkness, the unknown
- **Blue:** sanctity, peace, water
- **Coin:** money, wealth, offering
- **Diamond:** strength, endurance
- **Dove:** the Holy Spirit, peace
- **Full moon:** wholeness, completion
- **Grove of trees/forest:** the unconscious mind, chaos
- **Heart:** compassion, love
- **Lingam:** fertility, regeneration

- **Ouroboros (snake swallowing its tail):** complete cycle of birth, death, and rebirth in an endless round
- **Pearl:** secret knowledge, hidden truth, wisdom
- **Rainbow:** a bridge between heaven and earth
- **Red:** life force, anger, war, Christ's passion
- **Snake:** deception, sexuality
- **Sun:** success
- **Three:** the Holy Trinity; birth, life, and death; past, present, and future
- **Two:** balance
- **Valley:** feminine symbol; also death and the unknown
- **Violet:** sorrow, mysticism
- **Volcano/tower:** destructive energy

Some symbols have represented a specific meaning for centuries. Symbols such as a wheel, rose, key, cross, and lotus still represent a mystical entry into transcendental states of consciousness and hidden knowledge or wisdom. However, such symbols may also have other meanings associated with them, depending upon the culture in which they are found. For example, the cross, a sacred symbol for Christians, is also the symbol of earth to the Chinese.

Find a Potent Symbol with Personal Meaning

Perhaps there is some object that has deep personal meaning for you that you wanted long ago and still do not have. Perhaps there is a certain symbol that always reminds you of that object. If, one day, you find yourself cutting out a magazine picture of a red Porsche convertible, just know your subconscious still wants that car. Go for it. The magazine picture will be a good reminder for you to work with the Law of Attraction to manifest it.

The same is true if you have a recurring dream about, say, searching for a key while climbing to the top of a mountain. Such a dream might be pointing to a search for the wisdom key and higher states of consciousness as represented by the mountain. It could also mean the challenges you have faced to reach the top.

You may find a powerful symbol in your dreams to use as a touchstone for your work of consciously manifesting. Working with your dreams can be fun, intriguing, and instructive. To discover meanings of symbols that may be appearing in your dreams and also in your conscious waking thoughts, check out David Fontana's book *The Secret Language of Symbols*, Barbara Walker's *Women's Dictionary of Symbols and Sacred Objects*, or any of the numerous Internet sites devoted to symbolism, including *altreligion.about.com/library/glossary/blsymbols.htm*.

CHAPTER 3

Source, Energy, and Infinity

Humans require love to flourish. Love energizes thoughts, empowers individuals to dream and follow their bliss, and enables their efforts to manifest. In his best-selling book, *Think and Grow Rich*, Napoleon Hill explained that it is by our predominant thoughts that we thrive. Many people might agree that our thoughts of love leave a deep imprint in our psyches and hearts. We become powerful creators when we learn to transmute negative thoughts into positive ones—for example, anger into appreciation—and then magnetize our thoughts with love.

Love as a Magnetizer

Love can serve as a powerful magnetizer for manifesting. Here's the way it works. Because of the hormones that are released in your body when you are in love, your thoughts become highly magnetized. When you first fall in love, you may feel crazy and even somewhat obsessive. All you can think about is your beloved. The other person may, in fact, be thinking of you at the exact moment that you are thinking of her.

Whether it is altruistic, romantic, or compassionate, love seeks expression. Passionate love is the driving force behind magnificent works of art, architecture, literature, and music as well as procreation. Many of us became the expression of our parents' love for each other. Love can draw into your life a romantic partner, meaningful work, pets, and friends.

FACT

Mexican artist Frida Kahlo depicted her suffering, anger, and loss in her work. At the core of her life was a passion for art and love for muralist Diego Rivera, and her work intimately reflected this. Some of her pieces are difficult to look at, yet her work is well known and collected.

Some artists who have not yet experienced success may feel a love for their craft but do not have the optimism, confidence, and sense of expectancy that they can create something unique and exceptional. Perhaps their love for their craft is not as strong as their sense of defeatism or failure, which can sabotage their efforts. And yet, others use their pain and suffering as images in their work. Love pulls them into their work and passion serves as the catalyst that ignites their vision for what they desire to manifest. Such artists may become highly successful, turning out magnificent and unique works as their gifts to the world.

When you calm your mind, cultivate a positive mood, center your thoughts on the outcome of your desire, and love what you are doing, you are in a position to optimally manifest that which your heart most desires. Wallace Wattles, in his 1910 book *The Science of Getting Rich*, noted that when you live closer to the source of wealth and abundance and align yourself in harmony with that, you get more of what you seek from the source. Living closer to the source, as Wattles calls it, might prompt thoughts of appreciation, gratitude, and love toward the unnamed, unknowable source. Such emotionally charged thought attracts more of the same to the individual.

QUESTION?

How can an artist use love to create?
A passion for mosaics, for example, can lead the mosaicist to learn everything involved in the craft, study classical works, and develop a vision for creating his own masterful and unique works.

Pseudo Versus Scientific Law

Critics assert that the Law of Attraction is not a scientific law that can be observed, quantified, qualified, or otherwise measured or proven using the steps in the scientific method. In nature, some things have been observed to behave in a certain way with regularity over a long period of time and thus laws were formulated to describe those behaviors or actions.

FACT

There are many scientific laws. Einstein's special law of relativity, the law of conservation of energy, Newton's law of gravity, and the laws of thermodynamics are just a few examples.

Critics say that the Law of Attraction has nothing to do with the physics of attraction but rather represents a metaphysical philosophy. Others say it is little more than esoteric mumbo jumbo. Although Law of Attraction proponents say that the law works every time, people who have tried it with little or no result complain that it doesn't. When it doesn't, those people say that they are frequently informed that the fault lies not in the law itself but rather in how the law was applied. In other words, the fault lies with the person trying to manifest a result: the individual wasn't focused enough, didn't believe strongly enough, didn't take the proper action, or neglected making a space in her life for the result she sought.

While some critics shrilly denounce the Law of Attraction as being pure bunk, others temper their remarks with a reminder that positive thinking and instilling hope are good things. If believing in the Law of Attraction inspires one to have a better life, set some goals, and reach for treasured dreams, so much the better. French-born diarist Anaïs Nin once remarked that a life shrinks or expands according to one's courage. Sometimes it takes courage just to believe in something and allow for its unfolding in your life.

The mind/emotion connection that figures into the Law of Attraction has resonance in spells. Successfully casting a spell means the mind must be sharply focused and the emotions must be appropriate—no love emotion for a banishing spell, for example. All the necessary props or ingredients for the spell must be exact and the words spoken for the spell must be correct.

The Energy of Manifestation

For manifestation to take place, energy must be expended. The process begins with a desire to have something—let's say, a new friend who will become your romantic partner and possibly your future husband. In a measured and thoughtful manner, you think about what you want as clearly as you can. Eventually, you might develop a mental checklist that could go something like the following:

Criteria for My Ideal Mate
- Is intelligent and articulate
- Loves books, dogs, and children
- Is approximately my age

- Is athletic and physically healthy
- Is emotionally available
- Is fiscally responsible
- Has sound ethical values and high moral standards
- Is spontaneous
- Has a terrific sense of humor
- Dances like Fred Astaire

Next, your imagination wraps around new qualities, traits, or skills that you hope he will have. The more you think about exactly what you want, the more refined the image of your new mate becomes—he can cook, dance the salsa, and romp with the kids and dog with a wild spontaneity. Imaginative thoughts of interacting with such a person give you pleasure, and your thoughts of him become charged with positive emotion. Now you begin to anticipate meeting him. He's not in your life yet, but you feel certain that he's moving toward you—and you feel you deserve him.

Do Things to Bring Him In

You decide to take some action, perhaps type the checklist of your mental image of him and make multiple copies. You post a copy on your bathroom mirror where you imagine him standing near you while you apply lip gloss or comb your hair. You stick the list on your refrigerator and imagine he reaches past you for the dessert he's preparing to serve with coffee. You walk the dog and imagine he walks beside you, talking about the latest book he read. You almost love this guy already.

Up to this point, you have been using energy in your thinking, imagining, visualizing, and making lists. Now you decide to put yourself into situations where you might actually meet him. You attend a speed-dating event with a friend, sign up for a month on an Internet matchmaking site, frequent bookshops and grocery stores, and take a cooking class. You start taking your dog on extended walks, believing that at any moment he may soon walk toward you. You tell your friends and family members you are ready for him to show up and believe he's near.

Wait and Have Faith

Using mental, emotional, and physical energy, you have sown the seed of desire. The task of a seed sown in fertile ground is to sprout and grow. Let the universe do the work. It takes time for a seed to germinate and push up so you can actually see it growing. Even though you cannot see the germination and growth process, you must nourish it and have faith that it will spring forth in fullness.

Another parable put he forth unto them, saying, The kingdom of heaven is like to a grain of mustard seed, which a man took, and sowed in his field: Which indeed is the least of all seeds: but when it is grown, it is the greatest among herbs, and becometh a tree, so that the birds of the air come and lodge in the branches thereof.—Matthew 13:31–32

See the Result

According to the Law of Attraction experts, your expectation and anticipation will now pull the mate you seek into your life. A mustard seed at first appears tiny and inconsequential, but once it is sown in nourishing soil it can spring forth to become the greatest herb in the garden. So, too, will the dream in your heart sprout in its fullness. In the New Testament, Jesus explained in the parable of the sower the unseen power of the tiny mustard seed to grow into something great.

Explore the Realm of Infinite Possibility

Most of us have a materialistic side and go crazy when we see must-have items in our favorite catalogs or in the windows of neighborhood stores. We live in a credit card society where plastic can buy nearly every tangible thing known to humankind. Still, most of us hold off buying big-ticket items such as houses and cars until we can afford them. In some cases, that may mean waiting years. But what if we set aside factors such as cost and considered the possibility of having anything our hearts desired? What if we didn't have to figure out how to get it and left that up to the universe to arrange? What if our job was simply to go shopping in the storehouse of the universe and reveal to the Source our desires? What if it were that simple? The Law of Attraction experts say it is.

Expanding your consciousness is not difficult. It just takes a little patience and practice if you have never done it before. The mind is restless. Your job is to simply observe the thought process. As your relaxed state slows your breathing and heart rate, your thoughts will become quieter as well. Sit comfortably in a chair or lie on the floor on your back in a quiet, safe place with eyes closed. Do the following steps:

1. Inhale and exhale three deep, cleansing breaths. Feel your body filling with warm light with each inhalation. Release negativity and tension with each exhalation. Return to normal breathing.
2. Observe the mind without trying to control it until it finally settles into a quiet state.
3. Mentally recite your attribution for the Creator (Om, God, Source, Father/ Mother, Lord, or some other name) with your inhaled breath. As you exhale, mentally note a number designating each exhaled breath. For example: Om-one, Om-two, Om-three, etc.
4. Allow yourself to sink into a deeply relaxed state. When you lose count or feel like you are ready to move to the next step, do so.
5. Allow thoughts of all the things you desire to surface. Select one object, circumstance, or person you want to manifest in your life.
6. Focus on that one thing that you want to begin working on. Believe you deserve it. See yourself having it. Feel the joy and pleasure of that desire finally manifesting in your life. Feel gratitude and mentally thank the Creator for bringing it to you.

The topic of manifesting will be covered more completely in Chapter 9, but for now learning how to relax and let go of tension and potential blockages is an important first step for those who intend to deliberately work with the law.

Source as Infinite Potential or Abundances

The great sages and saints of all religions learned to rely on the Unseen Power at work in the universe. That power not only provided them with wisdom and enlightenment, but it also took care of their physical bodies' needs for food, clothing, and shelter.

In India today, yogis or rishis still do pilgrimages to the forested mountains of Rishikesh in order to meditate undisturbed in natural settings, in caves, under trees, or near water. Some remain until they reach enlightenment or the end of their present incarnations. They depend upon the Unseen Power of the universe to take care of them while they perform their sadhana (tasks associated with devotion to a deity), do penances, undertake anusthans (spiritual practices to achieve a specific result), or spend untold hours in meditation, contemplation, and the recitation of chants such as the Gayatri Mantra on their japa mala beads (a string of prayer beads, usually numbering 108 beads).

FACT

Many yogis chant the holy word *Om*, alone or as part of a chant, because it is considered the primordial sound of the cosmos, from which all things within vibratory creation are manifested. It is the holiest of sounds, and listening to the cosmic vibration of Om is itself a path to enlightenment.

Streams of Divine Power

According to the teachings of Hinduism, five streams of energy emanate from the cosmic Om. While Om itself is considered a manifestation of God, omnipresent in the form of Shabda Brahma, three of its five energy streams are known as Brahma (Creator), Vishnu (Sustainer), and Shiva (Destroyer). Yogis understand how to tap into the streams of Divine Power to achieve certain objectives.

The Gayatri Mantra, perhaps the most sacred of all mantras and considered the primordial mantra by Hindus, was projected into manifestation by the will of God in order to bring about the current cycle of creation, say

Hindu religious scholars. The Divine energy known as Brahma then manifested all animate and inanimate objects in the universe.

According to Hindu thought, all of creation expands and contracts in cycles. Certain cycles are characterized by lightness and darkness. When darkness is upon the earth, holy beings such as the Buddha, Mohammed, and Jesus appear on earth as light-bearers to lead humankind out of darkness, depravity, and despair back to light and truth. Some people believe that great and holy beings are always present and anonymously working to manifest good for the well-being of all.

One Man's Quest

The Buddha, a holy being who lived approximately 500 years before Jesus, was the son of King Suddhodana, ruler of the Shakya people in ancient India. His childhood name was Siddhartha Gautama. Until the age of sixteen, when he married, he lived the privileged life of a prince. Against his father's wishes, he left the royal palace to visit his subjects. It was then that he first witnessed human suffering when he met an old man whose life and health were waning, an invalid, and a begging ascetic.

Desiring to find a way to defeat suffering, poverty, and infirmity, Siddhartha renounced his life, left his wife and son, and became an ascetic. Through meditation and the breathing technique of observing the in/out breaths (anapana-sati), he discovered the Middle Way, a spiritual path without extreme asceticism or sensual indulgences. He had followed his desire to its end. By achieving enlightenment, he defeated suffering, poverty, and infirmity.

Tap the Source

The Source of all things is available twenty-four hours a day, seven days a week. To work with the Law of Attraction is to trust that we can go to that divine Source for anything we desire at any moment. Saints of different religions have said in different ways that we are children of the Divine or God. No parent would want her child to live in suffering and poverty. On the contrary, consider instead the possibility that we are to live in abundance, in good health, surrounded by love.

Replace Negative Self-Talk

What is keeping us from living the kind of life we only dream of having? Perhaps nothing more than our own negative self-talk. If we don't believe we deserve the good things in life, the Law of Attraction won't bestow good things upon us. If we believe that we can't do any better, and that we can't lift ourselves from under a mound of debt or free ourselves from destructive habits, then the Law of Attraction keeps us right where we are.

The twelve-step programs that are often key to the recovery of substance abusers advocate that people must take responsibility for their actions but that they can always find help by trusting in a higher power. Those who suffer addictions must learn to let go of negative self-talk, as it defeats the good they are trying to manifest in their lives. Self-talk is the perpetual driver of behavior. It tells half-truths and untruths. Replacing negative self-talk with the statement reworded into a positive affirmation can literally change a life.

Seek Joy

Joy, according to several dictionary definitions, is the emotion of happiness or delight. It is triggered by the expectation of something good or satisfying. Joy, it has been said, is at the core of our being. A peaceful joyful countenance reflects a corresponding inner life. Seek joy for yourself and others and give the gift of silent blessing to all—especially those experiencing lack in their lives—that they will experience joy and success in every aspect of their lives.

The Gestational Period

Sometimes when you really want something specific in your life, the waiting can trigger frustration and you may begin to doubt that it is ever coming. Those times are periods when you must learn to trust that the universe is doing its work. Your desire is known. Your intent has been proclaimed. When you cook, isn't it true that some types of dishes take longer to prepare than others? When you write an e-mail, isn't it true that some compositions take longer than others?

Part of working with the Law of Attraction is letting go of the need to control the time frame during which your desire manifests in your life. You have the capacity to let go of that compulsion, and as the noted psychologist Carl Rogers once observed, "You can't push the river."

The Law of Attraction works with momentum. Things can manifest instantly or take a long time. Why? The reason has a lot to do with the strength of your desire, the clarity of your vision, and the power of your intention. Remember that the universe is rearranging itself to bring you what you want but that it also allows you to wrangle with your choice and all the different aspects, elements, and options your mind conceives.

To every thing there is a season, and a time to every purpose under heaven: A time to be born, and a time to die; a time to plant, and a time to pluck up that which is planted.—Ecclesiastes 3:1–2

For example, you may be thinking you want something and then later experience doubts about having it. Let's say you have always wanted a dog. You begin thinking about what it might feel like to own a dog. You might smile whenever you think of the happy yelping welcome when you get home each night. You imagine warm fuzzy feelings just thinking about him curling up with you on the couch. You even have a name for him—Mr. Peabody.

But while cutting flowers in your garden one day, you begin wondering how Mr. Peabody would like the flowers. What if he digs around your flowerbeds, chews on the sprinkler heads, chases away the ground-feeding mourning doves? You begin to wonder if having a dog is such a good idea. What if he destroys your garden, your sacred place of peace and renewal? Suddenly you ask yourself which is more important—a beautiful garden with wild creatures or the company of a pet? Why hadn't you thought of these things before?

Napoleon Hill, author of *Think and Grow Rich*, warned that indecision and doubt work together to become fear. The process or blending of the two, though steady and insidious, may not be obvious to the conscious mind. The end result is fear. But fear is a state of mind that can be altered by conscious thought.

Your indecisiveness and fear block the pet from your life. The Law of Attraction allows you to change your mind or shift your desires around. Perhaps you decide a bird might make a better choice for a pet and eventually you greet the new parakeet that has made its way into your life. The Source has brought it to you because you abandoned ambivalence and instead formed and held a clear vision for the bird that was so strong it became your reality.

CHAPTER 4

What Critics Say

If you break your leg, did you attract that into your life? A plethora of books and DVDs have ignited a national discussion about the Law of Attraction and the simple premise that you attract everything into your life through your thought. Yet some scientists and critics disagree with that concept. They say it blames the patient to suggest that she attracted her ailment.

4

An Overstated Promise

At best, detractors say, the Law of Attraction overstates a promise that just thinking about something brings it to you. Further, critics argue, you cannot have irrefutable proof of the nonscientific claim that you can gain whatever you dream about or long for—it is not a hypothesis that can be proven through scientific method. Instead, they point out, savvy marketing, attention-grabbing buzzwords, catchy phrases, and the promise of getting something for (almost) nothing seem to have caught the imagination of Americans and the media.

Hype for Vulnerable and Gullible People

The disenfranchised, poor, aged, infirm, and gullible, critics say, have always been targets for schemes that claim to make their lives easier. When thoughts about great wealth, a Bentley, or a miracle cure don't materialize, disappointment doesn't begin to describe the feelings of the person who had believed in the promise of the Law of Attraction. Yet believers of the law have faith that it is always working to bring the fruits of your thinking into your life.

QUESTION?

Could a single fearful thought passing through the mind manifest in your life?
It's unlikely that you would attract into your life the parallel of an isolated thought about something frightening. However, the more you experience the fear and allow it to build around a specific idea or image, the more likely you are to attract it.

Resonance with Older Ideas

The Law of Attraction has resonance with older books that contain similar ideas. *Think and Grow Rich* and *The Law of Success* by Napoleon Hill, *The Science of Getting Rich* by Wallace Wattles, *The Power of Positive Thinking* by Norman Vincent Peale, and *How to Win Friends and Influence People* by Dale Carnegie are just a few titles from other eras that preceded the current offerings of the Law of Attraction. The new works often feature a personal growth, self-help, or New Age focus while the earlier books targeted a different type of audience with content that was practical and inspirational.

Those earlier works explored ideas of positive thinking, the necessity of taking action, and the importance of having a belief in a higher power working with you. Hill's inspirational book was published almost three-quarters of a century ago. Although totally appropriate for its time in 1937, his book addressed a mostly capitalistic white male audience and gave many Depression-era people hope for a better life through application of certain principles.

QUOTE

The difference between perseverance and obstinacy is that one comes from a strong will, and the other from a strong won't.—Henry Ward Beecher, nineteenth-century minister and abolitionist

Napoleon Hill interviewed five hundred of the wealthiest men of his lifetime. Born into a poor Virginian family in 1883 and orphaned by the age of twelve, Hill overcame poverty to become a journalist and lawyer. Scotsman and steel titan Andrew Carnegie became his mentor. Carnegie felt that others could create wealth for themselves if they understood his formula for building a stupendous fortune. He urged Hill to interview successful American businessmen like him to find out their success secrets. Hill did and shared his findings in books, lectures, and speeches.

Hill learned that any formula for wealth and success had to include such things as formulating a precise purpose, cultivating the desire for it to manifest, recognizing opportunity whenever and wherever it showed up, being persistent, cultivating success consciousness, perceiving advantage and new opportunities in every obstacle and adversity, and—perhaps most importantly—having a desire that is fueled by faith and charged with emotion. He also believed it wise to surround oneself with like-minded persons.

In his books, Hill wrote about his belief in the power of autosuggestion as a law of nature and suggested that our thoughts are like vibrations in the ether that are either negatively or positively charged by our emotions. The subconscious mind, according to Hill, must be influenced by emotionally charged thought mixed with faith if such thought is to bear results. Detractors believed that Hill's thinking was flawed. They asserted that it was foolhardy to believe that desire could turn into its tangible equivalent. Further, they argued that it was impossible to create something out of nothing.

Great leaders from myriad backgrounds have expressed their belief in the role of persistence in achieving success. Calvin Coolidge, the thirtieth president of the United States, once remarked to a group of school children that "nothing in the world can take the place of persistence." He noted that talent, genius, or education could not. "Persistence and determination alone are omnipotent," he emphasized.

Infinite Potential for the Many or the Few

Law of Attraction teachers and coaches say the law is always working and once you know how to work deliberately with it, you can draw whatever you want from the storehouse of the universe. You have the potential to manifest $1 or $1 million. You could establish a hospital, fund an orphanage, or build a social club for senior citizens. Anything you want to create is possible, provided you have desire, intention, and persistence. You already have the means—your thoughts—assert proponents of the law. Your potential for manifesting is limitless.

Detractors say that the potential to acquire money and material things exists for a few but not everyone. Money is to be made by those who know how to capitalize on the Law of Attraction. Those who can create a product like the best-selling books and DVDs or become personal coaches, seminar leaders, and lecturers are cashing in on a pop culture phenomenon. Critics add that like most trends, interest will diminish or die out altogether.

Proponents of the Law of Attraction argue that people can create their lives on purpose. In every age and era, there are those who form a strong desire to do something important or meaningful with their lives. In some cases, the desire is simply to build a better mousetrap. In others, it's to give something back to the universe or to do something for the greater social good. Those individuals believe so strongly in what they want that they think about it all the time, perhaps even praying about it and seeking help from the highest Source.

FACT

Agnes Gonxha Bojaxhiu, more familiarly known as Mother Teresa, desired to care for the "poorest of the poor." She dedicated her life to realizing her dream even though she had no money. She challenged the world to help her. It did. Her order, the Missionaries of Charity, was established in more than 100 countries. In 1979, Mother Teresa received the Nobel Peace Prize for her humanitarian work. She died in 1997 and was beatified in 2003.

Danger for Desperate People

Critics of the Law of Attraction ask why the Law of Attraction doesn't work for everyone, even those trying their best to work with it. For example, a young man with a family had been busy building his business while also helping his aging father and mother financially. One day, he took ill with a virus that settled in his liver. As he grew weaker, doctors did many tests and finally told him he needed a liver transplant. The young man remained optimistic and followed his doctor's orders but also took up yoga and meditation to draw healing energies into his body.

When it came time for the transplant, he was ready. He was certain that the power of positive thinking could prepare his body for a rapid and complete recovery. He listened to self-healing tapes and did yoga for stress reduction and relaxation. He even had his wife read him a Buddhist prayer each evening to help him visualize perfection in his body and the universe. He felt certain his health would be restored and he would continue doing the work he loved.

The surgery was successful. Elated, the young man and his wife shared his story with others they had met who were facing dire circumstances. Christmas came and went, and the couple looked forward to going dancing on New Year's Eve. The young man was much stronger and had supreme confidence in his new liver. He celebrated the holiday with prayers for the gift of the new liver and for blessings on the donor's family and his own.

On New Year's morning, he awoke with a fever. Two months later, he passed away from an aggressive cancer that had quickly spread throughout his body because his immune system was suppressed. His wife had been more prepared for his death before the transplant. After her husband had received his new liver, she had dared to dream again of their life together, more children, and travels to exotic lands. His death from cancer shocked her.

Even the Bible suggests that when faith is not strong enough and doubt creeps in, a desired healing may not take place. The Gospel of Mark 6:5 states that even Jesus had difficulty: "And he could there do no mighty work, save that he laid his hands upon a few sick folk, and healed them. And he marveled because of their unbelief."

Although the mind/body connection is still being studied, detractors of the Law of Attraction say the law represents a danger to people in desperate situations. The young man had sought help from alternative therapies and had followed all his doctor's orders. He had followed a course of positive thinking and yet it had not saved his life. Skeptics say that it is fallacy to believe that thoughts about having good health can bring about a cure. When, they ask, did wishful or magical thinking ever bestow life for the terminally ill? Yet believers in the working of the law might argue that no one knows what really goes on in another's mind, what kind of doubts creep in, what kind of fear might be blocking the cure.

Believers in the Law of Attraction argue that miracle cures, which doctors and science cannot explain, do, in fact, occur. They assert that it is nothing short of arrogant for us to believe that we humans know everything and that the power of healing isn't possible without drugs and medical treatments. People in dire situations often feel helpless and want to do something. Encouraging them to have positive thoughts and focus on the best-case scenario certainly offers a better option than dwelling on the worst-case scenario.

Blaming the Victims

According to its proponents, the Law of Attraction mirrors your interior world, manifesting your thoughts in your life experience. The law is always working, whether you are conscious of it or not. This idea, argue the law's critics, suggests that a person who has been a victim of adverse circumstances has brought calamity upon herself. Whether she fell prey to identity theft, was laid off or recently fired from her job, or was attacked by a bobcat while running on a woodland trail, she became a victim. Critics assert that Law of Attraction believers fault the individual for such misfortunes. How, skeptics ask, does an unsuspecting person draw such calamity upon herself?

Random Act of Violence

A young woman crossing her college campus at night became the victim of a man, high on drugs, who physically and sexually assaulted her. The woman lay in a coma for a month before recovering. She was so traumatized that she could not face returning to the school, so she moved across the country and began her life anew. Those who believe in the Law of Attraction suggest that her thoughts attracted the incident. Others, who believe in reincarnation, might suggest that her attack somehow represented the fruit of a seed planted in a previous life. But critics of the Law of Attraction ask how could anyone say to the young woman, "Why did you do that to yourself?"

Replace the Negative

A woman developed a mass in her breast. Doctors performed various tests, including an X-ray and an ultrasound. Believing the best course was to remove it, they scheduled her for surgery. On the day of surgery, they rechecked the lump. It was gone. While skeptics decry blaming the victim for the onset of disease or other unfortunate circumstance in a person's life, proponents of the law assert that if a person can attract a negative event, she might also have the same power to eliminate it. The woman was able to restore her health through the power of her belief and positive thoughts.

FACT

In Buddhism, whether good or bad happens, it is not God or the Creator causing those things but karma. Every thought, word, and act has a consequence, according to Buddhists. A person must let go of attachment, be still and observant, and discover what is real and what is not.

Criticism, Countercriticism, and Claims

As the Law of Attraction ideas gained widespread attention, critics emerged from various corridors to voice concerns and divergent points of view. Those who believe in the power of the universal law found themselves defending their belief in the powerful working of the law. They advised those who doubted to at least try to set aside their opposition and be open to the possibility that the law could work wonders in their lives. Their basic premise, they would tell skeptics, was that if positive thinking and a grateful attitude attract the things you want, then the flip side of that idea is that negative thinking will draw to you the things you don't want.

Attract or Alter

Some Law of Attraction proponents have even explained that war and famine might be the culmination of a widespread pattern of negative thinking sending forth negative vibrations that attracts negative events. As Rhonda Byrne noted, the vibrational frequency of people's thoughts match the frequency of the event thrust upon them even though they may not have been thinking about a specific event.

Hindu and Buddhist philosophies teach detachment and the avoidance of judging experiences as either good or bad so as not to be impacted by them; however, Law of Attraction practitioners assert that it is, in fact, your thoughts that draw life experiences to you. You are not altering your relationship to or perception of an event. Instead, you are making it possible for it to take place through your emotions and thoughts.

Critics Find Similarities Elsewhere

Some Law of Attraction critics have noted that the idea that positive thinking can bring about well-being has resonance with the nineteenth century and twentieth century philosophies known as the New Thought Movement and Mental Science, respectively. In the latter philosophy, living things are originated from the world of thought and feeling, not out of physical matter. See *www.tomorrowlands.org/edinburgh* for more information.

Some critics liken the Law of Attraction ideology to the New Thought Movement of Phineas Parkhurst Quimby and his teaching about mental healing. Quimby espoused beliefs that emphasized the importance of thought in the healing process. Others suggest the law resonates with Mental Science ideas of Thomas Troward: the "livingness of life consists in intelligence" and "the power of thought."

Historical Figures Taught the Law

Even as critics' voices have been rising to confront the basic tenets of the Law of Attraction and verbalize concerns about blaming victims, teachers of the law assert that many historical figures—specifically, Buddha, Hermes Trismegistus, Plato, Aristotle, Beethoven, and Isaac Newton—knew about the law and secretly taught it. They say other teachers included Winston Churchill, Thomas Edison, Carl Jung, Albert Einstein, and Andrew Carnegie. More recent teachers include mythologist Joseph Campbell and civil rights leader Martin Luther King Jr., whose most famous speech was built around the positive statement "I have a dream."

Critics say that some Law of Attraction teachers are ridiculous to suggest that creative imagination, visualizations, affirmations, and the power of positive thinking can help a person manifest circumstances, objects, or healings. However, practitioners of the Law of Attraction point out that miraculous healings, even from seemingly incurable diseases, can and do happen. The Roman Catholic Church also acknowledges the regular occurrence of miracles. Before a person can be canonized as a saint, three miracles have to be attributed to him.

FACT

Mythologist Joseph Campbell made knowledge of ancient archetypes accessible through his television series *The Power of Myth*. Influenced by Jung's work with symbols (the language of the mind) and dreams, Campbell said to "follow your bliss." His now-famous statement exemplifies the positive thinking expounded by Law of Attraction followers and they claim him as a "secret teacher."

It is often difficult to assess whether an ill person has experienced a miraculous cure. Certainly, doctors can attest to the recovery, but explaining such a sudden (sometimes instantaneous) recovery in someone who has been diagnosed with a chronic affliction or terminal disease can be impossible. Still, many people do recover through the power of their faith and unshakable belief that they will become healthy again. When they have such faith and belief in having excellent health, they set up a powerful force for attracting recovery through the Law of Attraction. One of the most famous places for healing is in Lourdes, France. For a healing to be deemed miraculous, the church undertakes a thorough investigation to rule out other possible explanations. When there is no explanation, the person's cure is deemed a miracle.

In ancient Greco-Roman times, people often believed that their rulers were born of gods. Whether or not rulers truly did possess the gift to heal, their subjects believed that the mere touch of an emperor's hand could cure an ailment. Perhaps their positive thoughts generated the healing they believed was coming.

Wallace Wattles observed in his book *The Science of Getting Rich* that you shouldn't waste time daydreaming or building castles in the air but rather stick to a vision of yourself and your purpose with all the strength of the mind you are capable of mustering. There will always be those who believe in the power of positive thinking, whether they call it the Law of Attraction or another name. Critics will also likely continue to weigh in on whether the Law of Attraction is actually a force at work in the lives of humans. It will be up to the individual to decide to believe the critics or the advocates of the law.

CHAPTER 5

The Law of Attraction in Ancient Traditions

Some people working with the Law of Attraction assert that any deliberate and concerted effort at manifesting involves nothing less than a new alchemy of transforming thought into physical matter. Further, they say that the application of ancient wisdom can clarify and intensify efforts of deliberate manifesting in alignment with the Law of Attraction. Such practices draw upon traditions borrowed from the ancient Babylonians, Greco-Romans, Egyptians, Aborigines, Asians, and Aztecs and include working with dreams, studying mythological archetypes, and even working magic.

Babylonians

Sometimes getting the thing you most desire comes about only through first achieving some other goal that makes possible the manifestation of what you seek. For example, a Babylonian named Hammurabi (1792–1750 B.C.) deeply desired to unify the scattered cities of Babylon into some kind of cohesive empire. Hammurabi offered to militarily protect cities if the residents would pay taxes and swear loyalty to him, but that had been done by others and was not enough to bind an empire together. He formulated a group of laws that came to be known as the Code of Hammurabi.

FACT

The Code of Hammurabi was chiseled into stone tablets and displayed for all in the ancient world to see. The Code contains 282 laws that were forerunners to modern tort law. Hammurabi's system was fair and clearly articulated and, most importantly, made possible the manifestation of his deepest desire, the unification of Babylonia.

The establishment of his code of simple and clearly articulated laws meant that contracts between people were honored, the treatment of women and slaves was regulated, and everyone, regardless of class, received protection from abuse and maltreatment. The establishment of Hammurabi's laws radically shifted the status quo. Everyone lived by the same rules.

QUOTE

Forasmuch as thou sawest that the stone was cut out of the mountain without hands, and that it brake in pieces the iron, the brass, the clay, the silver, and the gold; the great God hath made known to the king what shall come to pass hereafter: and the dream is certain, and the interpretation thereof sure.—Daniel 2:45

With his dream actualized, Hammurabi led the ancient Babylonians into a positive and productive period that scholars refer to as Babylon's golden age. Among other things, the Babylonians are known to have studied mathematics and the movement of the stars and are credited with inventing astrology, the twelve signs of the zodiac, and the 360-degree circle. Some Law of Attraction teachers say the law was understood by the ancient Babylonians, and their collective consciousness set up positive vibrations for good things to come to them.

Nebuchadnezzar, a Babylonian with Dark Dreams

According to the Old Testament book of Daniel, Nebuchadnezzar II was a Babylonian king with dreams of negative images that only a young Israelite captive named Daniel could correctly interpret. Just as the Law of Attraction enabled Hammurabi to achieve his dream of a great and unified empire, it could also have brought about the decline of Nebuchadnezzar's empire because the law always responds to positive and negative vibrations of a person's magnetized thoughts. Perhaps Nebuchadnezzar worried about a power shift taking place, and Daniel's interpretations, as clear and seemingly irrefutable as they were, surely struck fear into the heart of the ruler.

Dreams can be incubated to elucidate some problem you may be encountering in a deliberate manifestation effort or to ensure that you are on course to achieve a goal. Likewise, dreams have been known to uncover illness, foretell births and deaths, and reveal breakthroughs in self-help and spiritual work.

Daniel had predicted the fall of Babylon and the breaking up of the mighty empire into smaller and weaker kingdoms. Nebuchadnezzar's worst fears manifested within seventy years as the Persians invaded Babylon. Persia then fell into the hands of the Greeks, led by Alexander the Great. Some might say that the Law of Attraction was simply bringing to

Nebuchadnezzarwhat his fears and nightly dreams had attracted. Nebuchadnezzar ordered his advisers killed when they couldn't explain the meaning of the images of his dreaming mind and summoned Daniel, who correctly explained the dreams prompting the king to call Daniel a "revealer of secrets."

Jews of the Ancient World

There are many stories in the Old Testament about the desire, intent, dreams, faith, and will of the ancient Israelites to lay out a course for their destiny as children of the Lord. Many stories reveal how the Israelites held on to a vision and had unwavering faith and belief in it until it manifested. Perhaps one of the best-known stories of the Bible is how Moses led the Israelites out of slavery to the Promised Land.

Moses and the Promised Land

Moses' faith compelled him to follow God's instructions, no matter what they might be. The Israelites believed that Moses had been chosen by God to lead them from their enslavement by Pharaoh to the land that the Lord had promised them. "Strong and steady" characterizes their belief and faith that their dream of having their own special place in the world was sanctioned by the Lord. They also believed that they were the Lord's chosen ones and that He remained ever near them. Their attitude that God would not abandon them kept their faith strong, and that, in turn, kept fear and doubt in abeyance.

When a leader and a group of people hold a common vision for a goal, feeling expectant and joyful about the possibility of achieving it, remaining focused, and putting energy toward accomplishing the goal every day, they are following a powerful recipe for success in manifesting their collective desire.

The Jews' goal was to get to the Promised Land even though it meant they had to walk for forty years in the desert. Nevertheless, their belief that God was guiding them remained strong, steady, and focused. It allowed for their miraculous crossing of the Red Sea, safe passage through lands owned by their enemies, and, finally, entry to the Promised Land, the cul-mination of their jointly held dream.

Deborah's Intent to Vanquish Sisera

Among the ancient Israelites was a woman judge named Deborah. Like Moses, she, too, hoped to achieve a goal. Most days, Deborah could be found holding court under a palm tree located between Beth-El and Ramah. She heard much about the goings-on around the countryside and knew that an enemy of the Israelites named Sisera maintained a formidable army with 900 iron chariots. Deborah sent for Barak, one of her people's military commanders, and laid out a strong and decisive plan for defeating Sisera.

Barak initially had doubts that he could win the battle against Sisera. Deborah, however, had no thoughts of defeat. She believed the time had come for them to win. She must have been exceedingly confident, perhaps even excited, because Barak's doubts vanished. The adversaries faced off in a riverbed. With Deborah looking on, the Israelites won decisively. Although all of Sisera's men were killed, Sisera escaped on foot. Still, Deborah's belief in a positive outcome never wavered. She had hope and expectation in her heart that Sisera would not live another day to cause pain and suffering to the Israelites.

No force is more subtle in its workings, nor more powerful to bring results for good or ill than the steady output of thought from one or several minds combined, on one person to effect some desired result, and whether this is done intelligently and consciously, or blindly, the force works the same result.—Prentice Mulford, *Thoughts Are Things*

Sisera sought a shelter in a safe place. Jael, the wife of Heber the Kenite, noticed him approaching from her position just outside her tent. She offered him milk and allowed him to sleep while she guarded the doorway. When she was sure he was asleep, she took his life by hammering a tent peg into his head.

Deborah's profound belief that she and Barak could manifest her intention of freeing the children of Israel from the oppression of their enemy culminated with the death of Sisera and the destruction of his army. The joyful spirit of the Israelites and the gratitude they felt for overcoming their oppressor surely enabled them to feel more positive about their life because the Bible says they prospered. The more positive and joyful they felt, the more the Law of Attraction would have brought them.

Greeks and Egyptians

In a discussion of the Law of Attraction, a transliterated word of Greek origin stands out: *eudaimonia*, meaning "bliss and felicity" or as some Law of Attraction teachers have expressed it, "human excellence and flourishing." In ancient Greek history, a man named Alexander the Great epitomized the use of focused intention for beginning a new goal and developing a strong belief in personal excellence to manifest great things. Alexander's dominant desire in life was to conquer the world and establish one universal monarchy.

Alexander, Formidable Leader

Before he died, Alexander managed to conquer the vast majority of the ancient world that was known to the Greeks of that time. He remained undefeated in battle. He clearly knew what goal he wanted to manifest in life, and through the power of his thoughts, the intensity of his desire, and the Law of Attraction working with his thoughts and feelings, he became a formidable foe against his enemies.

A Dream to Unite a Divided Egypt

Did the ancient Egyptians understand the secret to attracting wealth, power, and influence in their lives through the harmonious alignment with the Law of Attraction? It would seem so. One leader of the ancient world, King Narmer of Egypt, desired to unite Upper Egypt with Lower Egypt and lived to see his desire manifested.

King Narmer was the first king to wear the white crown of Upper Egypt and the red one of Lower Egypt. He was called the King of Both Lands and Bearer of Both Crowns. King Narmer's unification of Egypt had a profound and positive impact on all aspects of Egyptian life. His prosperity was revealed in a mace head discovered by archeologists. It showed the king with his bodyguards and provided a list of all his assets. His people likewise experienced a glorious period as a unified Egypt saw the building of pyramids and the development of hieroglyphics, increased stability, and expanded trade. Some might say those achievements stand as a powerful testament to the positive thinking and the hopes, dreams, and deeds of the Egyptian people and their visionary leader.

FACT

Before Alexander's birth, both of his parents dreamed about the nature of their unborn child. Alexander's mother had dreamed of the sound of thunder and lightning tearing through her womb. Alexander's father had dreamed he had placed the seal of a lion upon his wife's womb. A seer told them their child would be born with a lion's character.

Rosicrucians

The Rosicrucian Order asserts a spiritual linkage to the profound, sometimes secret, teachings of the mystery schools of ancient Egypt and Europe that emphasized self-mastery to gain spiritual results. Rosicrucians believe that the key to gaining the mastery of life lies in your personal power and that the source for all power is found within.

With such mastery, you also attain strength, peace, and wisdom. The Law of Attraction works to help you achieve that mastery when you are attuned to the source. Harmoniously in tune with the universal spiritual laws, such as the Law of Attraction, you draw to you that which you need to further your spiritual unfolding.

To study the Rosicrucian way requires that a person seek truth and possess an open mind, a positive mental outlook, and clear aspirations for spiritual understanding. In other words, positive thinking and clarity of life goals can greatly impact the results you seek.

For those seeking better health, abundant career opportunities, better family relationships, or stepped-up personal growth, the Rosicrucian Order and other spiritual traditions can reveal how to actualize those desires. People can literally reset a new course for their lives once they understand the wisdom of the ways taught by the Rosicrucian Order. The path believers walk is necessarily an inner path into the secrets of the self, and it is the path that mystics have walked for centuries.

The Rosicrucians (*www.rosicrucian.org*) teach that spiritual seekers in their organization will learn about the workings of the natural laws over all realms, discover the interconnectedness of all metaphysical teachings, and increase self-understanding.

Psychics and Shamans

Psychics and shamans have traditionally been people who claim to sense the unseen, see into the future, work with the supernatural in lower or higher realms of existence, or have the ability to influence unseen energies or spirits through spells, incantations, magic, dream work, music, ecstatic trances, and sacred dance. Ancient peoples called psychics and shamans by other names—medicine man/woman, priest/priestess, sorcerer/sorceress, necromancer, and magician, for example—depending upon their particular cultures. Shamans often occupied places of high position within a village or culture.

Whether Aborigine, Asian, or Aztec, such individuals were especially consulted when negative things happened or when something good was needed by individuals or the community. To achieve the manifestation of the greater good, a spell might be cast, a blood-letting undertaken, a sacrifice made, or a dream incubated. The desire was usually coupled with an action to achieve the intended result. For example, the shamans of several Native American tribes did vision quests, performed shamanic healings, sat in sweat lodges, and engaged in sun dances. They chanted incantations to ward off attacks by aggressors. Although they did not label their effort as a purposeful attempt to align with the Law of Attraction, they were trying to accomplish something important through desire, intent, and action, and the Law of Attraction responded. That's not to say that they always got what they wanted. The law, when opposite poles of attraction are set up, responds to the more powerful vibrational pull or yields a weaker or, in some cases, a mixed result. Native Americans performed incantations but were still attacked and lost battles to their powerful enemies whose forces, goals, and intentions proved stronger.

Australian Aborigines

For the Australian Aborigines, alignment with the Law of Attraction was alignment and access to the Dreamtime's energetic realm, where they believed all creation takes place. Australian Aborigines are descended from groups of people who migrated from the Asian continent to settle in Australia. Their tribes have a variety of cultural practices but share a deep reverence and connection to the land. Their view of the world's beginning is known as the Dreamtime, and their shamans or sorcerers place great emphasis on dreams, sand drawings, and music played upon a didjeridoo, among other instruments.

FACT

A. P. Elkin, an Australian anthropologist, called the Aboriginal medicine men of Australia "men of High Degree" in his book *Aboriginal Men of High Degree*, and he admonished against devaluing the importance of their emphasis on psychic power as primitive magic.

The Australian Aborigines did walkabouts to a belonging place—a spiritual place—where they sought access to the Dreamtime. In such practices, they could tap into a great power much as a Law of Attraction practitioner might move into harmonious alignment by undertaking a spiritual journey and a specific meditation practice in order to manifest a desired result.

Asian Shamanism

The ancient peoples of Tibet, Siberia, Laos, and elsewhere practiced shamanism, often within the context of their particular cultural belief system. As intermediaries between the world of matter and spirit, shamans were able to control malevolent spirits by accessing the spirit world to effect healings and interpret dreams. Their special knowledge of the workings of the unseen world—alignment, surely, with the Law of Attraction—empowered them to deal with the invisible spirits or forces of misfortune and bring out the manifestation of peace, health, and positive change for the greater good.

Aztecs

The Aztecs manifested the greatest and most powerful civilization of the Americas in central Mexico during the fourteenth century until being conquered in 1519 by Hernando Cortes, a Spanish conquistador. Poor and despised because of their barbaric cultural practices, the Aztecs aligned themselves with the Law of Attraction through their determination not only to survive but to prosper and become militarily strong. Their legacy of cities, pyramids, a Sun stone calendar, sacrificial platforms, and other architectural creations say much about their accomplishments and in-depth knowledge of mathematics and astronomy—and yet the empire of the Aztecs completely disappeared.

Anthropologists estimate that the Aztecs sacrificed or killed a quarter of a million people, or 1 percent of the population every year. Some Aztecs—soldiers, for example—considered sacrifice to the gods to be an honorable death, just as death in battle, and so they might volunteer to be sacrificed for an important occasion.

Perhaps the element of violence within the Aztec culture through imposition of terror and tribute, ritual human sacrifices to their gods, and emphasis on extreme militarism created a vibration that eventually drew to them the demise of their civilization.

Hermetic Magicians

Magic is known to have existed in the Hellenistic society of the Greeks and Romans, and mention of magic in the Bible suggests that it was known within early Christian societies as well. The word *hermetic* is used to convey relevance to Hermes Trismegistus (known also as the Egyptian god Thoth and the Greek god Hermes) or the writings that have been ascribed to him, including alchemical, theosophical, astrological, and mystical doctrines.

Whether or not an ancient hermetic magician was cognizant of the workings of the Law of Attraction, he was assuredly engaged in practices with resolute intention and desire to draw forth a specific situation, event, or circumstance. Magicians utilized many devices and objects in their spells for good or for curses.

FACT

Dating from Hellenistic times to late antiquity, artifacts included handbooks of papyruses about magic, as well as gems, tablets, figurines used for curses, and amulets. Archeologists have also found Jewish metal amulets, texts of incantations in Aramaic, and magic incantation bowls from Iran and Iraq.

Magic may have emerged out of ancient religions in response to a need for individual empowerment. People needed to deal with cultural and societal pressures, concerns, and anxieties. Some suggest that the practice of magic enabled people during ancient times to have a greater sense of self while simultaneously revitalizing their spiritual and religious beliefs. Magicians were considered powerful individuals in their societies, and some even had followings.

Hermetic magic has been credited as being the forerunner of several magical and mystical orders and medieval alchemy. The hermetic path encompasses eclectic spiritual beliefs and even finds some resonance in pagan Gnosticism. The Masons, the Hermetic Order of the Golden Dawn, and Aleister Crowley's Ordo Templi Orientis (O.T.O.), to name a few orders, all follow the hermetic tradition.

Alchemy to the hermetic alchemists meant change or transformation. They were fascinated by change, and their alchemical symbols, according to psychologist Carl Jung, have been welling up for centuries from the collective unconscious into sensitive souls. Jung spent the later years of his life fascinated by and absorbed in research on alchemy.

Ancient hermetic texts include the *Splendor Solis*, the *Emerald Tablet of Hermes*, and the *Corpus Hermeticum*. The text of the Chinese book on meditation, *The Secret of the Golden Flower*, addresses the process of unfolding toward perfection as "circulation of the light," and it uncannily parallels the ancient writing in the *Emerald Tablet of Hermes* that is paraphrased "as above, so below."

Hermetic alchemists were sometimes thought of as practitioners of black magic because they attempted to turn base metal into gold. They were seeking ways to speed up nature's evolutionary process, as they understood it. Metals were believed to be living things that underwent a process of change to become perfect—in short, to eventually become gold.

Alchemy blurs the lines between science and philosophy, between the magical and the spiritual. But always, in the end, alchemy is about change and transformation. When a person desires to undertake personal growth work, she is in some ways joining the ranks of ancient practitioners of magic or spiritual shamanism, for she holds a deep desire to evolve and attempts to manifest the result through desire, intent, and action. Such transformation can bring a sea change in her relationships with others. As psychologists point out, it only takes one person to shift a paradigm. In relationships, that means that when the individual changes, everyone around that person necessarily has to change too.

CHAPTER 6

The Law of Attraction and Religion

Through the ages, many people have turned to religion to search for wisdom about their life's meaning and purpose. Even the ancients understood that knowledge is equated with power. During the Middle Ages, some who sought spiritual insight joined religious orders where higher learning was accessible. In the last century, seekers increasingly turned to Eastern philosophies. The 1970s witnessed people's use of mind-expanding drugs to enter alternative states of consciousness where they believed the secrets of the universe would be revealed. Today's wisdom-seekers mine ancient traditions, science, and other sources.

Christianity

The Law of Attraction works in the pursuit of spiritual desire just as it does for worldly things. Christianity emphasizes total submission of one's will to the will of God. Christian mystics have understood how the twin engines of faith and belief could merge the spiritual self into alignment and even unity with its Source. Some say that through divine grace, they entered transcendental realms and moved closer to God.

Mystics of all religions have exhibited paranormal powers, gained knowledge, and perceived truth through an inner knowing. That is not to say that all mystical experiences are pleasant. That would be too simplistic a way of defining mysticism. However, the understanding that mystics gain from time they spend in transcendental states has sometimes enabled them to manifest or create from spiritual desires, often to help others. Think about how much money Mother Teresa raised in her life or about the charities founded by Vincent de Paul.

And the serpent said unto the woman, Ye shall not surely die: For God doeth know that in the day ye eat thereof, then your eyes shall be opened, and ye shall be as gods, knowing good and evil.—Genesis 3:4–5

Christians believe that eternal salvation is secured by acceptance of Jesus as the Son of God and the Savior of humankind. Jesus counseled that God knows all the needs of his children. In Matthew 6:33, Jesus says to seek first the Kingdom of God and his righteousness. After that, all else will be added.

Contradicting Christian Beliefs?

Many Christians are divided on whether the Law of Attraction aligns with Christian beliefs. Those who are against the law assert that when people believe they create their lives and everything in them, they diminish or eliminate God as Creator and practice self-deification. In the Garden of Eden, the serpent promised Eve that she could have ultimate knowledge and become godlike. Eve apparently formed a strong desire to have what the serpent promised her, and so she defied God's command not to eat from the tree of the knowledge of good and evil.

Eve ate the apple and offered some of it to her mate Adam. Some people feel strongly that only God creates and that humans who desire the knowledge of universal laws and attempt to call upon the universe to help them manifest or create their lives anew put the universe before God. For some deeply devout Christians, the idea of creating a spiritual or religious life is admirable and credit should be given to the Lord. Others might say that the Lord's ways are mysterious and the Law of Attraction may be a divine mechanism to give people what they want, including drawing spiritually inspired souls closer to Him.

Pursuing Wealth or Poverty

People in religious orders may take a vow of poverty rather than a vow to acquire wealth and material possessions. Poverty has somehow always been equated with deeply held spiritual aspiration, whereas the pursuit of wealth often has been perceived as a selfish desire for things of the flesh instead of the spirit. The Law of Attraction, as you have already learned, is indifferent; it gives you whatever you think and feel you deserve. When you give yourself over to increase in your life, you are giving fuller expression to the abundance of the Divine Intelligence within you. However, if you seek poverty, the Law of Attraction will make it so. Proponents of the Law of Attraction say it is up to you to choose.

Christian advocates for implementation of the Law of Attraction in people's lives say, "God helps those who help themselves." They assert that people possess a powerful tool for creation, the human mind, and to not use it to better their lives and those of others wastes that precious God-given gift.

Jesus and the Law of Attraction

During his years on earth, Jesus exemplified a way of living in harmony with universal laws and in keeping with his divine purpose. Today, his life and words continue to offer hope and direction for suffering souls lost in darkness or weary from their battles in life. When Law of Attraction teachers speak of the power of faith, trust, belief, vision, and declaration, they frequently cite Jesus.

The Mustard Seed

Three of the New Testament gospels—Matthew, Mark, and Luke—attribute to Jesus the comment that the kingdom of heaven is like the least of all seeds, the mustard seed that grows into the greatest of all herbs, a tree with branches to shelter the birds. Likewise, great accomplishments start with intent and small actions. When you nurture the seeds of divinity within, the Law of Attraction makes possible an unfolding of your spiritual consciousness and brings to you or guides you to the means to help yourself and others.

Verily I say unto you, If ye have faith, and doubt not, ye shall not only do this which is done to the fig tree, but also if ye shall say to this mountain, Be thou removed, and be though cast into the sea, it shall be done. And all things, whatsoever ye shall ask in prayer, believing, ye shall receive.
—Matthew 21:21–22

Jesus and the Fig Tree

In the New Testament Gospel of Matthew 21:21, Jesus, hungry, spied a fig tree. Noting only leaves but no fruit upon it, he said, "Let no fruit grow on thee henceforth forever." When his disciples marveled at the speed at which the tree withered, Jesus told them how they, too, could do such things. He explained that what they required was an unwavering faith and unshakable belief. They must not have any doubts that whatever they commanded to happen would occur. By believing that their desires were not only possible but probable, they could do even greater things than making a fig tree barren. They could take down a mountain and move it into the sea simply by the power of faith and belief behind their declaration of desire or intention.

Jesus explained the means by which you can manifest. He said you must have faith, not doubt; clearly state your desire (for example, "Be thou removed"); ask for it; and believe that it will be done.

Jesus' Teachings

The Gospel of Luke contains a passage detailing how Jesus taught his disciples to pray. He said, "Ask, and it shall be given; seek, and ye shall find; knock, and it shall be opened unto you. For every one that asketh receiveth; and he that seeketh findeth; and to him that knocketh it shall be opened." (Luke 11:9–10)

In the Gospel of John, Jesus offers what has come to be known as the Sermon on the Vine and the Branches. A passage within that sermon has Jesus saying, "If ye abide in me, and my words abide in you, ye shall ask what ye will, and it shall be done unto you." (John 15:7)

For God so loved the world, that he gave his only begotten Son, that whosoever believeth in him should not perish, but have everlasting life. For God sent not his Son into the world to condemn the world; but that the world through him might be saved.—John 3:16–17

Living his life in tune with the purpose for which he had been sent to earth, Jesus showed through example how to love all, give much, believe all things are possible when your own power is aligned with God, and pray often with a heart of thankfulness.

In The Secret, Rhonda Byrne and her associates advocate seeking prosperity, abundance, inner joy, and peace and counsel that the job of each person is to decide what she wants. Mystics have always desired to draw nearer to God and to learn how to express His love to others.

That longing for the Divine has found resonance in the lives of Christian saints from the earliest days of the church. Indeed, the manifestation of the Divine in the physical world is represented by the myriad expressions of divine love. Jesus' words in the New Testament's Gospel of John encapsulate the depth of God's love.

Jesus Showed People How to Be Whole

Jesus served as a spiritual beacon—"I am come a light into the world . . . that whosoever believeth in me should not abide in darkness" (John 12:46)—and an exemplar of how the power of God works through the human heart and mind. According to the New Testament Gospels, Jesus performed many miracles that seemingly defied the natural laws of the universe. Among other things, he fed 5,000 people with five loaves of bread and two fishes, exorcised demons, showed a mastery over nature by cursing the fig tree that then withered, raised the dead on three occasions, and healed sick people.

Jesus emphasized having faith in God's power to bring about a particular result. He never told people that his faith had healed them, but rather that their own faith had made them whole. The power of their own minds was key. The Law of Attraction teaches that a clear vision of what you desire to manifest aligned in harmony with the Source, coupled with faith and magnetized by thought, attracts the result.

Catholic Mystics

The mystics strove to develop a closer relationship with God by looking within. They believed that God revealed Himself in ways that were not readily apparent to those who did not know what to look for or were simply unaware.

Teresa of Avila

Teresa of Avila was a medieval Spanish Carmelite nun whose desire for a deeper relationship with God eventually manifested as a result of her longing and effort. Teresa shocked many people, even the most devout, with her ideas about strict reform that included austere poverty, flagellation, and the wearing of sandals instead of shoes, giving rise to the term *discalced* ("unshod") Carmelites. For two years, she was convinced that she was in the physical presence of Christ, although she could not see Him. When she died, she left behind a rich legacy of devotional observations in her writings and her autobiography. Inspired by the Holy Spirit, Teresa yoked her desire to manifest a closer relationship with the Lord with an intention and action, that is, her adherence to a physical life of strictest poverty and renunciation. Aligned in harmony with the Law of Attraction, she got what she wanted and more. In time, she shared her spiritual gifts through her books *Life*, *The Way of Perfection*, and *The Interior Castle*. She became the second of only three women to be named doctors of the Roman Catholic Church.

John of the Cross

Teresa sought help from John of the Cross to bring about reform of the Carmelite Order that involved monks. Like her, John became a mystic. He longed for silence and time for contemplation and got both when he was incarcerated in a jail in Toledo. There, he endured both regular public lashings and isolation. During his incarceration, he wrote poetically about his suffering and love for God. His ideas and writings about the maturation of the soul and the necessity for becoming deeply attached to God would eventually result in the church also recognizing him as a doctor of the church.

Hildegard of Bingen

Yet another Christian mystic, Hildegard of Bingen, who lived several centuries before John of the Cross and Teresa of Avila, experienced visions that started in childhood and continued until her death in a.d. 1179. During medieval times, women didn't keep journals or jot down their spiritual or ecclesiastical ideas, but Hildegard became convinced that she was being instructed by a heavenly voice telling her to record the information she gained during her ecstatic states of consciousness. Hildegard worried that she might be ridiculed by others and was reluctant to do as she was told. Eventually, however, she began dictating to her scribe what her inner visions unveiled for her. She also created musical compositions, a morality play, poetry, and works of art that revealed what she called mysteries and secrets of the Divine. Her body of work earned her high regard in the church.

When Hildegard was forty-two, a blinding light passed through her brain and conferred upon her the ability to know the meaning of religious texts. Her powerful intellect easily grasped an understanding of theology that most likely surpassed the best minds of male clerics of her time. With the blessing of Pope Eugenius, Hildegard produced her famous text, *Scivias* (translated alternately as *Know the Paths* or *Know the Ways of the Lord*). She likened herself to a feather lifted by the breath of God.

FACT

The Catholic Church has conferred the title of Doctor of the Church on only thirty-three individuals. Three are women—Catherine of Siena, Teresa of Avila, and Thérèse of Lisieux. Various popes through the ages have bestowed the title of Doctor upon individuals who have contributed ecclesiastical works that have defended, explained, or expounded upon the beliefs and truths of the faith.

Hildegard perhaps exemplified the Law of Attraction's ages-old idea that "as you think, so you become." Some might say that Hildegard's prodigious works during her lifetime sprang from an inner world in which her thoughts, observations, reflections, and mystical revelation found fecund ground. Her desire to serve the Lord meant following the instructions of a heavenly voice telling her to reveal her knowledge even though her fear of condemnation literally made her ill. Nevertheless, Hildegard worked in tune with her calling and perception of truth—all in alignment with deeply held spiritual beliefs, and the Law of Attraction ensured that her inner contemplative process bore even more fruit. Her desire to serve the Lord meant expressing the knowledge she was being given.

From the interior world where she retreated to pray, meditate, and commune with the Lord, Hildegard brought forth a legacy that included more than 100 letters to religious clerics, seventy-two poems, nine books, and numerous works of art and musical compositions.

Hildegard wrote with insight and understanding about the human body and its illnesses and cures. She asserted that healing could come about through the use of things found in nature such as rocks, trees, animals, herbs, and even stones. Like a scientist, she knew how to attract knowledge of the workings of the natural world through observation. Her intellectual fortitude, some have said, grew stronger upon a foundation of combined comprehension of religion, science, and art. Miraculous healings were attributed to her intercession.

Augustine of Hippo

Augustine of Hippo was endowed with a great mind and oratorical skills, which he used in his service as a bishop in the early Christian church. He wrote, preached, and taught in Roman North Africa during the latter fourth century. He successfully manifested a powerful image of himself as an intellectually vibrant and powerful orator. He made the most of his genetic endowment for intellectual inquiry and oratory and was able to attract the means to further develop them. But Augustine was willful and intensely attached to sensual pleasure, and the Law of Attraction gave him more of that too. He developed a relationship with a young girl who became his concubine for fifteen years. When Augustine deeply desired to overcome the sensual things of life that bound him and kept him from having a more personal relationship with God, he translated his desire into conviction and action. When the law began to fulfill his desire for that experience, he wrote an intensely personal account of his struggle to come to terms with his sensual nature and to know God.

In his book, *Confessions*, Augustine wrote that he came to God too late. He expressed regret that he had thrust himself upon the beautiful things that God had created instead of turning within to seek God, the Creator. According to *Confessions*, it was only after sensing a voice telling him to "take and read," was Augustine compelled to pick up a

Bible where he read and obeyed a passage that instructed him to follow Christ. The Law of Attraction was at work at all times to give Augustine whatever he set his heart upon and felt driven to get—at first, stature as a hedonist and powerful orator; later, as a denunciate of hedonism and devoted follower of Christ.

Hinduism

The Hindu faith is rooted in ancient Vedic philosophy with its inherent ideas of karmic law or the law of retribution—what you sow, you reap; also, what you send out comes back. These ideas dovetail into the Law of Attraction because what you think about most is what you draw into your life experience. Throughout an average day in your life, are you thinking lovingly of the welfare of others or falling into a pattern of criticizing others for everything that makes you unhappy and stressed out? According to the tenets of Hinduism, your thoughts are as powerful as a spoken word. Words, like your actions, are creating your karma, and when the elements are ripe for those words and actions to bear fruit (whether good or bad), they will.

Although Hinduism is considered a polytheistic religion with as many as 33 million gods and goddesses, it teaches that at the core of all living things is Brahman, the one god who is really three gods in one—Brahma (the creator), Vishnu (the sustainer), and Shiva (the destroyer or one who brings about dissolution). Other gods and goddesses are simply manifestations of the One; this concept is summed up as unity of the Godhead.

Hindus achieve enlightenment through attunement to and alignment with the indwelling God. By becoming enlightened, individuals can attain release from the endless cycle of reincarnation, which takes place because of the karma they have created. In their spiritual work and practices, Hindus endeavor to transcend thinking in terms of duality or opposites.

The Law of Attraction principle that good thoughts and actions return good things to the doer while bad thoughts and bad actions bring more negativity and misery is an example of duality thinking. The idea that from one Source all things come and at their core those things are God is another example of the transcendence of duality of thought. One sees unity in the many. The following is a list of beliefs that are common to many Hindu sects.

- There is one Supreme Reality (Brahman) and ultimately all souls will realize it as Truth.
- The reality of human existence is that it is nothing more than a dream in the Divine Mind.
- There are many different paths to the realization of Brahman.
- Karma is created by a person's thoughts, words, and deeds (for good or bad) that cause the soul to reincarnate; reincarnation will continue until a soul's karma is exhausted.
- Ignorance of the innate divine nature of humans and the unity of all things creates dualistic thinking.
- Salvation (*moksha*) comes about in three ways: works, knowledge, and devotion.
- Nirvana is the complete liberation from karma, endless cycles of birth and death, and dualistic thinking.
- Liberation takes place when an individual loses her sense of self that is separate from God and instead becomes completely absorbed into the reality of the Supreme Godhead.

Spiritual well-being for most Hindus comes as a result of living a clean and decent life, observing *ahimsa* or nonviolence, serving their families, performing *dharma* (their worldly duties) and *sadhana* (spiritual practices) in the right way, and showing respect for all life forms as sacred things. Most Hindus are vegetarians. Also, they often place high value on selfless service to others. Respect for elders is culturally ingrained in most Hindus. Mohandas Gandhi, a famous Hindu, once said that we must be the change that we seek in the world. Many Hindus seek to create a better world by first turning to the divine within to change themselves before trying to effect change in the world.

Exercising Power over Nature

Certain Hindu yogis, sages, siddhis, and holy persons through the ages who have committed their lives to the pursuit of truth have purportedly been able to travel through time and space at will, shrink or expand in size, abstain from food and water without damage to their physical bodies, control their heartbeat and breath, effect miracle healings, and instantly produce tangible objects through the power of thought. Some sources say the Law of Attraction finds resonance or has roots in tenets of Hinduism and shares the belief that an underlying unifying force of energy in the cosmos governs all that exists.

Chanting, Prayer, and Devotional Practice

Hindu spiritual practice consists often of daily *puja* or worship at the shrine of the *ishtadeva* (one's chosen deity or form of God). To focus the mind on the spiritual realms and God, the devotee might chant a mantra or the word *Om*, considered to be the cosmic sound of vibration in creation. Similarly, the core of the Law of Attraction might be summed up as thoughts having vibrations and those vibrations attract similar vibrations. To Hindus, even the name by which you are called sets up a vibration for your life.

Scholars have dated the origins of the Hindu religion to roughly 4000 B.C. to 2200 B.C., whereas circa 2500 B.C. has been suggested as the date for the Old Testament story about the flood and Noah's ark.

Doing an Anusthan

To attain a specific spiritual result, a devotee, often with the guidance of a teacher or guru, will undertake a penance or fasting or an anusthan (specific practice often coupled with chanting, visualization, fasting, pilgrimage, or other action). This is not too different from working with the Law of Attraction with clear intent and conviction to manifest a specific result.

Buddhism

During almost any discussion of the Law of Attraction, the wisdom of the enlightened sage Gautama the Buddha (563 to 483 B.C.) is inevitably quoted as proof that the law has survived from ancient times until now. A favorite quote of Buddha, paraphrased here, is that each of us is the result of what we have thought. Another quote states that a person's work in life is to discover his work. Then he is to throw his whole being into doing that work. This advice, though it was offered more than 2,000 years ago, is as true today as it was then and has particular significance for understanding the psychology of the Law of Attraction, say proponents of the law.

Buddhism also says to let go of ego-centeredness. But to release the "I," you first must know the self. Practitioners must strive to understand their interconnectedness or interdependence with others and, in fact, the entire universe. These two positions seem to be opposite: me or us. The polarity must be understood—do you live your life focused purely on yourself or do you live your life aware of your interconnectedness with others and the world?

FACT

The Buddha expounded four noble truths. Suffering exists; put another way, impermanence exists. Attachment to desires or craving is the origin of suffering. When attachment to desire ends, suffering ceases. Freedom from suffering is possible by following the Eightfold Path: right view, right thought, right speech, right action, right livelihood, right effort, right mindfulness, and right contemplation.

Buddhist philosophy aligns beautifully with the Law of Attraction due to its emphasis on perception, thought, speech, and action. Right thought, for example, means to harm no person or thing through negative thought, including yourself, and to avoid desire and cravings and ill will. Instead,

Buddhism emphasizes cultivating thoughts of goodwill, love, joy, and gratitude. Speech should never be critical, harsh, or malevolent; instead, it should be gentle, kind, truthful, and appropriate for time and place. Having a generosity of spirit and gratitude for the blessings you already have are as important in Buddhist practice as they are for deliberately working with the Law of Attraction.

QUESTION?

What is generosity of spirit?
Dana is the word used in Buddhism to mean generosity of spirit. It is perhaps best illustrated in a person's relationship with others in the form of mutual aid, trust, kindness, and commitment. Never to be obligatory, dana carries with it positive karma in spiritual benefits that can stretch over many lifetimes.

The idea of dana or generosity occupied an important place in Buddha's teachings. The act of selfless giving for the welfare of others means giving even more than is required or customary. The Buddha emphasized that attitude toward giving was far more important than the actual gift and, further, that the greater spiritual benefit comes to the poor person who has little but gives much than to the rich person who has much and gives something that is personally insignificant. The Buddha did not abjure the acquisition of wealth; on the contrary, he considered it a source of happiness and peace of mind if the money was gained in a morally just way.

Taoism and Other Eastern Religions

In China, ideas about manifesting emerged in the beliefs of ancient Chinese people who were Taoist. The *Tao Te Ching* (or Great Book of the Way and Virtue) by Lao Tzu states that nothingness named the beginning of the universe and haveness named all objects. The book reveals that a person makes an individual choice to have nothing and know the great wonder of the Tao or to have objects and know abundance. Another passage says that the sage has nothing, yet lives to help others and in so helping grows richer. The sage gains even more abundance by giving to others.

FACT

The date of composition of the *Tao Te Ching* has been disputed, but many sources list 6 B.C. as likely. Lao Tzu, whose name means "Old Master," is widely accepted as the author of the book. He was a Taoist sage who served in the Zhou Dynasty court.

Taoism contains the idea of effortless manifesting. Achieving your goal is not as important as the process that unfolds from the inception of an idea to the completion of the desired result. The miracle is that you can draw to you something you deeply desire out of the chaos, obstacles, and confusion that are all around you every day.

Taoism stresses living life from an open and loving heart space. Be attentive. Be positive. Be happy. Observe the Tao at work. Know what goal or desired object you desire to manifest and let that be the result you aim for, but focus on observing how the Tao operates to make it happen. You don't have to be action-oriented and try to figure out how to get that thing you want. You simply allow for the manifestation to arrive in its own perfect time. The process of its coming to you should be the focus rather than achieving the object, according to practitioners of *wu-wei*, as the art of effortlessly manifesting is known.

QUOTE

He who knows (the Tao) does not (care to) speak (about it); he who is (ever ready to) speak about it does not know it. He (who knows it) will keep his mouth shut . . . blunt his sharp points and unravel the complications.—Lao Tzu, *Tao Te Ching*, 56:1–3

Tao Emphasis on the Yin

Although the Tao acknowledges the importance of male or yang qualities, it emphasizes the female or yin. Female is the polar opposite of male; yin opposes yang. Each person should, according to Lao Tzu, find a balance between yin and yang. When faced with a problem, instead of responding with a knee-jerk aggressive action (yang), remain calm and find power and peace in the stillness. Then you will know the right course to the solution. Your thoughts often propel your body into action as a response to a problematic situation. Use your thoughts and the working of the Law of Attraction to draw to yourself solutions and opportunities by remaining in a quiet mindful (yin) place. That is the way of the Tao. You are neither advancing nor retreating. You are not buffeted about by emotions. Instead, you are anchored at the center of inner strength and power.

To Polarize or Not

Some teachers of the Law of Attraction talk about polarization, an idea that finds resonance in the *Tao Te Ching*. They assert that you can choose to live your life with a focus on none other than yourself (independent) or you can choose to live in a way that understands and accepts your interconnectedness with the whole or everything in the universe (interdependent). To choose the latter requires an understanding and acceptance that you are one part of all things that make up the whole and that all you do affects the others. To choose to polarize either way requires a measured thoughtfulness, a decision, and a commitment to live by your choice for your lifetime. Choosing one pole or the other can strengthen your intent and clarify your work with the Law of Attraction. Of course, you can also choose not to choose.

Shintoism

Shinto literally means "way of the gods" in Japanese. It can trace its roots back to antiquity in animism and nature worship. Practitioners share a deep respect for nature, believing that spirit powers live in nature and natural settings, and thus, they strive to live harmoniously alongside nature and all its creatures. The notion of living in harmony with all other things, respecting and even honoring their sacredness, aligns with the Law of Attraction because such a way of living attracts more harmony, respect, and sacredness into your life.

A primary element of Shintoism is a belief in *kami*, or spiritual presences. Shintoists focus on four main areas: family (because of Shinto's linkage to tradition and the preservation of traditional beliefs and practices), sacredness of nature, bodily cleanliness (baths, mouth-rinsing, and hand-washing are done often), and celebrations to honor the kami. The Shinto considers nature sacred. When the Shintoists honor nature, they may create beautiful gardens and protect the places they consider to be sacred. Their respect and love for the natural world and its inhabitants, through the Law of Attraction, ensures that those special places endure and flourish. Law of Attraction practitioners could take cues from Shinto belief about the sacredness of the earth if they desire to do more for the planet, such as curbing cutting of the rainforests, aiding efforts to reduce toxic waste, working with others to find solutions to global warming, and preserving species of plants and animals.

Judaism and Kabbalah

Kabbalah, the set of ancient mystical beliefs of Biblical Judaism that was once the intellectual domain of only Jewish patriarchs and prophets, is built upon precepts akin to those of the Law of Attraction. Students of Kabbalah claim that the teachings of the Kabbalah and the spiritual work they do enhances their understanding and draws them closer to God. Through the Law of Attraction, their efforts also pull to them other people who stimulate sharing of ideas and insights. Some say that the once-secret teachings may have originated with the Bible's first human—Adam. However, others assert that God gave the wisdom teachings not to Adam but rather to Moses.

The Way of Kabbalah

Kabbalists say that the teachings contain the secrets of the universe as well as the human heart. Right understanding enables people to observe the chaos of the world without becoming entangled in it as well as to maneuver through or remove the minefields of pain and suffering. The stress is upon sharpening the mind to gain clarity of thought. Teachers emphasize that all humans possess the seeds of greatness. Through Kabbalah, those seeds' potential can manifest.

The Kabbalist idea of self-actualization (we are each accountable for ourselves, our thoughts, and our actions) resonates with Christian, Buddhist, and Hindu thinking as well as the Law of Attraction. Kabbalists believe that faith and certainty become stronger when we connect to God's light and draw down the manifestation of good into our lives.

QUESTION?

What texts are helpful in the study of Jewish mysticism?
The Book of Formation (Sefir Yetzirah) elaborates on the ecstatic experience of the divine. The *Book of Splendor* (Zohar) was written in thirteenth-century Spain and expounds upon occult and metaphysical ideas. Along with the Torah and Talmud, these two texts form the basis for the study of Jewish mysticism.

Importance of Mental Certitude

Practitioners of Kabbalah believe that they can lift themselves closer to the light of the divine by respecting and viewing others as equals— seeing no hierarchy in humankind—and by treating others with dignity and loving service. The softening of the heart, possessing certainty of will or mind, coupled with positive action, allows greatness to manifest. This, too, seems like a reiteration of the Law of Attraction.

Rabbis from roughly the seventh to the eighteenth centuries developed the mystical method of Kabbalah to interpret and explain Scripture. Two main ideas of Kabbalah state that all of creation emanates from God and that the soul is eternal. Another important concept is that humankind (the microcosm) mirrors the divine (the macrocosm). Finally, an understanding and use of Kabbalah can enable us to transcend our karma.

Opening Up to the Sacred

When you desire to gain deep spiritual insights, study of such sacred books draws you deeper into the world of ideas of spiritual thinkers and holy people. These are people who may have spent their lives in an intellectual and heartfelt pursuit of the divine. Aligning your mind with those whose ideas appeal to you draws in more sources for similar thought because you are open to seeing such ideas everywhere. Your conversations with others may drift to a particular spiritual concept that confuses you. You may pick up a book that elucidates a concept or philosophy perfectly. The Law of Attraction is at work at all times to help you find myriad sources to fulfill your desire for more knowledge, insights, and understanding when you feel passionate about a topic.

Since ancient times, rabbis and students of Kabbalah have turned to the symbolism of numbers, images, colors, and words to decipher and explain the ecstatic experience of God. One important and necessary image for the study of Kabbalah is the Tree of Life with its ten orbs and twenty-two paths.

FACT

The word *Kabbalah* means "to receive, to accept." Many translators attribute the meaning "tradition" to the term. Some sources say the Kabbalah, which offers an esoteric interpretation of the Scriptures, was given with the Torah, but whereas the Torah was meant for the masses, the Kabbalah was intended for the holiest ones who then orally passed on its secrets to Jewish mystics.

Ecstatic Kabbalah

There are different paths for the study of Kabbalah. The path known as Ecstatic Kabbalah emphasizes recitation of divine names or combinations of the pure forms of the letters of the Hebrew alphabet. The iteration or chanting of divine names, fueled by a noble desire to attain greater understanding and insights into the divine, causes loftier spiritual thoughts and thus sets up a corresponding attraction with the universal

Law of Attraction to draw to the Kabbalist an expansion of consciousness, perhaps even a state of ecstasy.

New Age

New Age philosophy, according to some people, is nothing less than a religion. Others say it lacks the attributes of other established world religions, most of which have some type of dogma or creed, traditions, and specific teachings that bind believers together. New Age thinking, in comparison, stresses an individualistic approach to spirituality that includes an eclectic melding of religious, scientific, self-help, psychological, and ecological ideas, among others. Although experts on the Law of Attraction say the principle of the law is ancient, the popular use of that universal law fits well within New Age thought and its emphasis on the connection between the body, mind, and spirit.

The Human Potential Movement, popular in the 1970s, was a New Age movement that emphasized the notion that humans possessed infinite potential and were limited only by negative thoughts or traditional beliefs. The main goal in the Human Potential Movement was to replace a negative mindset with positive thinking. Today, that goal encapsulates the idea of how to best work with the Law of Attraction to be all that you can be and to have abundance.

One of the most controversial and popular programs to emerge out of the New Age Human Potential Movement was est (Erhard Seminars Training). Founder Werner Erhard advocated est as a way for people to undergo personal transformation and attain empowerment. People were taught to take responsibility for their lives and what they were manifesting, good and bad. Erhard reportedly gave credit to his study of Zen Buddhism to create the space in which the concept of est was to emerge.

Magick

Pagan magick is a religion to many. A report by the *Chicago Tribune* stated that Neo-Paganism is one of the fastest-growing religions in the

United States today. The Wicca religion is a form of pagan witchcraft that espouses belief in a Goddess and God, dual but complementary polarities, and is based in nature. It is difficult to estimate the number of Wiccans or Neo-Pagans because many are solitary practitioners. Some, however, do band together to practice their rites. Their spells often utilize special magickal tools to manifest the desires of an individual or group.

QUESTION?

What is *theurgy* and what is its relevance to manifestation?
Theurgy was a system of magic based on the belief that practitioners would be aided by the gods with whom they communicated. Platonists (followers of the Greek philosopher Plato), for example, believed that physical objects were merely representations of unchanging ideas. They thought it possible to communicate with the gods and to receive divine help in manifesting.

Magick has its origins in the ancient world, but modern experts on the Law of Attraction say the law itself is nothing less than magick. Perhaps you could find the pot of gold at the rainbow's end or be like King Midas of Greek mythology and turn everything you touch into gold by working with the law. However, skeptics might ask why the medieval alchemists, who were using all the knowledge about magick available to them, were unable to produce gold out of base metals. Was it really that their belief was not strong enough? Did they not have faith? Did they not magnetize their thoughts enough?

Such questions seldom faze proponents of the Law of Attraction. If you want gold, some proponents of the law suggest writing a blank check for a certain amount of money and signing it *The Universe*, *Keeper of the Universe's Storehouse*, or *God(dess) of Abundance*, for example, and to expect it to manifest. Working along with the Law of Attraction for wealth, you might try to express enthusiastic optimism while thinking positive thoughts about the money coming and have faith that financial prosperity is going to manifest in your life by the power of your thought even if you can do nothing else.

Origins of Magick

If you were to attempt to trace the lineage of magicians back in time, you would most likely discover stories about the Magi, the Assyrian-Babylonian learned men and high priests of what was once a Mesopotamian tribe. In ancient times, magick and religion were co-mingled Zarathustra, who lived circa 600 b.c. in what is now known as Iran, for example, is considered the father of magick in ancient history. The Greeks knew him as Zoroaster and the religion by which he was associated as Zoroastrianism.

FACT

Shamanism possibly had primitive beginnings among the ancient Egyptians, who believed in nature magic and fiercely protected their wisdom traditions relating to such. In Iraq and Iran, archeologists found earthenware vessels (Babylonian demon bowls) featuring nature motifs that may have been used to cast spells or trap or protect against demons in nature.

Egyptian magic utilized the power of names. To name something was to have the ability to claim its power or exercise some authority over it. They held dreams to be communication from the gods, believed in dream incubation, and even understood how to place an order for a dream. Mummification involved both a religious practice and rituals of magic. Modern practitioners of the law say you can use the Law of Attraction's power to draw to you something you desire by naming it, declaring and writing its name often, affirming your desire to have it, and expressing gratitude that you know it is on its way to you in this moment.

The polytheistic Egyptian magicians participated in spell-casting and loved talismans and sacred objects. Because their priests were the keepers of ancient wisdom and the only ones who could be magicians, they were reluctant to share such knowledge with others. Perhaps they understood the Law of Attraction, because under the pharaohs, Egypt experienced increase—at least for a while.

Celts

The ancient Celts of Wales, Ireland, Scotland, and parts of Western Europe perceived magic everywhere and in everything. Celtic Wiccans worshipped the earth mother and the horned god. They shared a deep reverence for the earth, believed in faeries, elves, and gnomes, and often invoked in their spells the four elements of nature (air, earth, fire, and water). The Celts willfully suspended disbelief and saw magic manifested in their daily lives. Scholar, poet, and philosopher John O'Donohue noted in his book *Anam Cara: A Book of Celtic Wisdom* that the Celtic people in the west of Ireland had legends and stories in which there were bridges between the visible and invisible worlds. For example, the locals might not cut down a bush in a field for generations because they knew the faeries had long ago built a fort in that place. Their prevailing thoughts came about through a strong and powerful tradition and undoubtedly brought, by means of the Law of Attraction, incidences and manifestations that further enhanced and deepened their magical beliefs.

Carl Gustav Jung, the Swiss psychiatrist, writer, and student of Sigmund Freud, studied magick and alchemy, presumably for insights into human psychology. Likewise, the prolific English writer Aleister Crowley, a contemporary of Jung, studied astrology, the occult, and sex magick and was a member of a number of secret societies.

Modern Magick

Long before the Gaia Hypothesis and the modern philosophy of integrative medicine, with its emphasis on the mind/body connection, Paracelsus, a sixteenth-century alchemist, astrologer, and occultist, proposed a radical idea for his time. He asserted that the natural world was a living organism that expressed the One Life. Further, he postulated that humankind and the universe, in essence, were one and that a magnetic attraction existed between each part of the human and the corresponding part in nature.

Health depended upon a harmony between man and nature. Paracelsus wrote his ideas in a treatise, *Doctrine of Signatures*. He did not think of himself as a magician, although others did.

Just as medieval alchemy blurred the lines between magic, religion, and science, the boundaries between modern magick and religion also are blurred. A student of modern magick may learn about not only rituals, gems, spells, symbols, Hebrew letters, Kabbalah, occultism, and alchemy, but must also understand the power of declarations, incantations, and intention.

Modern magick, like the magic of the ancients, represents a spiritual path for some seeking wisdom and higher truths. Getting specific results involves utilizing the power of one's thoughts, words, and deeds, something it shares with the Law of Attraction.

CHAPTER 7

The Law of Attraction in Popular Culture

When Oprah Winfrey, the popular television personality and radio host who can turn almost anything into an overnight sensation, featured Rhonda Byrne on her show, millions of viewers and listeners took notice of Byrne's book and DVD, *The Secret*. Follow-up shows with other guests discussing the pros and cons of the Law of Attraction generated even more interest. Suddenly and unabashedly, publishers, music industry executives, film producers, and others were creating products to appease the public's seemingly insatiable appetite.

Various Names for the Law of Attraction

Various authors of articles and books on the Law of Attraction mention the fact that in the early part of the twentieth century, a dozen or so books were published about the subject. Such texts make note that the law in times past has been called by various names, including the law of affinity, the law of abundant return, mind over matter, the power of positive thinking, the law of harmonious vibration, and the law of attraction in the thought world (the last is also the title of a book written by William Walker Atkinson).

The Secret is perhaps the best-known name for the concept. Certainly, marketers of products to the modern consumer understand that the packaging of any product can contribute to its success or failure. Byrne's mindset of "I can achieve anything" was also a likely factor in the phenomenal success of her book about the law of attraction. Her personal story of going from deep despair to the pinnacle of success just by implementing the Law of Attraction in her life meshes with America's love for rags-to-riches stories. The premise that there exists an affinity and causal relationship between people's thoughts and what manifests in their lives is an easy concept for nearly everyone to grasp.

Treatment in Literature and Film

The Law of Attraction is everywhere in books and film. To find works of fiction about manifesting a new reality through the power of thought doesn't take much effort.

Literary Fiction and the Law of Attraction

Revisit some favorite classics such as *Alice's Adventures in Wonderland*, written in 1865 by Lewis Carroll. The story is about a girl named Alice who imagined a new reality as she slipped down a rabbit hole. She repeated the words "curiouser and curiouser" as she descended. She met intriguing characters, including the White Rabbit, Queen of Hearts, Cheshire Cat, March Hare, Dormouse, and Mock Turtle, among others.

Alice's journey was an adventure that coupled magical thinking with wonder and marvel, bringing her a glorious fantasy experience.

Other authors have created works to show how the mind can create alternate realities, attracting fantastic characters. Consider, for example, *The Wonderful Wizard of Oz*, written by L. Frank Baum in 1900. Young Dorothy was transported from Aunt Em's farm in Kansas to the Land of Oz. En route, she met the Tin Man, the Scarecrow, the Cowardly Lion, the Munchkins, the Good Witch Glenda, the Wicked Witch of the West, and, of course, the Wizard. The story has been studied by scholars as an allegory for 1890s America and the political, social, and economic themes and circumstances. However, the tale could be considered an example of how the mind, given free rein, creates imaginatively and draws to itself even more fantastical ideas through the Law of Attraction.

FACT

Law of Attraction teachers advise that people can envision themselves in a movie of their own making, daring to imagine a different life than the one they are living. Using Law of Attraction strategies for deliberate manifestation, they can then draw in the opportunities and means for starting anew.

Yet another work of fiction is *A Wrinkle in Time*, written by Madeleine L'Engle. The book features Meg Murry, her brother Charles, their friend Calvin O'Keefe, and three transcendental beings known as Mrs. Whatsit, Mrs. Who, and Mrs. Which. The book, considered science fantasy and one of the first during its time to feature a female protagonist in that type of book, seemed doomed to remain unpublished. L'Engle said she received rejections of the manuscript from twenty-six publishers. Holding on to her dream of seeing the book in print, L'Engle finally gave it to John Farrar, who agreed to publish it. The book garnered wide acclaim, received several awards, and has been continuously in print since it was first published in 1962. Such was the result of the power of L'Engle's belief in herself and in the work.

Film and the Law of Attraction

The film industry, too, has produced dozens of movies in which the protagonist uses the power of positive thinking to conceive and manifest a new reality. In fact, in film school, screenwriters learn to take characters out of their lives or their familiar world into a new world. Their journey into the new world begins when something radically changes the story direction, often brought about through the power of the character's own thought or action—the Law of Attraction at work in facilitating a character's desire for a new beginning.

Proper phrasing makes a desire more attainable. If you were an aspiring writer, your affirmation might go something like, "I am in the process of becoming a successful writer because I am creating more compelling and believable scenes for my play every day." This imprints upon the conscious and subconscious mind that the individual is already working toward the result.

Peter Pan, adapted from the 1904 play by J. M. Barrie, features Wendy Darling and her brothers John and Michael, who learn to fly to a magical place called Neverland. They are helped along in their journey by Peter Pan, who refuses to ever grow up, and his little friend Tinkerbell.

Tom Hanks's character in Big is a boy who, by making a wish before a magic wish machine, awakens the next morning in an adult body. In *Thelma and Louise*, the women finally find freedom on a road trip through their resolve and desire to radically change things in their lives. Shine, a movie based on a true story about Australian pianist prodigy David Helfgott, showed how indomitable the human mind can be when it has suffered tragically but determines to prevail. The protagonist, though suffering a breakdown, returned to play in concert halls again. In *Under the Tuscan Sun*, the protagonist, recently divorced and deeply depressed, took a trip to Tuscany. Her decision to buy a house and to have a different life set the Law of Attraction in motion to not only bring her a new life but new love and success in her writing career.

Citizen Kane, the American classic based on the life of William Randolph Hearst, tells the story of Charles Foster Kane's rise to power and his accumulation of unimaginable wealth after being sent away by his beloved mother when he was a child. The film mirrored the life of the wealthy media magnate Hearst, who had grown up believing that he could have anything. *Citizen Kane* showed that the Law of Attraction brings abundance when one desires it, but if one is overwhelmed by feelings of lack, regret, remorse, and spiritual bankruptcy, the law brings more of those. In the film, the multimillionaire ends up unhappy and alone, living an isolated existence in his castle surrounded by priceless possessions. These do not, however, fill the emptiness in his life that he brought on by his own domineering personality and ruthless use of power.

The romantic comedy *Laws of Attraction*, starring Pierce Brosnan and Julianne Moore, pitted two people at opposite poles before the Law of Attraction brought them together. Two hotshot New York divorce lawyers—who have seen the worst possible situations in which couples battle it out in divorce court—try to outfox, outthink, and outmaneuver each other. The case takes the lawyers from a courtroom to Ireland, where they attend an Irish festival, drink too much, and end up married to each other. Does their marriage end in the courtroom like so many others or will it last? The premise that one divorce lawyer could be attracted to another is the Law of Attraction at work: like attracts like and a happy ending seems assured.

Nonfiction and the Law of Attraction

In the area of nonfiction books, readers interested in the Law of Attraction are rediscovering authors who lived in the nineteenth and twentieth centuries and contributed knowledge and works in the New Thought Movement, especially books incorporating a success strategy that we now call the Law of Attraction. Notable among them are James Allen, William Walker Atkinson, Mildred Mann, and Napoleon Hill.

James Allen apparently found inspiration and insight in one verse and used it to title his book, *As a Man Thinketh*. The work was published in 1902, and in it Allen asserted that humans attract into their lives the circumstances that provide for what their souls secretly long for or fear.

Believing that Allen's premise was right, William Walker Atkinson elaborated upon it and expounded some of his own theories in a book titled *Thought Vibration or the Law of Attraction in the Thought World*. The work, published in 1906, became a cornerstone of the New Thought Movement and included ideas on transmuting negative thoughts and patterns, utilizing emotional psychology, and developing immunity to harmful thought attractions.

Mildred Mann contributed to the New Thought Movement through her active participation, metaphysical teachings, and writings. Her book *How to Find Your Real Self* asserted that humans are not here by accident and that every life has meaning, purpose, and value. Mann believed we are the cause and effect of all that happens to us. She outlined steps for manifesting, including having desire, deciding on what you want, asking for it, believing it is yours, working for it, expressing gratitude, and being expectant that you will get it.

There is nothing, absolutely nothing, that has ever happened to you or to me or to any other human being in this world, except that we have consciously or unconsciously brought it to pass, be it good or bad. There is no sense blaming the other fellow . . . he was merely an instrument, brought to you by the Law which you set in motion.—Mildred Mann, *How to Find Your Real Self*

Modern Media Images

It's no secret that television and radio advertisers rely heavily on Law of Attraction messages to sell memberships in organizations that promise healthier food choices, well-being and good physical conditioning, great retirement living with all the amenities, and safety and security in certain wealth investment plans. The emphasis for many of the media messages seems to be "Other smart Americans are doing this; shouldn't you?" Such advertisers, using the "like attracts like" philosophy, tell you that they have what others want. You are in the demographic the advertiser is targeting. Notice in the commercials how the actors targeting people like you are in your age range (or appear to be). They need to look as much like someone your age as they can, otherwise their message will seem to be directed at a different audience.

FACT

Experts on the Law of Attraction say giving thanks for what you have and desire to manifest is vital to successfully working with the Law of Attraction. In his groundbreaking book *The Hidden Messages in Water*, Dr. Masaru Emoto noted that exceptionally beautiful frozen water crystals were produced when the words *love* and *gratitude* were spoken together. View images of his work at *www.life-enthusiast.com/twilight /research_emoto.htm*.

Buzzwords and phrases such as "intentional thought," "thoughts are things," "energy goes where attention flows," and "believe and make it so" now have become part of the pop-culture vernacular. This might be due in part because Law of Attraction teachers such as Joe Vitale, George Pratt, Bob Proctor, Reverend Michael Beckwith, and Jack Canfield have been beamed into living rooms around the world while doing television and radio appearances in which they promoted *The Secret* and shared their insights and words expressing the language of the Law of Attraction.

Popular talk show hosts such as Larry King, Montel Williams, Ellen DeGeneres, and Oprah Winfrey have given plenty of airtime to the subject of the Law of Attraction. Newspaper and magazine journalists, bloggers, and e-zine writers have also done their part. Who in America doesn't want what the law promises—anything that a heart desires? Viewers are told that everything—love, prosperity, the big house, the fast car, and unbelievable wealth—can be theirs and that success in every endeavor and abundance of every kind is possible if they know the secret and work with the Law of Attraction.

But what about achieving a lasting world peace, ridding the world of scourges such as HIV/AIDS, and feeding the hungry? Those concerns don't get as much play as the desire for middle-class worldly luxuries. Still, Law of Attraction teachers say that all things are possible when people align their feelings, thoughts, and actions. The Law of Attraction responds to the more intense vibration created when people unite their minds and hearts toward a common vision and purpose and work together to achieve it.

Cottage Industry

The groundswell of support for *The Secret* and other books like it has spawned a cottage industry of products and intellectual offerings about the Law of Attraction and spiritual laws for success, not only in the physical world but also in cyberspace. You can choose from a plethora of books to read and motivational recordings to listen to. There are seminars, lectures, and conferences to attend, with some sessions being held on cruise ships or at exotic travel destinations.

You can also order pamphlets, subscribe to newsletter mailing lists, listen to the soundtracks of radio and TV talk shows featuring experts on the law, purchase empowerment tapes, or read postings on blogs. For those who really need help in sifting their thought energy, there are personal life coaches, facilitators, and trainers more than willing to help—for a price, of course.

New Age Centers

People who share common New Age interests often form groups with other like-minded individuals. Internet sites listing such organizations sharing common interests in everything from astrology and metaphysical and esoteric topics to New Age healing practices, music, art, literature, the environment, and other topics are proliferating on the World Wide Web. You can find Usenet groups for virtually any subject in which you are interested and read or post information or participate in discussions with people the world over.

Self Help

If the Law of Attraction failed to bring individuals the empowerment they sought, people would most likely not continue to spend money on self-help workshops, books, tapes, CDs, conferences, and videos. Self-help giants like Anthony (Tony) Robbins, Oprah Winfrey, Dr. Phil McGraw, and others have helped thousands of people with their optimism, motivational insights, and self-help advice.

Dating/Relationship Connection

Cyberspace dating sites and real-world matchmaking services are capitalizing on the principles of the Law of Attraction by facilitating the introduction of people who desire to attract potential dating partners or matches. From eHarmony.com and Match.com to dozens of other Internet sites, online dating is hugely popular, drawing about 40 percent of single Americans.

Music and Magnification

Music that aids in deliberately working with the Law of Attraction has proven to be a useful tool for many. Consequently, it's possible to find a plethora of offerings in different musical genres, all intended to aid practitioners of the law. CDs of songs with upbeat lyrics to motivate and inspire the achievement of dreams and goals can be found alongside works created to accomplish healing through sound and soothing accompaniment, regardless of where a practitioner may be in his journey.

There are not more than five musical notes, yet the combinations of these five give rise to more melodies than can ever be heard. There are not more than five primary colors (blue, yellow, red, white, and black), yet in combination they produce more hues than can ever be seen.—Sun Tzu, *The Art of War*

Law of Attraction teachers say that clarity of mind is of paramount importance in the process of manifesting desires. When a person's mind is restless, it will lack calm and focus. Listening to beautiful music can lift the vibration of the spirit. Some teachers assert that because music is itself a vibration, it shifts mood at a cellular level and helps redirect the mind into a singular focus. Further, when music is used as part of a visualization process for manifesting, it can help magnify desire and intention.

The conscious mind worries about the future or dwells on the past, while the subconscious mind is always anchored in the present. Music can draw conscious thoughts away from thinking about the past and future back to the present. The conscious and subconscious parts of the mind can be in harmonious alignment when listening to and emotionally feeling beautiful music. That, according to the law teachers, is the optimal state for establishing the clear desire and intention to manifest. Doctors who work in integrative medicine with emphasis on the mind/body connection say music is also healing.

FACT

Andrew Weil, M.D., a pioneer in integrative medicine, is the author of numerous books, publishes the monthly *Self Help* newsletter, and maintains a website that offers medical advice and insights on everything from using integrative approaches to deal with disease to aging well, staying on track with health goals, and keeping the mind sharp. Visit *www.drweil.com for more information.*

Sites on the Internet offer musical suggestions of songs in pop culture that offer hope that humankind will triumph over adversity, gain clarity of vision over the fog of confusion, meet the challenges of life with success, find meaning and abundance in simple things, and restore optimism and light where negativity and darkness have prevailed. Other sites tout the bubbling optimism found in strains of ethnic music as the means to change emotional attitudes and thinking styles.

Popularity of Optimistic Thinking

Optimistic thinking has entered mainstream society. Oprah, Dr. Phil, and other self-help advocates and many Law of Attraction teachers advise getting to the bottom of negative moods because negativity hurts a person's efforts toward achieving life goals. The subconscious mind may be sabotaging any and all efforts to improve. The experts say past issues such as old hurts and resentments must be dealt with so they don't hold an individual back. Further, they assert that people have to move beyond the blame game. Some teachers of the Law of Attraction suggest that an individual can shift her relationship paradigms by letting go of anger, disappointment, and the desire to get even. They say change can happen in three steps: Forgive, forget, and move on.

Desire, according to some Law of Attraction teachers, begins the process of manifestation; a declaration of intent gets the ball rolling, and optimistic thinking sustains it. They advise that an optimistic attitude is the best way to work with the universal law, and they advocate cultivating an abiding sense of optimism to achieve success. Some assert that it is nearly impossible to experience the awe and wonder of life when you are in a bad mood, and say it is paramount not to allow situations or other people to steal one's joy.

Optimists and pessimists see life differently. Take, for example, the proverbial example of a glass of water. The optimist will see the glass half full while the pessimist will see it half empty. The pessimist anticipates the worst. He doesn't want to raise his hopes and be disappointed, and he usually isn't. But the optimist's expectation of good becomes a self-fulfilling prophecy.

The bookstores in the physical world and also in cyberspace offer texts galore on the subject of optimism and happiness as well as optimism's role as an agent in manifesting everything from deeper spiritual experiences to great sex, love, financial security, and happiness.

Law of Attraction practitioners and teachers ask why anyone would want to continue living with old, habitual negative ideas. They advocate drawing in the good things in life by getting rid of mental clutter and outmoded ways of thinking. Learn to open your mind, heart, and life to receive the good things you desire and deserve.

Find People Who Share Your Interest

Increasingly, virtual meeting sites are being established on the Internet for optimistic people to share interests. One such site is Meetup.com at *www.meetup.com*. It provides tools to help people organize meetings around their interests. There are plenty of sites for people who desire to connect with others to put the Law of Attraction to work in their lives. People can find support in banding together with like-minded locals in their regions or communities. Sharing ideas and feedback with others can reinforce individual effort and make it easier to stay positive.

FACT

Some religious traditions teach that humans are spiritual beings in physical bodies. The spirit is eternally happy. However, the human body conceals the innate happiness of the spirit; the mind constantly seeks to experience that happiness. At the moment of peak happiness, thinking stops (at least momentarily). In a moment of happiness, the ego is silenced and thoughts yield to inner peace and warm and joyful feelings.

People who want to try working with the Law of Attraction might look around at causes within popular culture to find one that most interests them. People are able to make a difference with other like-minded individuals by coming together to manifest results through their commonly held desire, intent, optimism, and mutual attraction to the cause's ideals.

CHAPTER 8

Implementing the Law of Attraction

Perhaps you are someone who likes to start projects on a small scale, see some results, and then go for ever bigger results, sort of like the kid who sticks a toe in the shallow end of the pool and moves gradually into the water until she's comfortable enough to start diving off the deep end. This chapter is designed to help you get started working with the Law of Attraction, but the choice is yours to move as slowly or as quickly as you want.

Know What You Really Want

If you like to shop, you will love the first step in the Law of Attraction, which is to decide on what you want. How do you decide? Close your eyes and think of something that you either want or need that would make you incredibly happy. Set aside your doubt and pretend for a moment that anything you want is possible. If doubt floods your mind, start small and continue taking baby steps in your manifesting efforts until you have proven to yourself how easy it is.

Is what you want to manifest an object, such as a new lipstick, a paella pan, or a fountain for your garden? Is it a situation you'd like to bring about, such as improving your health, securing a promotion, or mastering a tennis serve? Is it something you want to do for the world, such as write a book, establish a business, or create a masterful work of art?

QUESTION?

What if I don't deserve the thing I want?
If you deny yourself permission to have the object of your desire, you will block its arrival. Reasons you might deny yourself permission include feeling that you don't deserve it or your income doesn't support the purchase or thinking that someone else is more deserving.

It's best to develop a crystal-clear idea of the object of your desire and stick with it. Indecisiveness may render you some wild variant of what you really want. Consider the following example.

Lena, a young advertising executive, spotted a beautiful pair of Stuart Weitzman heels while shopping for a wedding present for a friend. The shoes came in several colors, and the blue color perfectly matched the dress she planned to wear to the wedding. But Lena fell in love with the pair of red heels. The shoes were quite expensive and her credit card was maxed out. To buy the red shoes meant she would also have to purchase a new dress. Every time Lena visualized those heels on her feet, the color changed—red, blue, red. Finally, a wealthy older friend cleaned her closets and gave Lena a bag of shoes containing the Stuart Weitzman heels she had wanted—in purple.

Since Lena could not be certain about shoe color, she got a color she didn't want—or did she? The universe may have simply been giving her the shoes she had wanted in her favorite colors, red and blue. Mix them together, and you create the color purple.

Shopping in the Storehouse of the Universe

Think of how much you enjoy browsing through the pictures in your favorite catalogs, spending a day at the outlet stores, or whiling away an hour or two at a Costco or Sam's Club warehouse. Now consider all the offerings of every store, merchant, or collective. Remember, you are shopping in the warehouse of the universe. The promise of the law is that if you can imagine and desire something clearly enough, using high levels of creative energy, you can swiftly attract it.

Perhaps you already have something in mind to bring into your life experience. The following is an example of how one young woman saw what she wanted and used six steps to deliberately work with the Law of Attraction. Lupe had grown up poor in Puerto Rico and found work in New York. While she dreamed of having many things, mostly basic necessities, she also longed to have a diamond-studded watch like one she'd seen an actress wear in a movie.

Lupe had little discretionary income, but on the streets of New York almost anything could be had and the price was always negotiable. She soon discovered that there were many fake brand-name items, including watches, from which to choose. Separated from her family and alone as the Christmas holiday approached, she decided to purchase a watch from the street.

Step One: Desire

What you fervently desire is sure to manifest when you give yourself permission to have it, think about it often and with feeling, consider ways to acquire it, and set in motion the acquisition of it through your intent.

Lupe purchased the fake with an abiding hope that one day she would get the real thing.

Step Two: Intent

When you desire something deeply and form an intention to acquire it, you will begin to turn over in your mind ways that you might have the object of your desire. Intent to have something usually triggers strong emotional feelings such as excitement and happiness. You feel motivated to work for it. Although her new watch was a designer knockoff, Lupe wore it with pride. She just knew that someday she would own the real thing. She intended to have it even if she had to work extra shifts. She vowed to work hard to make getting the watch a probability instead of a possibility. She imagined herself as the star of her own movie, wearing it.

Step Three: Belief in Attainment

When desire is coupled with intent and motivation, you begin to believe that you can attain the object you desire. When the fake watch broke, Lupe stopped wearing it. Instead, she kept the watch displayed on the bathroom windowsill in her one-room apartment. She never told herself, "I can't afford a real diamond watch"; instead, she allowed her mind to wrap around the happiness and pride she would feel when she would finally wear the real thing.

Be ready to receive. Sometimes that means making space in your life, your home, your business, or your jewelry box for the object of your desire. Always be prepared for your desire to come to you.

Step Four: Positive Attitude

Belief that you can have your desire must be sustained because there surely will be a period between dreaming of having it and the physical manifestation of it in your life. Seldom are manifestations instantaneous. In Lupe's life, several years came and went. Yet she never gave up hope that in the right time and the right way, her watch would arrive. She believed that it was already en route to her, as if she had paid for it and it was simply a matter of waiting until it showed up. She never questioned how or when, but just kept her faith and saved her pennies.

Step Five: Gratitude

Intensify your efforts of deliberately working with the Law of Attraction by feeling and expressing your thankfulness at what you already have. Feel gratitude for the power that is working to bring you the object you fervently desire. In Lupe's case, she became a little sidetracked. Love and marriage came into her life. She and her husband moved into a new, slightly larger place as her husband anticipated taking over his father's jewelry business. Lupe finally put the broken watch away in a dresser drawer. Each day as she walked to work, she spent the time thanking God for her many blessings—her new husband, their deep love for each other, and their small but darling apartment only a few blocks from her work. Though there were many things she and her husband needed, she felt grateful for what they already had. She had a list of needs. The watch remained on her list of wants.

Step Six: Receive

From time to time, Lupe took her broken watch from the drawer to look at it. She didn't buy a new cheap watch or another fake. She trusted that when the time was right, her dream watch would arrive.

On the morning of their second wedding anniversary, her husband gave her a red box. Inside was a diamond-encrusted watch by Cartier. It wasn't one of the newest designs, but it had been in his father's store for several years as if waiting for just the right person to claim it. At first glance, Lupe immediately recognized the watch she had been visualizing since the first time she'd seen it at the movies. Through tears of joy, she told her husband that his gift was perfect, just what she had always wanted.

Clarity of Intention

Clarity of intention brings faster and stronger results. Don't engage in wishful thinking and then forget about what you wanted. Be clear about your intention to have exactly what you want. Hold in your mind the image of your desired object. See the colors, the detailing, the size, the weight, the opacity or clarity, and even the time frame in which you want it in your life. Do whatever you can to mentally see it in its totality. Think of all the ways it might arrive in your possession, how you will enjoy it and use it. Know with certitude that it is already in the universe on its way. Lupe knew precisely what she wanted. Lena, in the earlier example, couldn't decide on the exact color.

QUESTION?

How can intent become energized to achieve greater personal success?
When your thoughts, emotion, and intention are aligned 100 percent on achieving the optimal outcome, you will achieve greater success. Conversely, when you slide into a place of lower expectation and dilute the intention to have the best, then you may fail to achieve your desired goal.

If you don't like what you are attracting to yourself (negative friends, undesirable business situations or clients, loser boyfriends, and the like), change your energy. Clarify your intention to send out different vibrations and watch how the Law of Attraction will begin to bring you new friends, fantastic business associates and opportunities, even possibly a new romantic partner with the qualities and moral values you desire.

Energize Your Intention

One way to energize intentional thought is by mapping out an action or to-do list. Think about some of the things you might do to set up a powerful magnetic attraction, drawing to you the object of your desire. Clean the garage, for example, to make possible a space to park that new sports car you want. Throw a party and invite single people; ask everyone to bring a friend. Who knows—that new romantic partner you desire might just show up.

Thoughts become more powerful when they are magnetized by your emotion. Intent becomes energized through repetitious thinking of the same thoughts and by clarity of focus. It's also important to know your reasons for wanting something. Usually, it will have to do, in part, with how it makes you feel. Dare to dream larger than life itself.

FACT

In *The Fabric of Reality*, David Deutsch wrote that the veracity of the external reality of a dream within your mind cannot be disproved. Perhaps all humans are collectively dreaming this dream of existence or are merely actors playing roles in the dream of Divine Mind that spun itself outward from the one into myriad forms and beings.

By allowing your thoughts to frequently visit your desire and by opening your heart to feel the positive emotions of joy and happiness, you are supporting your intention and strengthening the pull of the Law of Attraction. You are drawing toward you that which is already in infinite potentiality. But it bears repeating here that you must be vigilant about your thoughts. Negative situations, people, and objects drift into your life when you worry, are afraid, and feel stressful. But when you are happy, are grateful, and feel empowered, more good things manifest.

Express Desire in the Right Language

When you are asked about your desire, if you say, "I want to stop dating losers," you are putting yourself in position to continue attracting them. *Loser* is an emotionally potent word for people. It's so negative that it is the strongest word in that sentence. Find other words and phrasing to express your desire for a healthy relationship with an emotionally mature individual who is right for you. Think carefully about how you are asking for things. Instead of saying, "I need to get out of this lousy job," try saying instead, "I am manifesting meaningful work in my field of _____ that pays three times my current salary of _____, and I'll be working in that position by _____."

According to teachers of the Law of Attraction, when you form a strong intentional desire, you shake up the status quo. Even if you aren't doing things to fulfill your desire, you have initiated a shift in your thinking. That, in turn, sets up a new vibration that opens the way for new objects, opportunities, and individuals to show up in your life.

All about Attitude

Do you believe that most humans are innately good? Do you think each person has an awesome power to have the life he chooses? Do you seek the lesson in every good and bad experience that comes into your life? When you experience a moment of high drama, do you remember to take some deep breaths, try to depersonalize the situation, and see what there is to learn from the way the situation is unfolding? These are all examples of having a positive attitude.

When you have a great attitude, are focused on and energetically pursuing your goal, and always have a bright smile and a kind word for others, who do you think will want to align with you? Who wouldn't? You will attract everyone on your way up to the top because everyone wants to be around a winner.

Having a good attitude when life is beating up on you can be challenging. When your finances are going south, when your wife has dumped you for her personal trainer, when your car has just been keyed, it's difficult to see any good. But that is exactly the time to cultivate a positive attitude. When the darkness swirls around you, look for the light.

As the dark gets darker and more powerful, that's the best time to seek and generate light. Make yourself into a beacon of bright light and optimism. Express positive feelings and a grateful attitude for what's good in your life and let those feelings extend outward into the lives of all those you know and love. Don't give much energy to the things that aren't working for you. Try to be an observer in the drama and, as you seek whatever goodness you can find, watch how the energy begins to shift. At times, it can be positively palpable.

Generosity of Spirit

A generosity of spirit is symbolized by trust, mutual aid, kindness, respect for others, and a commitment to do as little harm as possible and assist others in their journey through life. In short, generosity means giving and is often synonymous with charity. The Buddhists believe that even the smallest act of charity can yield great merit, either the moment it is performed or in the future. For example, King Ashoka reportedly avoided any suffering associated with his death because before dying he had shared a portion of a piece of fruit with the priests who were tending him.

When I was a child, I spake as a child, I understood as a child, I thought as a child: but when I became a man, I put away childish things. For now we see through a glass, darkly; but then face to face: now I know in part; but then shall I know even as also I am known. And now abideth faith, hope, charity, these three; but the greatest of these is charity.
—1 Corinthians 13:11–13

Three Great Virtues

Charitable acts, in which the giving is unconditional and self-sacrificing, are often equated with *agape*, the Greek word translated to mean "love." In the New Testament, the apostle Paul wrote in his first letter to the Corinthians that of the three great theological virtues—faith, hope, and charity—the last is the greatest.

Show Generosity of Spirit

Cultivate generosity if you want to powerfully express and implement the Law of Attraction in your life. Give generously to receive generously. Be like the Hindu goddess Lakshmi, whose prayer states that the goddess is "generous to everyone." Her devotees rise early at dawn to chant the thousand names of the goddess with the intention of drawing her blessings of wealth into their lives. Attracting wealth into your life does not mean you are depleting someone else's reserve.

FACT

Law of Attraction teachers and practitioners say that the power that brings something to you out of infinite potential can deliver the same thing to another. There is no corresponding loss to infinite potential. When you give from a place of loving kindness, your gift, some say, returns in a magnified form.

Harmony

In Chapter 6, Taoism's concept of not doing, or *wu-wei*, was introduced. In a discussion of generosity of spirit, *wu-wei* has a place because of its emphasis on living life from the spirit and expressing harmony and love in all you do. Andrew Carnegie demanded his employees work together in a spirit of harmony because he believed it was a critically important factor in achieving success. The power behind *wu-wei's* "action without action" is synchronicity. When you set forth an intent or desire in your mind and are harmoniously aligned with the energy of the Tao, your power, invisible and strong, works with the laws of the universe.

CHAPTER 9

Reinforcement Tools

You may already be working with the Law of Attraction and have been trying to maintain a positive mindset, but doubts have been creeping in. Perhaps you are moving through a transition period, feeling pushed outside your comfort zone, and experiencing fear accompanied by lack of focus and scattered flow. This chapter will discuss methods for dealing with those issues, but first you must have a full understanding of the role emotions play in impeding or furthering your work.

The Role of Emotions

An effective reinforcement tool for working with the Law of Attraction is an understanding of how your mood affects your ability to attract the results you desire. It may be more difficult than you think to understand how external and internal thoughts can trigger feelings that translate to good or bad moods. Yet such knowledge can be a powerful aid in your manifestation efforts. You'll know what your mood triggers are, and recognizing them can help you to quickly redirect a negative mood or reinforce a positive one.

Mood is the best indicator of your emotion. The happiness and passion you feel when you do work you love can quickly change into hurt when someone criticizes you. You may even become angry and desire to lash out at that person. In a short span of time, you've just experienced three emotions.

The words *emotion* and *motivation* derive from the same Latin word *movere*, which means "to move." However, defining *emotion* proves difficult. *Emotion* can be applied to a vast array of feelings or states of being, both positive and negative.

Everyone feels emotions as various bodily sensations. In a dangerous situation, you may feel the instinctive fight-or-flight reaction due to your body's sudden release of adrenaline. People behave according to the emotions they feel in their bodies, and many personality disorders have an emotional component. While psychologists differ in their opinions about how many basic emotions people experience, most agree on six.

Basic Types of Emotions
1. Love
2. Surprise
3. Happiness
4. Fear
5. Sadness
6. Anger

Any emotion can affect the way you make decisions. A subgroup of emotions known as social emotions include pride, jealousy, guilt, and embarrassment. Negative emotions such as anger or fear and self-defeating thoughts can keep you from taking advantage of opportunities when they show up in your life. Psychiatrists say that anger turned inward (internalized) can become depression and that emotion can surely paralyze the decision-making process. Sharpen your understanding of social emotions; recognizing when you feel them can be a powerful tool in your box of attraction and manifestation aids.

Grief, fear, hopelessness, shame, and disgust can also render you unable to logically reason through all the factors to effectively make a sound decision. When it comes to deciding to manifest something in your life, making the decision to do so is easier than making a life-and-death decision because of the anticipatory feelings associated with getting something you desire.

Managing Emotions

You must learn to identify the state of mind that is best suited for making decisions. Many feelings and emotions can impede your ability to make good decisions, and learning to control them can be very helpful in working with the Law of Attraction.

Distorted Decision-Making

You don't want to be asked to make a decision when you are in a bad mood. Why? If you are in such a mood and are asked to decide something, you are likely to revisit negative memories and anticipate negative consequences to your decision. However, if you are in a good mood when you are asked to make a decision, you may anticipate a positive outcome to your answer based on your good feelings. Make important decisions when you are in a neutral mood. Then neither positive nor negative emotions can unduly wield influence over reasoning and logic in your decision-making process.

When you feel strong visceral sensations such as hunger, pain, sexual desire, or a craving for a substance such as alcohol, powerful neurophysiologic mechanisms may be driving those feelings. Likewise, your subconscious fears, needs, and wants color how you experience life and make decisions when the future outcome is uncertain. Decision-making is often done in the presence of thoughts about whether the decision will generate benefit or harm in your life.

FACT

The fight-or-flight reaction is a biological stress response to fight or flee when there is the perception of imminent threat. Think of a caveman resting under a tree who suddenly spots a deadly cobra in a threatening posture. The man's nervous system releases adrenaline and stress hormones to rapidly adapt to such a dangerous situation.

Was Descartes Wrong?

In *Descartes' Error: Emotion, Reason, and the Human Brain*, neurologist Antonio Damasio wrote that the idea that the human mind was simply an organ of thought separate from the processes and functioning of the body, as Descartes believed, is wrong. Descartes proclaimed "Cogito ergo sum"—I think, therefore I am. Damasio's book, based on his work on the mind-body connection in brain-injured patients at the University of Iowa College of Medicine, suggests that "I feel, therefore I am" might be more to the point. Emotions and feelings play a central role in directly influencing a person's reasoning and decision-making abilities, according to Damasio. In particular, damage to the prefrontal cortex may mean that a person can no longer produce the emotions to effectively make a decision.

Healthy Expression of Emotion

Mental health professionals say that it is unhealthy to "stuff" your emotions. Instead, you are encouraged to express feelings in positive ways in order to process them. Getting to the root of anger, for example, is an important precursor to working with the Law of Attraction because once you know what triggers it you can deal with the cause and then forgive and release. Working on your self-esteem proves easier once old issues have been resolved. It's important that you feel worthy and deserving of the good things in life and that you develop a success consciousness.

Emotion Not Processed

Your brain is a repository of memory and feeling. It takes a lot of energy to hold resentment, shame, hatred, and ideas of retribution inside. Seek professional help before probing emotionally potent psychological wounds because the process can sometimes trigger mental health issues. Your brain is the most powerful manifestation tool you have. It needs care and attention for it to perform its role in working with the Law of Attraction.

Eye Movement Desensitization and Reprocessing (EMDR) has proved to be an effective tool in helping patients suffering posttraumatic stress disorder. The technique allows the patient to reconnect with the anxiety state and reprocess the events that were so terrible or occurred so quickly that his brain was not able to process all the information. Visit *www.emdr.com* for more information.

Expectation and Anticipation

Expecting to receive what you desire is vital to getting it. A heightened sense of expectation intensifies the vibration of your thought whenever you dare to expect that the thing, person, or circumstance you desire is yours to be had. Allowing yourself to feel a sense of expectation reinforces the attraction or pull of it to you. Expectation evolves into a sense of anticipation when you believe so strongly that what you desire is on its way to you that you accept it without doubt. Pleasure levels rise within you. You are excited, eager, and happy. Consider the following example of simple pleasure: A toddler, separated from his loving parents during their long workday, looks up to see one of them entering the room. The child's sudden recognition causes him to feel happiness.

When your anticipatory feelings of expectation coincide with the actual event finally occurring, a heightened state of pleasure sets in. Think of a time when something wonderful happened to you. When you recall that experience, how do you feel? Happy again? Now think about something you deeply desire that you know at some point is going to show up in your life—for example, getting a promotion with a huge pay increase, finding the love of your life, conceiving a child, receiving a scholarship, or buying your dream house. The happiness grows in intensity, doesn't it?

When working with the Law of Attraction, whether you simply imagine positive feelings or really feel them doesn't matter. But if you spend five minutes imagining the elation you'll feel at getting your heart's desire and then fifty-five minutes of every hour doubting that the law is really going to work, you are sabotaging your efforts. Further, you are blocking the manifesting of what you want. Feelings of failure, fear, worry, and resentment may remind you that it's always been that way and nothing you can do can break the cycle of negative bondage. Such thinking has resonance in the Greek mythological story of Sisyphus.

FACT

In Homer's *The Odyssey*, the tale is recounted: He engaged in chicanery and trickery with the gods and they punished him by forcing him to eternally roll a huge boulder up a steep incline. Each time Sisyphus neared the top, the stone toppled back down, forcing Sisyphus to begin again. He was doomed to a life of frustrating repetition without ever reaching the goal.

Test for Emotional Ability

Close your eyes and imagine a tragic event—the loss of a loved one, the hurt of rejection, or the suffering of a pet or your child, for example. Think of a future event that could also make you heavy-hearted. If you felt your eyes welling with tears, a lump in your throat, heaviness in your chest, and unmistakable waves of sadness washing over you, the good news is that you will also likely be able to feel the opposite emotion of happiness, joy, and delight.

Release, Replace, Repeat

You can call up a negative emotion, examine where it came from, try to understand what it might be teaching you, and expel it from your subconscious in numerous ways, including EMDR, self-hypnosis, dream work and lucid dreaming, art therapy, mask-making, and other self-help methods. Replace patterns of thinking such as self-doubt or self-criticism with appreciation of your body and mind. Practice self-forgiveness, self-patience, self-understanding, and self-love.

Get Ready for Limitless Potential

The limits of your abilities, according to many psychologists, are based on your limiting beliefs. The good news is that you can challenge those beliefs and replace them with more empowering beliefs about yourself. Think of expanding your brain in a way that allows your imagination to stretch and set goals that you may have once believed unattainable. Then let your thoughts create the optimum environment for manifesting those goals from the storehouse of the universe.

Being established in truthfulness, the yogi gets the power of attaining for himself and others the fruits of work without the work. By being established in non-stealing, the yogi obtains all wealth.—*The Aphorisms* (*Yoga Sutras*), Patanjali, sutras 36–37

Use Self-Help Tools

The average person uses only about five to ten percent of his mind, mostly for thinking, feeling, reasoning, and storing memories. With the aid of some techniques for developing creativity and intuition along with other New Age tools—such as lucid dreaming, psychic development, and energy manipulation for healing, yoga, meditation, and communication with higher consciousness, among others—you could use more of your mind for self-discovery, innovative and new ideas, and personal growth.

Attraction and Energy

A desire sets up an attraction. You have the power to intensify that attraction. A variety of ways to accomplish this have already been discussed, including the use of music, visualizations and other visual cues, declarations and incantations, spells, dream incubations, and affirmations.

If you find that your affirmations are not working for you, do a little introspection. Are you spending five minutes each day affirming and the other twenty-three hours and fifty-five minutes in negative self-talk or doubtful "reality" mode? Try flipping the equation.

FACT

Affirming the belief that what you desire is coming to you is the best way to deflect doubt when it creeps in. Trust that what you want is on its way, and give thanks for that. Sidestep the details of how and when it's coming. Let the Source handle those. You focus on reinforcing desire and intention through all means available.

If you want something badly enough, what do you do? You tell everyone you meet. Let's say it's a baby grand piano. You talk about it, think about, look at pictures of it, visit piano stores, run your fingers up and down the keyboards, dream of what it feels like to finally have one of your own, and go to sleep with the piano on your mind. You listen to piano music, read the biographies of great pianists, and dream of playing your own baby grand at parties or recitals. You feel shivers of delight at the mere thought of owning such a beautiful piano. You may even jump up and down and exclaim, "My piano is here!" That's creating heat around your desire. You are going to pull that piano into your life.

A draftsman who worked for a company that was closing took an art class. Working with glass soon became his passion. He had a great idea for a project using a technique that involved glass fusion. He made a few small pieces using a friend's kiln. A local gallery offered to exclusively represent his work after he showed them small prototypes of a large piece he intended to create. First, however, he had to purchase a kiln, a computerized glass-cutting saw, and special materials—but he didn't have the money.

Anxiety about raising the money for the tools and materials soon replaced his excitement. Self-doubt began to erode his belief that he could actually do the big project. Still, he did not cave in. He wrote a short affirmation to say several times throughout the day. Upon awakening and at bedtime, he visualized his art project in the gallery where buyers were purchasing it. He allowed himself to sink into the excitement of showing his work and the happiness upon learning that his work had sold. He thanked God often throughout the day for inspiring him with the project idea, for his friends who supported his art, and for all the blessings in his life that he could enumerate.

Within six months, the man's dream became reality. A builder saw his work and liked it so much that he hired the artist to use a variation of the project in the sales office of new homes that his company was building.

Four Basic Techniques for Manifesting

Although you have already learned the basics for manifesting, you can reinforce and intensify your efforts through an understanding of the four techniques for manifesting. A cautionary word about bad habits might be useful here. Bad habits such as overindulgence in food or drink sabotage your efforts to lose weight and manifest a sleeker, healthier self. Chronic tardiness decreases your chances for manifesting success at school or work. Lack of focus scatters your energies and undermines your efforts to produce the results you desire in every area of your life. Avoidance issues impede your ability to solve problems and clear the way for the manifestation of your dreams. Overlay your bad habits with good ones. Make a commitment to repeat the good habit until it takes hold, displacing and eventually replacing the bad one.

Implementing the Techniques of Manifestation

1. Habitually focus on having abundance rather than lack in your life. Technique: Establish a routine of setting aside certain times throughout the day to consider the abundance that already exists in your life. Discover what makes you feel alive and passionate. Pursue that and the universe will support you. Count your blessings and feel grateful, but also expect that your desires await you if you summon them through emotionally charged positive thinking.

2. Establish the intention to manifest your desire with goals and then magnetize your intention with confidence and certitude of achieving positive results. Technique: Allow your mind to wrap around your desire and all the various ways you can help the Law of Attraction bring that person, circumstance, or thing into your life. It doesn't hurt to develop specific goals and ideas about opportunities to watch for in order to attain your desire, but don't get too bogged down with how your desire can manifest. That limits the universe's options in bringing it to you. Don't forget to consider why you want to manifest your desire, what you will do with it, and how it will make you feel. Also consider whether or not your desire is going to hurt someone else; for example, coveting your best friend's car or boyfriend is a not a healthy choice and should never be the object of your desire.

3. Cultivate conviction and make ready to receive. Know with your heart, mind, and soul that the object of your desire is en route to you at this very moment. This does not suggest a total passivity on your part. Refer to Technique 2. Allow the object to come into your life. Technique: Because you claim the destiny of the object of your desire, practice seeing yourself having it. Let yourself experience joy and the satisfaction of finally having your desire wash over you again and again.

4. Develop an attitude of gratitude and express appreciation often—not only to others (even pets) for their gifts of love and friendship but also to the Source or the Creator. Technique: Allow yourself to feel as if you have forever been and always will be in the protective and capable hands of the Divine. Let go of all worry and feel serene, peaceful, happy, and grateful.

Knowing the steps for deliberately creating something is necessary, but so, too, is an understanding of other metaphysical laws that may directly affect the outcome of your spiritual work with the Law of Attraction. As you go through the steps of working with the Law of Attraction, consider how these others laws are working.

Universal Laws Affecting Manifestation

1. **The Law of Intention:** To work with this law, know why you are doing what you are doing as well as how your actions attract good and bad to you.
2. **The Law of Karma:** Be aware that your every thought, word, and deed triggers a reaction in the universe. Think of it as "you reap what you sow" or "what you send out returns to you."
3. **The Law of Continuity:** Remember that energy and matter do not die but can be transformed.
4. **The Law of Synchronicity:** Take notice of how, once you've decided to manifest something, references to it start showing up in your life frequently in a multitude of ways.

You may feel as if you don't have anything to be grateful for, but think again. You have eyes to read this text and a mind to grasp the meaning of the words.

Take a Break from Negative Messages

Reduce the amount of negativity you will tolerate. Americans are bombarded every day by advertising messages that emphasize dissatisfaction and lack in your life. Some sources say that the average person receives more than 1,000 negative messages each day. You are constantly hearing that you need a better mattress, you need a faster car, you need to switch your hair color product, or you need the purple pill to salvage your sex life. Ask yourself how you eliminate negative messages in order to raise your level of life satisfaction.

Psychologist Martin Seligman, Ph.D., noted for his contributions to the idea of learned helplessness and depression, decided to study the factors that enable people to have positive emotional health. His research led to an area of psychology known as positive psychology or optimal human functioning. People are more likely to experience vibrant physical health and feel less stress when they have a high level of life satisfaction.

In his research on optimism, Seligman discovered five primary factors out of twenty-four associated with high levels of life satisfaction. The five were optimism, curiosity, the ability to give and receive love, a zest for life, and gratitude. Seligman asserted that of those five factors, gratitude was the most important one associated with happiness. Visit *www .authentichappiness.org* for more information.

Positive Thinking

Engaging in positive thinking certainly makes life more pleasurable. One positive thought is likely to generate another, creating a cycle. The steady stream of thoughts will flow, whether you direct it or not. The happy and good life that may seem so elusive to some can become reality with a simple redirecting of thought. Positive thinking and goal-setting are now considered scientifically viable methods for changing a person's life.

Three Vital Components

Dr. Seligman and his associates have noted that there are three components associated with happiness: the pleasant life, the meaningful life, and the engaged life. These three components seem to be vital to having high levels of individual happiness.

RAS

Other scientists have researched the brain and identified a specific area called the reticular activating system (RAS). That part of the brain interfaces with visual mechanisms to enable you to disregard things that are not relevant to your goals and focus special attention on those things that are critical to attaining your goals.

Fast Results

Thoughts repeated daily become the instructions for your subconscious to carry out. The subconscious is also the site of your beliefs and habits. You can reinforce the instruction set by writing your goals, repeating affirmations, and spending time in creative visualization. You can impress upon your subconscious the belief that positive thinking brings you the good things you desire in life. In that way, habitual positive thinking yields faster results.

Watch your thoughts, for they become words. Choose your words, for they become actions. Understand your actions, for they become habits. Study your habits, for they will become your character. Develop your character, for it becomes your destiny.—Anonymous

People who win the lottery have managed to align themselves with abundance. Perhaps they followed the advice of Law of Attraction seminar instructor Michael Losier, who has been featured multiple times on *Oprah & Friends*, Oprah Winfrey's radio show, and offers worldwide training programs on deliberate attraction. In his article about how to win the lottery, he reminded would-be winners of three steps: desire, attention to desire, and allowing. Of the three steps, he noted, the one with which people seem to have the most difficulty is the third step, allowing.

Why that? You are a child of your divine Father/Mother/Creator. Your birthright is to have abundance in your life—not some paltry portion, not just enough and no more, but all that you desire. Grasping this with your mind and feeling the truth of it with all your heart enables you to establish a powerful attraction to manifest success consciousness. Open yourself to allow for the drawing in of the fruit of your dreams and deepest desires.

CHAPTER 10

The Impact of Negativity

Perhaps you know the impact of negativity from direct experience. For example, maybe you have had the experience of happily going off to work only to sink into a foul mood an hour later because of a coworker who never let a negative thought go unspoken. Negativity is both malignant and infectious. When you are in a negative environment, it is difficult to have the mental clarity and the positive outlook that are so necessary for intentional alignment with the Law of Attraction.

Blockages and Obstacles

The anxious mind can spiral endlessly along in melodramatic fashion, triggered by a single thought that acts as a catalyst for worry. For example, you just returned from the market, where you did a little banking and grocery shopping. Your teenage daughter approaches and asks for cash for a snack before going off to her after-school study group. You reach for your wallet, and it's missing. Your mind races.

"Where did I leave it . . . at the store? Oh, no . . . all that cash . . . the car payment. . . . Maybe the checker has it. . . . Yeah, right. Who'd turn it in? . . . Why would they? . . . My cash . . . my house payment . . . gone. . . . Oh no! . . . They could steal my identity!"

Mulling over a problem in order to come up with creative solutions is one thing, but when fear triggers the emotional part of the brain, worrying takes over, often obsessively. The worrying mind attracts more negative situations to worry about. Experts in behavior and brain science warn that worrying can overshadow and negate reason and logic.

FACT

In his book *Emotional Intelligence: Why It Can Matter More than IQ*, author Daniel Goleman asserts that while anxiety weakens the intellect and undercuts all types of mental and academic performances, a positive mood can facilitate flexible and complex thinking.

Your choice of words or use of language differs depending on whether you are in a negative or a positive mood. The brain cannot hold both negative and positive emotions at the same time, say Law of Attraction teachers. You will experience either positive or negative polarity, and it will be reflected in your inner dialogue word choices.

When you are in a bad mood and your mental thought vibration is negative, you use words like *no*, *not*, *can't*, *won't*, *don't*, and *impossible*. But when you feel upbeat and happy, you use positive expressions like *yes*, *can*, *will*, *do*, and *possible*. When you say *can't*, *won't*, *don't*, and *no*, you are focusing your attention on what you do not want because the mind sifts the negative contractions out of the statement and zeroes in on what remains. For example, the statement, "I don't want any more bills," brings you more bills.

Try substituting a positively phrased question like "What is my deepest desire?" Then express what you want using positive language and avoiding those negative words. For example, instead of saying, "I can't get the job of my dreams; I'm not good enough" say instead, "I am excited to be in the process of getting the job of my dreams because I am skilled at what I do and am passionate about doing it." Give focused attention and energy to your positive affirmation statements.

Some spiritual seekers who regularly spend time chanting a specific mantra each day have been known to awaken from a dream and remember that within the dream they had been chanting the same mantra, suggesting that repetitious verbalization or mental thought can be impressed upon the subconscious and emerge in the dreaming mind.

Create Desire Declarations That Align with Your Truth

The Law of Attraction responds to your feeling. When you say an affirmation that resonates with you, your affirmation becomes positive. But when you make a desire declaration or say an affirmation that is not true for you, your feeling is conflicted because you have doubts that it can really be true. Doubt cancels out your desire and blocks manifestation.

Clarity of desire and the absence of any doubt are of paramount importance in getting what you want from the universe. If necessary, write a list of what you don't want so that when you write of what you do desire, you can write it without obfuscation or words that evoke a negative vibration. You'll know by how you feel if what you've declared is true for you. You will feel relieved, possibly joyful, hopeful, and excited.

Remedy Blockages and Eliminate Subconscious Doubt

When the law takes too long or doesn't seem to work as you had hoped, you can assume that there may be blockages or obstacles that need clearing. Check your thought patterns. Are you experiencing skepticism, fear, anxiety, doubt, or worry? Check your feelings. Remedy blockages by asserting control over your conscious mind. Become quiet and permit your higher self or Divine Mind to take charge in quelling your mind's constant chatter.

You can exert control over your conscious thoughts to some degree, but your subconscious may be a wee bit more challenging. You may have the urge to declare that you can't possibly be responsible for any negative thinking that goes on in your subconscious, but the fact is that you are the only one who could possibly be responsible. It is, after all, your mind. Don't blame your parents, ex-wife, or others. Use frequent affirmations and creative visualizations to eliminate doubt and negative emotions that can block your alignment with the workings of the law.

QUESTION?

How can I use my senses of sight, smell, taste, touch, and hearing to work with the Law of Attraction?
Observe how your senses respond to various stimuli. What evokes negative or positive feelings for you? Use that knowledge to reset your mood or vibration. For example, an intense color or ear-splitting music may evoke a positive vibration in some people, but you may find it repulsive.

Reinforce Your Desire Through Journaling

If you are using personal affirmations, visualizations, and emotional magnetizing of your thoughts and you still feel blocked, try journaling your visualizations. From your visualization exercise, write down everything you observed with your mind's eye. Feel the positive emotions that come up for you when you read over your script. Record all the specific details as well as your feelings. Make your visualization and the journal entry as complete as possible.

Now take time to put everything together. Write, read, and recite a personal desire declaration and an affirmation. Make it true for you. Visualize your desire. Notice your positive emotions. Write about your visualization exercise in your journal. Allow the space in your life for the desire to manifest. When your desire comes into your life, be appreciative and bask in feelings of elation, satisfaction, fulfillment, and gratitude.

Victim Mentality

The Universe or Source has already given each person everything she needs in the form of consciousness and universal laws to be the creator of her own destiny. Creative manifestation simply requires an individual claiming that which she desires. People who complain about their misfortunes or illnesses or lack bring more of that to themselves. They are victims of their own patterns of habitual negative thinking.

FACT

Paramahansa Yogananda included a chapter in his book, *The Divine Romance*, about how he used to be extremely thin until his guru Sri Yukteswar changed his thinking, enabling him to be able to gain or lose according to his desire. In his book, Yogananda outlined how to think so that the mind will do it all without overlooking dietary laws.

Work with your mind to make it a powerful instrument on which you know you can always depend. The mind, properly trained against its tendencies to fall into the same ruts of thought, the same lazy patterns of self-criticism, can be your most powerful ally in whatever undertaking strikes your fancy. If you want to lose or gain weight, think beyond your eating patterns, physiology, and biochemistry and instead consider how your mind and the Law of Attraction could bring you down or up to your ideal weight.

Make Statements Resonate True for You

If you have a pattern of attracting unhealthy relationships but you make a desire declaration that you have healthy and loving relationships in your life, you won't attract such relationships because you know deep down that it isn't currently true for you. Focus on feeling and nurturing statements that can be spoken as true for you and focus on your desire as being in process and occurring right now: "I love that I am attracting . . ." or "I feel excited that I am . . ." or "I love the thought of. . . ."

You have formulated a clear desire. You feel fantastic every time you declare it. However, if you have doubt (the uncertainty that you can truly attract your desire to you), that doubt or limiting belief evokes a negative vibration and will cancel out the positive statement of your desire. Eliminate the doubt and rework your desire declaration until it rings true and makes you feel happy and excited.

Allow Manifestation to Occur

Perhaps the most important step in deliberate manifesting is the art of allowing something to come into your life. Believe that you deserve it and are worthy and ready to receive. Let your desire come in. In the twelve-step program there is an admonishment to "let go, and let God." It's that simple. When you allow, you feel relief and other positive emotions.

Negative Versus Positive Emotions

If you described your thoughts now, would they be negative, neutral, or positive? Are you thinking that being able to attract into your life exactly what you want is interesting but that it's really for others who engage in wishful thinking? Or are you thinking "Wow, I can't wait to get started"? How do you feel when you remember a time when your boss chastised you for some failing and did it in front of your coworkers? How do you feel when remembering a poignant moment when you were praised in front of others by a leader of a business or community organization? External events and memories of them can trigger negative or positive emotions, subsequently pulling your mood down or lifting it.

Michael Losier, a popular seminar provider who studied neurolinguistic programming, teaches students in his Law of Attraction programs that a person experiences positive or negative emotion every time he daydreams, pretends, remembers, or observes something.

Any time your attention focuses on a memory, thought, or observation, it triggers an emotional response, and that response is either positive or negative—but the response can never be both at the same time.

Some esoteric teachings stress that reincarnation is the means by which humans are able to work out all of their desires and also do all the kinds of things they desire to do, expressing themselves life after life as artisans, healers, shamans, scientists, and world leaders.

Break the Negative Thinking Cycle

Quiet observation of your thoughts will shed light on how much of your inner dialogue is negative in response to internal thoughts or external stimuli. Statements such as "I don't have time," "I can't help it," or "I can't afford it" are self-limiting. You remember an old hurt, and the negative feelings are now there in the present. You see a coat in the department store window and want it but it costs too much. You feel bad. Such instant, reflexive responses must be subdued and eventually replaced with positive responses.

Author Robert T. Kiyosaki, author of *Rich Dad, Poor Dad, What the Rich Teach Their Kids About Money—That the Poor and Middle Class Do Not*, advises in his books and lectures that people replace the negative, self-limiting phrase "I can't afford it" with the positive question "How can I afford it?"

Focus on Feeling

To create a positive statement for a desire declaration, focus on feeling. For example, "I feel excited that I have all the time I need" or "I am thrilled to know that my talents are in demand in the marketplace and I am attracting the perfect job" or "I am attracting into my life ideal friendships that are vibrant, healthy, nurturing, and stimulating" or "I love feeling abundant and knowing that money easily flows to me from myriad sources." These kinds of declarative statements establish desire linked with positive feelings in the present moment.

Behavior Modification: Avoid Old Patterns

The first step in modifying behavior is to get rid of old patterns of belief that limit you. Law of Attraction experts assert that limiting beliefs are responsible for your inability to work effectively with the Law of Attraction to creatively and deliberately manifest. The following exercise can help you identify limiting beliefs that you can then work on releasing.

Identifying Self-Limiting Beliefs

Fill in the blanks. Then make a list of other self-limiting beliefs you have. Rework the negative statements into positive declarations that are true and make you feel good.

- I'd like to start my own business but I can't because _____ _____.

- I would run the Boston Marathon but I can't because _____ _____.

- I would like to buy my own house but I can't because _____ _____.

- If I were just more _____ I could attract my perfect soul mate.

- I wish I could lose weight but I can't because _____.

- Because I don't have a college degree, I am prevented from _____.

- I don't dare attempt to _____ because I'm too _____.

Years of self-limiting beliefs may be sabotaging you without your realizing it. These beliefs reveal themselves in patterns that keep coming up again and again in your life. For example, you attract the wrong kind of romantic partner: "I can't attract a good man because I always fall for losers just like my Aunt Milly." Limiting beliefs are often so ingrained that they may seem to be at the heart of who you are, the very core of your being.

Self-limiting beliefs hold you back from most personal and spiritual growth. You may harbor a fear of failure, a fear of never finding Mr. Right, or the fear of success. Perhaps you have engaged in self-sabotage, working hard to achieve something only to undermine your hard work with persistent, self-defeating inner criticism. Or perhaps you have always equated success with "no pain, no gain." With the Law of Attraction, you can have success and abundance and you do not have to suffer to achieve it. You do have to recognize and release self-limiting beliefs.

If you feel stuck or trapped, set goals for various areas of your life—spiritual, health, family, work, personal. List specific reasons that keep you from reaching your goals, and include what has stopped you in the past. Know that you have the power to release even the most ingrained beliefs and turn them around into affirmations of unlimited potential.

Defy Logic

Proponents of the Law of Attraction assert that every person can create a life of wealth, abundance, and happiness that otherwise might seem improbable or impossible and defies logic and reason. If a review of your life and the goals you had established make you feel happy, it's likely you accomplished them. On the other hand, if you feel sad or disappointed, you likely did not accomplish them. Here's a little quiz that might get you motivated to leverage your life with the Law of Attraction.

Assessing Your Life
1. What do you like about your life?
2. What drives your passion?

3. What gets you energized and sets your head spinning with new ideas?
4. What personal growth do you desire for your life?
5. Where do you want to be in your career/job this time next year? In five years?
6. What do you desire your life to be like?
7. What do you desire to add to your life that is currently not in it?
8. What one new thing would you like to manifest right now?

Follow your passion, even if you have little money and no formal training or degrees to qualify you. You'll know you are on the fast track to success when you feel good doing that which fuels your passion. The Law of Attraction states that like attracts like. Feelings magnetize your desires, and magnetized desires attract more of the same and propel you forward in your passionate endeavors to success.

Kick Things Up a Notch

When you do spiritual work, you must learn surrender and listen to the voice within. Surrendering to that inner wisdom allows you to know with a kind of understanding that goes beyond logical thinking. Likewise, when you work with the Law of Attraction, you must set aside logic and reason, curry trust and faith, and know with an inner certainty that the law works. When the law gives you even a little indication that it is working, you will feel excited and your belief will be reaffirmed. Your excitement increases your joyful vibration, which, in turn, increases your level of trust in the law.

Make a Law of Attraction Journal

It is helpful to have a place to record your desire declarations, affirmations, visualizations, statements of evidence or proof, and prayers or statements of gratitude. Include images of your desires and dreams in your journal. As your desires manifest, place a symbol that has meaning for you upon your written declaration. In fact, make a note each time positive things flow easily into your life. Rejoice. When you rejoice and commemorate each manifestation, your vibration aligns with the law to bring you even more abundance.

Let the Law Work

Perhaps your desire has many steps that seem to boggle your mind when you ponder how much must be done in order for that dream or goal to manifest. Your work is not to figure out how the Law of Attraction has to work to manifest. Your job is to create the vibration around your desire and the intention and to stay in harmonious alignment with the working of the law. The Law of Attraction will do the rest.

When you are feeling happy and positive and suddenly someone with a dark and negative vibration visits you, you most likely will feel a palpable energy shift downward. Instead of staying in the lower vibration, remind yourself of what is in your best interest. You may need to leave the company of that individual in order to again feel happy and positive.

A yogic technique for ridding yourself of a bad habit, such as being judgmental or overly critical, is to close your eyes and focus your attention at the point between the eyebrows. Don't strain but focus gently and affirm the new good habit. Keep thinking about it until it becomes ingrained. Reinforce it daily.

Develop High Vibration

The higher your level of emotion and belief, the higher your vibration and the more likely you will swiftly attract into your life the ideal romantic relationship, more abundance, spiritual understanding, vibrant health, financial prosperity, meaningful work, or other desires. Since self-limiting thoughts and doubt slow or block the arrival of your goals, keep your energy and emotions high and use everything you have learned thus far to stay in alignment with the law.

Ask How You Can Make Something Possible

Hilda didn't even know that she was writing a desire declaration when she wrote in her journal about her dream to serve on a police force. Her entry included a description of herself dressed in a crisp blue uniform. She wore black boots, a leather belt, and a heavy silver badge. She described feelings of elation whenever she dreamed of herself in that uniform taking her oath. Even though she worked as a file clerk, she always thought about how she might achieve her dream and always wondered how she could make it possible. She heard about a local community police department that was seeking to fill a position. A year almost to the day from writing her desire declaration, Hilda was hired as a crime scene technician. She was issued a uniform and a badge and given on-the-job training. One evening while preparing to celebrate her new job with friends, she discovered her journal entry and was amazed that what had manifested fit almost exactly what she had written.

Activating Your Subconscious

As you learned earlier in this chapter, the Law of Attraction won't bring into existence something that you may be repeatedly affirming but do not really believe you can have. By asking "How can I have this?" you are activating the amazing powers of your subconscious to provide solutions and opening the way for the Law of Attraction to work.

Great ideas may begin percolating through your mind or you may begin to see opportunity everywhere because of your positive mental attitude and elevated vibration. Solutions or plans to circumvent obstacles may emerge unexpectedly.

CHAPTER 11

The Law of Attraction and Your Health

Modern experts in alternative medicine now assert what shamans and spiritual healers have perhaps always known—that the power of an optimistic mind can often heal the ailments of the body. It's well known that optimists live longer than pessimists. If you can accept that, at your most fundamental level, you are an energy being and that energy attracts like energy, you can begin to deliberately manifest good health. The Law of Attraction is always at work to bring you what you believe is true about your body and its health.

Good Health Begins with Healthy Thinking

If you want to get healthy and stay that way, start with healthy thoughts. Paramahansa Yogananda, founder of the Self-Realization Fellowship, wrote in *The Divine Romance* that sickness and health are both dreams of the mind. Cultivate joy, tranquility, optimism, and a sense of wonder. Laugh a lot, since laughing has been proven to produce health benefits. Become childlike in your view of life, nature, and the wonders that already exist around you. Minimize the amount of pessimism, doubt, and worry you allow yourself to experience. Do not be enslaved by the whims, desires, and demands of the body. Take care of it, but be its master.

Here are some ways to begin to implement healthy thinking. Cultivate feelings of self worth. Think about how you felt at a time when you were at the peak of good health. Ask yourself what brought about the decline in your health. Is it something that can remain in the past or is it still a factor? If it is still a factor, what can you do to get rid of it or minimize its impact? How committed are you to improving your health, stamina, and overall well-being? What steps will you take in the next moment, hour, or day to get on the road to good health? Remember, poor overall health can attract other problems and even shorten your life expectancy. Every thought you think, every act you do to achieve good health can bring huge health benefits and, in some cases, extend longevity.

Andrew Weil, M.D., a leading expert on integrative medicine and author of a plethora of books about health, believes good health is primarily in the hands of the individual. Like other health practitioners, he advises people to reduce stress (try breathing exercises, for example), eat right (consume lots of fruits and vegetables while reducing the intake of red meat), quit smoking, and engage in regular physical activity (take up walking). But he asserts that maintaining a healthy mind is equally important.

Change Your Thoughts, Improve Your Health

Find ways to engage your mind in interesting endeavors. A healthy mind is an engaged mind. For example, your mind is stimulated when you endeavor to learn how to speak a new language, play a musical instrument, and do crossword or Sudoku puzzles. A healthy mind also focuses on positive rather than negative thought patterns. Perhaps you have noticed in your own life a link between periods of positive thought patterns and feelings of wellness versus negative thinking and maladies.

Tools of Healing

You can use sound healing, aromatherapy, massage, breath work, herbal and hydro therapies, and guided meditation for mind/body healing. They are techniques found in virtually every medical tradition, including the ancient health teachings of Ayurveda, and increasingly Western-trained physicians may include those therapies along with medications and other conventional treatments. People working deliberately with the Law of Attraction may gain increased benefit from such treatments because of their optimistic outlook for improving their conditions.

FACT

Mind/body medicine is also referred to as behavioral medicine. Formerly labeled fringe medicine by conservative academic and medical establishments, mind/body medicine in recent times has gained such wide public support (one recent study showed that one in three adults have used alternative therapies) that the National Institutes of Health have established the Office of Alternative Medicine.

Aligning Your Mind and Body

Could you be bringing on your own illnesses or attracting misfortune in your life through the power of negative thought? If so, doesn't it make sense that changing your thoughts could change your life for the better?

The Tibetan Buddhist approach to healing necessarily begins in the mind. The Buddhist philosophy teaches that the mind is the creator of all problems and remedies, good fortune and bad, health and sickness. Buddhists believe in the law of karma. Each person is constantly sowing karmic seeds that persist until the right circumstances occur to cause the seeds to bear their karmic fruit. Negative karma manifests as problems, disease, and suffering, while positive karma shows up as success, good fortune, and vibrant health. To the degree that you can control your emotions and thought patterns, you can influence your karma and, thus, your health and vitality.

Avoid Harming Yourself and Others

Mindfulness means being present in each moment and noticing the quality of your thoughts even as you are being observant. Standing sentinel at the doorway of your consciousness to guard against creating seeds of negative thought (which, in turn, creates negative karma, according to Buddhism) is the way to avert sickness of the body and mind. The Buddhist philosophy states that you must avoid any action that is harmful to yourself or others and that you must remain vigilant in monitoring your thoughts. In that way, you avoid attracting ill health to yourself in this life as well as in any future incarnations. Negative thoughts, words, and actions are like poison arrows that are destined to return to the sender.

QUESTION?

What is Ayurveda?
Ayurveda is an ancient health care system that originated on the Indian subcontinent. It utilizes knowledge of the body, soul, mind, and senses to promote healthy living. *Ayurveda* means "knowledge of life." The principles of Ayurveda (associated with the Vedic culture) influenced Tibetan and Chinese medicine as well as Unani medical practices that originated in Persia in circa A.D. 980.

Align your expectation and desire with the Law of Attraction if you want good health; what your mind believes about and expects from your body and its mental, emotional, and physical condition is what you receive more of.

Make Peace with Your Body

Accept and appreciate your body. Think of it as your friend. Instead of constantly criticizing how you feel or look, decide on what positive things you can do to effect the changes you desire. When illness comes, don't think of the body as betraying you. Work with your body to rid it of wrong thinking and feeling.

> You praise the townsman's, I the rustic's state:
> Admiring others' lots, our own we hate:
> Each blames the place he lives in: but the mind
> Is most in fault, which ne'er leaves self behind.
> —Quintus Horatius Flaccus (Horace), "Villice Silvarum"
> (Letter to His Bailiff)

While self-love and self-respect are necessary for self-esteem, obsessive self-focus and selfishness can cause you to think and act in ways that can be detrimental to your health and well-being. The seeds of selfishness often sprout into anger, greed, and jealousy that, in turn, can fuel feelings of haughtiness or superiority over other beings. In Buddhist thought, selfishness is the root cause of all problems and disease. When you feel hostility, you attract more of it to you.

> Attentive breathing is a simple technique to help relieve pain. If you have pain from a pulled muscle in your leg, for example, focus your conscious mind upon the painful area, breathe in, and imagine the painful tension as a dark, hard knot shattering under the energy of your attention. Breathe out, releasing the broken pieces. Keep doing the technique until the pain subsides or completely dissipates, and you won't have to reach for your painkillers.

Practice Thought Transformation

Another Buddhist idea is the transforming of negative thought or labels into positive ones. For example, when a doctor tells you that you have a disease, you may react to her labeling of your affliction with fear, horror, and helplessness. You may see the disease as a problem, but you could also see it as a positive element in your life, the fruition of some karmic seed and the means to consciously alter your lifestyle in order to live in more balanced and spiritual ways. You could work on developing a compassionate mind. The transformation of negative thoughts into positive ones can effect changes in the body, restoring health. The body, after all, is our physical dwelling.

The Magical World Within

Imagination is much more powerful than reason. The magical kind of thinking that goes on in the imagination addresses the subconscious mind, which is childlike in that it does not question directives that are both simple and repetitive—for example, an affirmation that your left knee is in the process of healing so you can again dance the tango. To stimulate the mind's fantasizing abilities, use colorful imagery rather than dry data and facts.

FACT

According to the ancient practice of feng shui, you preserve your store of energy when you avoid people who leach energy from you. Since energy flows from high to low, think of people who drain your energy and others who seem to energize you. The body is like a battery that stores and dispenses energy, but when energy is depleted, proper functioning is impossible.

Become Healthy and Stay That Way

What do you do if you are ill? First you might rest and listen to what your body is telling you through its symptoms. Sometimes it takes a little time for an illness to declare itself or reveal what it is. But if you think you have a life-threatening illness or know you suffer from a chronic illness, you will want to see your doctor. You have to take care of yourself, do whatever you can, and seek professional help if necessary.

According to the principles of the Law of Attraction, the key to a long and healthy life lies in what you believe about yourself. According to some scientific studies and cultural beliefs, lifestyle choices and genetic factors are not the only indicators for longevity and health. Your dad may have lived to see his hundredth birthday or perhaps your mother died of breast cancer in her early forties, but that does not mean that you will have the same fate. Here are some ways to get healthy: Eat right, get plenty of rest, quit smoking, and follow your doctor's advice before undertaking an exercise regimen. But also remember the healing power of the mind. Your optimistic outlook, positive thinking, and reduction of stress should make up part of a regular regimen for becoming healthy and staying that way.

Martin Seligman, who investigates positive thinking and optimism at the University of Pennsylvania, noted in an October 2007 *Newsweek* article that optimistic people may be inspired to take better care of themselves because they believe that their self-care efforts result in good health. Seligman also stated that optimists are inclined to build better social networks than pessimists, a factor associated with longevity.

Reduce Levels of Stress

Stress can be a good thing. It triggers alertness when we need it—for example, when we give a speech or perform for others. Stress also prepares us to react instantly to danger. During a healthy stress response, norepinephrine, an excitatory neurotransmitter that is necessary to create new memories, is released.

Everyone feels stress from time to time, but unrelenting stress, the kind you might experience in a high-pressure job, can wreak havoc on your health. According to several sources, 75 to 90 percent of all visits to the doctor may be attributed to stress-related ailments and cost the U.S. economy in excess of $300 billion annually.

Stress-Related Illnesses

Doctors refer to stress without relief as distress. Patients suffering distress have a chronic oversecretion of stress hormones that exerts an adverse cumulative effect on brain function and memory. When the brain is constantly flooded with those powerful hormones designed only for short-term release during emergency situations, the result can be damage and death to brain cells. Some patients suffering a lifetime of chronic stress experience impairment of long-term memory. Distress can trigger emotional disorders and contribute to a plethora of bodily ailments, including the following:

- Anxiety
- Arthritis
- Asthma
- Decreased brain function and memory loss
- Depression
- Diabetes
- Headaches
- Heart problems
- High blood pressure
- Insomnia and sleep problems
- Skin problems

It is not necessary to eliminate stress, but rather to effectively manage it in order to attract optimum health in alignment with the Law of Attraction. Do you feel totally stressed out and exhausted at the end of your day? Have you overscheduled yourself? Have you taken on more than any one person could reasonably expect to handle in a workday? One way to assess whether or not you're trying to do too much is to work with a list of daily tasks.

According to the philosophy of feng shui, adding healthy plants to your environment—especially bathrooms—can increase the flow of healthy energy to you. Keep your home free of clutter. Take out garbage often. Keep toilet seats closed to ensure that your healthy energy isn't draining away.

Make a list of all the things you do each day. Prioritize your list into things that only you can do and work you can delegate to others. Of the things only you can do, reorder the list so that the tasks you dread the most (and are likely most stressful) are spaced out with other tasks that you love to do. The point is to create balance between work you dread and work you love. Evaluate how you feel after a day of using the new list to see if you managed to reduce your high levels of anxiety and stress.

Set Boundaries and Resolve Conflicts

Highly successful athletes understand (either consciously or intuitively) how to work with the Law of Attraction. They understand the role that a positive attitude plays in goal achievement. They deal with a potentially stressful situation immediately (putting off resolution allows the stress to continue building) and set professional and personal boundaries and goals. Although they are competitive, they usually display good sportsmanship in competition. That means they learn how to engage in healthy conflict resolution. All of these things aid in stress reduction.

When you cannot establish firm boundaries or say no to others' demands, you may feel that people such as coaches, friends, business associates, or family members are treading all over you. As a result, you may harbor feelings of hostility and resentment. Use the following techniques to reduce your stress and anxiety while resolving conflicts with others.

1. Stay focused on the present situation and be in tune with your mood and vibration. When your vibration is high and you feel good, you are in tune with the Law of Attraction and can more easily draw in a healthy solution to a conflict.
2. Concentrate on regular, slow breathing to help you remain calm, clear-thinking, and able to make good choices.
3. Attempt to truly understand the other person's point of view.
4. Show restraint when accusations and criticism are leveled at you, and respond with empathy for how the speaker is feeling.
5. Make it clear that you will work with him to find a solution.
6. Actively listen and avoid the tendency to interrupt or anticipate what the other person might say next.

7. Take responsibility for your words, attitude, and actions. If you are wrong, own up to it and release it.
8. Avoid defensive posturing.
9. Seek a compromise. If agreement cannot be reached, involve an impartial third party to help you resolve the conflict.
10. Request a break if the discussion has become too heated and the communication is no longer constructive. Agree to resume it later at a specific time after you've both had time to allow any aggressive feelings and anger to dissipate.

Set aside a little time every day to release the cumulative stressful feelings you have taken on throughout your day. Release the tension. Put on some quiet music or sit or lie quietly and just be aware of your breath. Let go of tension with every outgoing breath. Feel appreciation and joy for the gift of life and for a functioning body that is your vehicle for this incarnation. Be grateful in the knowledge that it is in your power to create vibrant health.

Healthy Body Visualization Techniques

What messages do you play over and over in your mind about your body? As previously noted, what the mind constantly focuses on with feeling, the subconscious tends to believe as true. Do you see yourself as too thin, fat, disproportionate, flabby, old, wrinkled, weak, frail, wracked with pain, or ill? Such messages may or may not be true, but you can change your health and sense of well-being by changing your thoughts and raising your vibration.

Your thoughts are magnetized by feeling, so if you feel you are weak, you cannot attract strength; if you feel that you are flabby and fat, you cannot draw to you lean and thin; and if you feel that a cold is coming on, it probably will. Conversely, if you feel lithe, strong, and full of energy, you attract those qualities when you frequently give them your attention and feeling of appreciation.

Prayer for Vibrant Health

Oh, Holy One, I appreciate the gift of my body as the vessel that carries my consciousness through life. Now, as I move my awareness deeply inward, my mind's eye examines this body from the feet to the head. I perceive it as a living mass of cells, like vibrating particles of light, each performing its function exactly as it was created to do to keep this body vibrantly healthy and strong.

The rays of thy holy light manifest through the prism of my mind as healing colors of the rainbow. I hear the cosmic vibration—OM—and feel blissfully alive and sustained.

Focusing my attention on the heart space, I enter the temple of peace. Resting in your restorative and loving presence, I give thanks.

Maharishi Mahesh Yogi, founder of Transcendental Meditation, told viewers of CNN's *Larry King Live* show in May 2002 that a person's own karma or actions bear the responsibility for their successes and happiness in life. Each individual has the potential for experiencing the ultimate reality of life, or pure intelligence, he explained, and it is from pure intelligence that creation emerges.

FACT

Holy men and women of various religious and cultural traditions saw the human body as little more than a vessel to carry humans through their incarnations. However, while some saints emphasized transcending the body and especially the senses (focusing instead on the work of the spirit), others viewed the body (and good health) as a divine blessing.

You can use Transcendental Meditation and many other types of wisdom practices to align with the Law of Attraction to create a better life or better health. The Maharishi counseled people to think better thoughts. And as Deepak Chopra, who once was a follower of the Maharishi, has pointed out, simply having better thoughts (or happy thoughts) can translate to having happy molecules and thus a better heart, healthier kidneys, more or less weight, and so forth.

Heal Illness and Disease

The statement "thoughts are things" finds repetition in New Age circles and at Law of Attraction seminars. A passing thought about diabetes might not cause the condition to manifest, but if you constantly worry and fear that you're going to develop it, you just might. Then what? How do you reverse the process, get rid of the illness?

If you want perfect health, affirm it by proclaiming that you want it and that you like the way your body feels when it is healthy. The beings known as Abraham in the Jerry and Esther Hicks book *The Law of Attraction: The Basics of the Teachings of Abraham* have stated that thinking such thoughts makes you feel good and such feeling places you in tune with the law to attract perfect health.

In his 1990 book *Quantum Healing: Exploring the Frontiers of Mind/ Body Medicine*, Dr. Deepak Chopra explained that quantum healing—the body's ability to cure itself of a disease—involves healing the mind to manifest changes in the body. Human bodies, he pointed out, are fields of information, intelligence, and energy. The mind need only focus on an area of the body that needs healing and the body sends healing energy to that place.

Where Western medicine most often treats symptoms with medications or surgery, holistic and Ayurvedic medical practices emphasize the mind/body connection and work to find the root cause of the disease. If, as Dr. Chopra has asserted, each of the 50 trillion cells of the human body knows how to heal itself, then your body should be able to effect a cure and restore its health.

When you let go of destructive patterns, release victimology thinking, take responsibility for your choices in life and the consequences, and forgive, you will be taking a giant step toward healing whatever ails you.

Dis-ease is just that—the lack of ease about your life, your body, your choices, or anything that troubles your mind and heart and brings discord to your comfort level. Have patience with your body.

It isn't necessary to go over and over again how, when, or why the body developed the illness, but rather to affirm that you are releasing it. Let go of old patterns of thinking and living. Embrace limitless potential in your health and your life through deliberate focus on the Law of Attraction and allow for your deepest desires for perfect health and well-being to manifest. Tell your mind that it is strong; tell your body, too. Banish doubt. Purify your body and strengthen your mind.

Get wisdom, get understanding: forget it not; neither decline from the words of my mouth. Forsake her not, and she shall preserve thee: love her, and she shall keep thee. Wisdom is the principal thing; therefore get wisdom: and with all thy getting get understanding.—Proverbs 4: 5–7

The following breathing technique has been practiced by yogis for centuries. Breathing techniques were known by the ancients and have been used in many cultures either alone or with herbs or other elements to restore balance in the body for health. If you feel ill, try the following breathing exercise.

- Sitting in a comfortable position with straight posture, place your right thumb against your right nostril. Breathe in through the left nostril slowly until your lungs are full.
- Release the thumb and press the first finger of the same hand against the left nostril and breathe out.
- Inhale through the right nostril, then close it off and breathe out through the left.
- Repeat the cycle three to five times. (Yogis advocated doing this exercise before sunrise, at noon, at sunset, and at midnight to achieve purity of the nervous system for spiritual practice.)

- When you feel calm and rebalanced, relax and resume normal breathing. Visualize your body's soldiers (white blood cells) proliferating and gathering in a specific area that is in need of healing, or circulating throughout the body if you are trying to heal something like the flu. Feel the breaking up of tension in the afflicted area and warmth filling it. Visualize the healing.

You Still Need a Physician

It's been said that health is much more than the absence of disease. With skyrocketing health care costs, the prevailing emphasis now is on prevention of illnesses or diseases. This means that a basic understanding of how to care for the body is important. Focused intent for good health aligned with the Law of Attraction can bring it to you. That does not mean you should avoid seeking treatment from a qualified physician or medical establishment if you develop an illness or other serious condition.

FACT

Neuroscience has shown that people who meditate are healthier than their nonmeditating counterparts. Those who meditate experience a mental shift of their brain waves away from the right frontal cortex, an area associated with stress, to the left frontal cortex, resulting in a decrease in stress and anxiety. People who meditate experience a decrease in the activity of the amygdala, the part of the brain that processes fear.

In a medical crisis and immediately after, it can be exceedingly difficult to think about feeling joyful and doing positive affirmations. For example, when you are feeling an impending asthma attack, the inability to breathe fuels your anxiety at what could easily become a quickly deteriorating situation. Your lungs feel like shoe leather, prohibiting the easy inward flow of life-sustaining air. Asthma can kill you, so you must follow the protocols and treatment that your doctors have prescribed.

Once the emergency situation has passed and your condition is stabilized, you can meditate, do creative visualization, and recite affirmations for perfect health. Then, your expressions of gratitude and joy will align truthfully with your emotions.

In working with the Law of Attraction, you need not dwell on what initially caused the problem nor worry about when the condition initially emerged. Your work is to believe that the condition or illness is gone and vibrant health has returned. Just by feeling good, you are in touch with the energy source of all that exists, and that high-frequency energy source is your lifeline to a lifetime of good health.

CHAPTER 12

The Law of Attraction in Wealth and Prosperity

How do you create wealth? Creation begins in the world of thought. To have wealth, you must first be able to imagine wealth. Monetary wealth is the accumulation of coins or currency in large amounts. Visualize it freely flowing to you in ever-greater quantities. See yourself possessing, investing, spending, and donating money. Imagine how others will greet you and treat you when you are loaded with dough. How does being wealthy feel to you?

Abundance Versus Poverty

Abundance is not just about money. Abundance represents the success and happiness in all of the various areas of our lives. Financial prosperity is just one aspect of abundance. You can have unimaginable wealth, but if there is lack or suffering in other areas of your life, you may not equate having money with having peace of mind and satisfaction.

Perhaps the only area of your life where you are experiencing lack is in the money sector. You may feel that the American Dream is passing you by. The only abundance you seem to be manifesting is debt—college loans, credit cards, mortgage and car payments. There never seems to be an extra quarter, much less a dollar, left over at the end of the month. At times, you feel beaten. You wonder if you'll ever get ahead. What you might be doing is blocking the flow of money into your life by your worries about your indebtedness.

QUESTION?

What is the effect of hanging on to memories of past actions such as a bankruptcy filing?
Focusing your attention on a negative event can pull it back into your life. Concentrate not on the errors of the past but rather on the good things that are now en route to you through the Law of Attraction.

Thinking about lack brings more of the same. So you have bills. Who doesn't? It's difficult to go from a poverty mentality to an abundance mindset, but that's what you have to do. Set aside a few minutes whenever possible to visualize yourself (literally) as a money magnet. Feel excited, jubilant, and elated—the way you would feel if you won the lottery. Visualize money flying to you from myriad sources, both known and unknown. Allow your thoughts to consider how you might create new income streams. Without giving in to the impulse to hoard your newfound money, focus on ways to begin building wealth. Learn about investing in assets and the importance of diversification. Learn how to make your money work for you so that while you are attracting more, the wealth you already have grows. You may think it's impossible to acquire and grow wealth, but it's not. Remember that you have an invisible creative power to call upon whenever you want it and as often as it suits you, and the Bank of the Universe never closes.

In *The Power of Positive Thinking*, Dr. Norman Vincent Peale admonished people, even those experiencing severe lack in their lives, to stop fuming and fretting over the obstacles they encountered. He encouraged his readers to take control of themselves emotionally, to be peaceful, and to expect the best . . . always! A good attitude and faith better aligns you with the Law of Attraction and allows you to lift yourself from lack or even poverty to the financial freedom you seek. That is not to say that you shouldn't do your part to create income streams and save, but you should not dwell on the negative.

When you incline to have new clothes, look first well over the old ones, and see if you cannot shift with them another year, either by scouring, mending, or even patching if necessary. Remember, a patch on your coat and money in your pocket is better and more creditable than a writ on your back and no money to take it off.—Benjamin Franklin, *Poor Richard's Almanac*, 1775

Start moving the energy of abundance by creating flow. You create flow by giving to others what you desire—for example, love, money, appreciation—and doing so without thought of lack or deprivation. Live from a sense of abundance rather than lack. Know that money is energy that must move or circulate. Be grateful for each nickel, dime, and dollar as it comes to you and remember to give something back to others. That old saying by Benjamin Franklin "A penny saved is a penny earned" and the wisdom of the saying "Give more, get more" don't cancel each other out; they are part of the cycle of the circulation of money.

Give Freely

If you go to the grocery store and see a bell ringer for charity standing outside when you leave, take the coins you got from checking out and drop them into the charity bucket. Mentally affirm that the money will return to you many times over to help you build financial prosperity for yourself and your family.

Giving what you desire to manifest more of it in your life is an important concept. If you want money, give money; if you want love or respect, then show love and respect to others. If you are stingy in your giving, then don't be surprised if only a little money trickles back. Your gift, however, is less important than your attitude about living an abundant life—giving and believing that you will always have more to give. Of itself, that is a powerful positive affirmation.

According to feng shui experts, placing a water fountain that can run twenty-four hours each day in the prosperity area of a room (located in the rear left corner as you stand in the doorway looking in) will stimulate the positive flow of money. Financial abundance will begin to circulate around you just as the water circulates around the fountain.

The Millionaire Mindset

Financial success comes even more quickly when you do the following three things: Imagine your monetary desire with strong intention to manifest it; frequently focus purposeful attention on your goals; and be involved actively in achieving your desired outcome. Be on the lookout and take advantage of new opportunities to create income streams and remain open to allowing the universe to bring you what you want.

Millionaires have something in common besides wealth. Here are some of the habits and beliefs that wealthy people share:

- When something doesn't work, they don't view it as a failure so much as an opportunity to learn how not to behave, so that during their next effort they are successful.
- They do not give up even before they've started.
- They use their money wisely.
- They take responsibility for what happens in their life and do not believe that things happen by chance.

- They have respect for others and will enlist help from others to ensure the success of an endeavor.
- Regardless of the potential for a negative (even disastrous) result in a situation, they will always look for the possible positive outcome.
- They believe strongly in the necessity of commitment, not only to others but to the project.
- They do not engage in self-limiting thoughts, and instead of saying "I can't afford it," they will ask "How can I afford it?"

Think about the word *money* for a moment and see what kind of emotional responses the term evokes in you. Do you have negative feelings about never having enough of it? Do you view having money as not compatible with your spiritual life? Your thoughts about abundance or lack of money create a vibration that magnetizes your mindset. That magnetic vibration either impedes or enhances the flow of currency to you.

The Difference Between Abundance and Financial Wealth

Abundance means different things to different people. For some, abundance is having the good things in life that money can't buy and for others it is financial freedom. For someone who has survived a natural disaster, lived under a tyrannical dictator, or escaped a war zone, abundance means something different than it might mean to an individual trying to raise three kids alone and having to work two jobs to do it. For the former it is about freedom, safety, and family, and for the latter it is about having money to care for her children.

FACT

In his second inaugural address, Franklin D. Roosevelt warned of the dangers of ruthless self-interest, dulled conscience, and irresponsibility, calling those symptoms of prosperity "portents of disaster." He noted that the real test of a progressive society was not whether its people heaped abundance upon those who already had plenty but if it provided for those with too little.

Perhaps you are someone who believes abundance means having it all—plenty of wealth, good relationships, excellent health, and family. The reality is that you can have it all. Purposeful, focused, and magnetized thoughts and feelings bring whatever you desire.

Suspension of Disbelief

When you see a movie or read a novel, you choose to suspend disbelief in order to go along with the experience. You will identify with the hero and, for the length of the film or book, you will experience his world and adventures as seen through his eyes. The suspension of disbelief is an important element. You have a vested interest in the outcome—the satisfying ending. There is little point in seeing the movie if you sit there reminding yourself that it's just a story with no relevance to you.

So, too, you must suspend the disbelief that you can have wealth, even if you know your sneakers have holes in the soles and your present financial hardships are oppressive and seemingly unrelenting. You can think like the pessimist that wealth is not and can never be part of your life, and your thoughts and feelings will make it so. Or you can become the optimist and see yourself feeling the elation of acquiring, holding on to, and increasing the currency flowing into your life right now. It takes only a necessary shift in consciousness.

Johann Wolfgang von Goethe once commented that the moment that you commit yourself is the magical moment Providence moves, too. Take that first big, bold step toward the money you desire to claim and the magic and power in that step forward can launch the process. Remember, money is an energy that flows like an electric current. Set up the attraction, avoid impeding its flow, and it must come to you.

"Magic is believing in yourself. If you can do that, you can make anything happen," Goethe asserted. He also said, "Destiny grants our wishes, but in its own way, in order to give us something beyond our wishes."

Get Out of Debt and Manifest Prosperity

Failure and lack in life are manifested first in the mind. Somehow you imagined lack and it found you. So how do you get out from under the weight of debt to manifest financial prosperity?

In the Old Testament, Joseph dreamed of having his brothers' sheaves of grain bow before his and the sun, moon, and stars paying tribute to him. Such dreams were harbingers of Joseph's future as a powerful man in service to Egypt's pharaoh, yet Joseph would first endure his brothers selling him into slavery. How does an enslaved person develop the type of thoughts necessary to leave the world of oppression and enter the one of abundance and wealth and power? You can accomplish it through the imaginative power of the mind and an attitude of gratitude.

Make a wealth poster. On the center of a piece of poster board, place or draw something that symbolizes the infinite source—for example, the infinity symbol (the number eight lying on its side). Around the perimeter, write the areas of your life, such as relationships, knowledge, and health. Add images and affirmations to symbolize the things you desire for each area and how money will help you achieve those desires.

Words You Must Never Use: **Debt** *and* **Bill**

Words like *debt* and *bill* are supercharged with negativity. If you try to formulate a positive affirmation such as "I am happy that I'm getting out of debt," the subconscious will key in on the word *debt* and bring you more. Ditto for the word *bill*. It is far better to write out an affirmation that excludes those two words. For example, "I am happy that my money increases every day and that I can now pay off my car." Or, "I am overjoyed that my wealth is growing daily, and I can easily make my mortgage payment with plenty of money left over."

If you spend even a little time reverting back to old patterns of thought about how little money you really have and how your financial obligations are so numerous that you may never get out of debt, you are sabotaging any positive efforts you may be making to attract money. Stay focused on what you want. Give your emotional and thought energy to that.

Money Is Not the End All, Be All

Beware of magnifying the importance of money so much that you begin to hoard it. Making money into your god will thwart your efforts to bring more of it to you. Remember that money must circulate. As it comes, express gratitude and share or tithe a percentage to your church, favorite cause, or someone in need.

Watch Those Mixed Mental Messages

The universe is rich beyond the human mind's ability to grasp just how abundant it is. It is counterproductive to flip back and forth between the extremes of being greedy or lacking money. Rather, cultivate a steady positive focus on joyful confidence that whatever you desire and intend to have is already on its way to you in this moment.

Become a Money Magnet

Wealth magnet John D. Rockefeller used to say that God gave him his money. Born in 1839 on a New York farm, Rockefeller was the second of six children born to William A. and Eliza Rockefeller. John's life was informed by his work ethic, family training, religious beliefs, and financial habits. Hearing a minister once say "Get money; get it honestly, and give it wisely," was a moment of epiphany for Rockefeller. Those words became the financial plan for his life.

After making his fortune as founder of the Standard Oil Company, he stepped down from the daily leadership of the company when he was fifty-seven. From that point on, he focused on giving away the bulk of his fortune in philanthropic efforts to do the most good for human welfare.

Everyone has a little adversity in life. Follow your passion, aligned with the Law of Attraction. Let your affirmations reflect your trust in a higher power. For example, try the following affirmation: "I am happy to be guided by the infinite wisdom that upholds all of creation in all my monetary affairs. As a child of the Divine, I am grateful for the blessings of grace through which money flows easily into my life. Just as I am receiving an abundance of money from sources both known and unknown, so do I give generously to others."

FACT

Some of the world's wealthiest people faced adversity before becoming money magnets. Oprah Winfrey grew up in poverty on her grandmother's farm. Apple cofounder Steve Jobs and designer Ralph Lauren were both college dropouts. Billionaire Bill Gates left Harvard before graduating to sell software. J. K. Rowling was on welfare when she wrote a little book about a kid named Harry Potter.

Make a Wealth Receptacle

Infuse this exercise with enthusiasm, happiness, and a sense of expectation, for completing it can help you focus on wealth and potential avenues (such as jobs or businesses) to generate it.

1. Find and decorate a tray, urn, hat box, coffee can, or some other receptacle in red and gold, colors that attract prosperity.
2. On a piece of paper, write out your declarations for wealth, making them clear and succinct and including the time frame during which you want your wealth to manifest.
3. Put the paper containing your wealth desires into a red envelope and drop it into the box.
4. Add other items that symbolize your wealth desires.
5. Place the box in the wealth sector of your home or office near a money tree plant and a small bubbling fountain or aquarium. Finally, place a small lamp or other light source with a red bulb in that sector.

In every culture, when people want to manifest something in their life expression, they often surround themselves with images of the things they desire to manifest. Symbolically, the items you place in highly visible areas stimulate your mind to turn toward thoughts of prosperity.

In your wealth tray or container, you could add a miniature statue of the Money Buddha or Lakshmi, the Hindu goddess of wealth. Other possibilities include the tarot deck's Ace of Pentacles since it represents wealth, money, luck, and the successful beginning of a new business or enterprise. You might add old Chinese feng shui coins—obtain them from a wealthy place, not one going out of business—or dollar bills in multiples of the number eight. Eight is such a lucky number for wealth that in China, businessmen strive to get that number in their addresses and phone numbers. It is believed to double their incomes.

You could also drop in a piece of jade, a semiprecious stone believed to attract good luck and fortune. If you think there may be obstacles in your path to wealth, install a small statue of the Hindu god Ganesh, the remover of obstacles. Hang a gold-colored wind chime from which are strung metal cylinders and Chinese coins. The movement of the chiming elements suggests the attraction and circulation of money. Light a red candle.

Watch for Signs

If you are endeavoring to attract prosperity, you should avoid spending money you don't have. Don't expect that you'll go to sleep at night and find your wallet will be miraculously full of currency when you awake in the morning. Do watch for the means of prosperity to suddenly start showing up in your life as job offers or business connections, alliances, and new opportunities. At first, they may seem like coincidences or synchronicity at work.

Do allow for money to flow in, even if you don't expect it or never considered it coming from a particular source. Do pay attention. Record the proof of the Law of Attraction at work by noting in your journal, diary, or scheduling book whenever you find a penny, get a gift certificate you didn't expect, receive a free coffee at Starbucks, notice a forgotten five dollar bill in the pocket of a jacket you picked up at a yard sale, or see some other sign that the law is at work in your life.

Avail yourself of the opportunities that feel right to you. Just imagine if J. K. Rowling had not allowed the inspiration for the adolescent wizard Harry Potter to lead her? What if Ralph Lauren had not decided to take his tie designs and found his own company, Polo Fashions, in 1968? And what if Oprah had decided that she could never hold her own in the world of daytime television talk shows?

CHAPTER 13

The Law of Attraction and Relationships

How do you find and choose one special person from a world of potential mates? Some say that the key lies in the human brain and the way it is wired for romantic love, sexual attraction, and the need for attachment. The desire to give and receive love may compel us to look for the ideal life partner, but finding the right one can be difficult. Still, humans were choosing a single mate with whom to bond long before Kabir, the fifteenth-century Indian poet, wrote that "the road of love is narrow."

Love Yourself

True love starts with self-love. You must love and respect yourself in order to unconditionally give and receive true love. The choice of a mate necessarily requires a deep understanding of who you are and what you desire as well as what you don't want in a lifelong partnership. Otherwise, you may tumble into a romance based on physical attraction and chemistry and only after you have become emotionally invested will you discover fatal flaws in the relationship.

The Law of Attraction will bring you excellent candidates for your life partner. You help it accomplish that goal by a thorough understanding of your personality, the aspects that drive your choices, and your most important core beliefs and values. Then you must decide what you seek in others.

The three stages of romantic love include lust, attraction (overidealizing and fantasizing about the other person), and attachment (where fantasy love is replaced by real love and commitment). Falling in love, your brain becomes flooded by dopamine (which stimulates blissful feelings) and norepinephrine (which produces heightened attention and excitability). Serotonin levels drop, which suppresses the neural circuits involved in assessing others.

Brain chemistry changes depending on how long you have been in love. Blind attraction does not necessarily ensure a long and lasting commitment. Relationships often end because one or both of the individuals in the relationship could not live with some quality, habit, or trait of the other once their brain chemistry returned to normal and the attraction stage of love shifted to the attachment stage at around thirty months. Lack of attachment during the cooling off may account for why divorces hit a peak at around four years. Anthropologist Helen Fisher, Ph.D., professor and human behavior researcher at Rutgers University and author of *Why We Love*, says that biological programming is why people get antsy after about four years of marriage. The drive for a couple to remain together to see a child through its infancy (or about four years) dates back millions of years. The normal duration for infatuation is two to three years, according to Fisher.

Probing Below the Surface of Who You Are

Psychologists say that emotionally healthy people who thrive in strong, committed relationships may have had the advantage of having healthy relationships modeled for them. Their interpersonal relationships include such elements as respect, boundaries, truthfulness, and transparency. Others, who don't seem to be able to make successful relationships, may have had less nurturing models or are driven by psychological factors (such as the need to rescue, seek father figures, or date bad boys or divas) to choose bad partners because their own self-esteem is low.

Carrying Forward Old Wounds

Those who have studied human relationships assert that on a deep subconscious level, we carry psychological patterns and wounds from previous relationships that can sabotage our current ones. These wounds may not even be ours; they may have been inherited from our parents.

Spend some quiet time reflecting on how your answers to the following questions might be impacting your current relationships. Then consider whether you desire to have someone in your life who triggers or engages in such behaviors.

- Were family members verbally abusive? Was that tolerated in your family?
- Did members of your family practice manipulation instead of truthful integrity as a means of winning?
- Did the adults in your family stoically conceal their emotions? On the other hand, were they emotionally volatile?
- Did either of your parents ever have an affair? If so, was trust ever restored?

- Did anyone withhold love or intimacy as a means to manipulate?
- Did someone suffer an addiction and hurt others as a result?
- Was hitting or spanking a child acceptable punishment in your family?

Evaluate the choices you have made in selecting romantic companions. Try to identify patterns. Do you keep attracting the same type of person? At first, you believe your new love to be the ideal romantic partner, but you eventually discover that you are not good together. Are you an incurable romantic who falls in love at first sight and all too soon has to accept the end of the relationship? Maybe you prefer romantic partners who remind you of someone in your past or in your family—a father figure, for example. Do you seek people whose attitudes are compatible with yours but whose personalities are not? Does it seem that you are always attracted to your mirror opposite?

Evaluating Relationship Choices

There are reasons why you selected your romantic partners, whether you knew it or not. Identifying the reasons—and the reasons why your relationships may have failed—can help you reshape the way you approach relationships. It will also help you identify what is truly important to you so you can have a clear picture of the type of relationship you want in your life.

Leaping Before Looking

You love staying home, reading mystery novels, and watching reruns of *Law and Order* with your cat. You haven't traveled outside of your state, don't drink, and eat a mostly vegetarian diet. But you find yourself attracted to a swaggering world-traveler who eats anything gourmet, belongs to several wine clubs, and runs three miles every day with his Doberman. Why, you might ask, are you attracted to someone who is so dissimilar to you? Someone whose life experience and beliefs are different from yours can inspire feelings of excitement, exhilaration, and risk. Yet differences in your opinions can become catalysts for heated debate or major departure points for high drama and conflict.

You may believe that you and your partner share an unspoken commitment to monogamy and demand absolute loyalty from each other. You soon discover that he professes his love for you but also believes that it's okay to chat with women he finds on international dating sites. He tells you he's not doing anything wrong because there's no emotional commitment; he's just socializing. You, however, feel totally betrayed. It's possible the two of you are viewing the situation through different lenses.

Lack of trust, anger, and resentment soon replace the love and commitment you thought you both shared. If you had a different cultural upbringing, you may have cultural as well as psychological minefields to navigate. That will require patience, understanding, and special communication skills. But as Mother Teresa once observed, love is a fruit always in season and within everyone's reach. A better understanding of your own core values, beliefs, and attitudes helps you refine ideas about what you desire in an ideal mate.

Figuring Out Your Core Principles

Read the following list, adding principles or values that are important to you and crossing out those that are not important. Narrow the list to the eight core principles that you believe are critical to your life. Eliminate five of the eight. The remaining three are your most important core principles.

- Self Acceptance
- Career
- Fame
- Family
- Friendship
- Happiness
- Health
- Honesty
- Inclusion of Others
- Integrity
- Joy

- Justice
- Love
- Peace
- Power
- Recognition
- Spirituality
- Status
- Wealth
- Wisdom

To create a mission statement, write a paragraph for each of these three values about what they mean to you when you experience success in them. Finally, merge the three paragraphs together to create a powerful mission statement for your life.

The University of Iowa's Shanhong Luo and Eva C. Klohnen assert that once people are in a committed relationship, their shared personality similarities positively impact marital happiness and satisfaction. In their research, opposites did not appear to attract each other. For the full article, go to *www.apa.org/journals/releases /psp882304.pdf*.

Finding Someone with a Similar Personality

When a couple can both give and receive unconditional love and respect, the relationship thrives. It suffers, however, in an atmosphere of deceit, or with an imbalance of power, unrevealed expectations, or betrayal. Psychologists say that the act of betrayal is often so damaging that roughly one out of every three people who are betrayed become clinically depressed. The key to finding that perfect mate lies in your deliberate work with the Law of Attraction to bring someone whose personality is similar to yours into your life.

Are You Sabotaging Your Romantic Relationships?

Every moment in a relationship, you have the power to feel positive or negative, beautiful or ugly, full of hopes and dreams or just hanging on. When you are with someone special and find yourself communicating with sarcasm, criticism, whining, or sniping, you are setting yourself up to elicit negative responses. Be the lover you want your partner to be. Remember that true love is taking care of the other person's happiness because it is essential to yours.

FACT

There are proven ways to attract someone good. For example, loving and respecting yourself makes you attractive to others. When you establish firm boundaries, you draw emotionally healthy people to you. When you demonstrate loyalty and trust, you attract those who honor commitments. Cultivating these qualities will attract others for whom these things are important.

Praising Behaviors You Want Repeated

When you attract people who respect and care for you, it makes you feel good about yourself. They appreciate you, and you know because they tell you and demonstrate their appreciation. That, in turn, endears them to you and raises your self-esteem. You are inclined to return the love and attention they shower upon you. Your praise and loving actions induce them to show more positive and romantic behavior. The cycle creates a healthy environment for your relationship to blossom.

Recognizing the Negative

Each time you find yourself in a foul mood and ready to pick a fight with your partner, think back to the exact moment you first began to feel negative. What triggered the shift? Understanding the triggers can enable you to choose to respond differently. Past hurts can cause you to slip into knee-jerk reactions to something your partner says or does. Take responsibility for your role in the argument. If it's part of an old pattern, watch for the triggers and shift the energy.

Attract the Perfect Romantic Partner

The Law of Attraction will bring someone perfect for you if you allow for that to happen in your life. Be aware that you cannot change anyone but yourself, so don't try to use the law for that purpose. It won't work because you don't own their vibration and thoughts. You can change only yourself.

A vital step in getting the relationships, things, circumstances, or life experiences you desire is to allow yourself to receive whatever you are intentionally creating. That is why the affirmations "I am open to receiving" and "I allow my highest good to come to me now" are so powerful and should be repeated often.

Focus on the life you want with the kind of person you want. Feel joy, gratitude, and peace to raise your vibration to draw that person to you. You have a choice in every moment to be available to love. Put your attention there and the attraction begins. Don't worry about when, where, or how it will happen. Know that someone special is en route to you at this moment. The speed of the arrival is directly related to the strength and magnetism of your thoughts, intention, and desire.

Focus On the Qualities You Desire

Make a list of the good qualities you seek in a partner and why. Or, if it's easier, list the qualities you don't want and then use each in a sentence that states the opposite, or the quality you do want. For example, this could be a negative statement: I feel insulted and disrespected when I hear profanity carelessly peppered throughout my date's vocabulary. Think about the opposite and use it to write a positive statement: I feel happy, loved, and respected when my date is thoughtful and considerate about word choices.

Do Not Tolerate Bad Behavior

Refuse to tolerate bad behaviors such as aggression, yelling, manipulation, deception, lies, threats, and intimidation. Recognize such actions for what they are—abusive behavior. Often such behaviors are by-products of addictions or emotional issues and are destructive to a relationship. Set boundaries. If they are not honored, end the relationship to protect yourself.

FACT

Some people find it helpful to do a tarot card reading to remind them to make affirmations or do visualizations to attract the perfect romantic partner into their lives. The Sun, a powerful card of the Major Arcana, symbolizes warmth, completion, and a successful outcome of an endeavor. The Two of Cups shows young lovers, symbolizing new romance, engagement, and marriage.

Turn On the Switch for Love

An omnipresent spiritual force begins to draw into your life the love you desire at the moment you decide to open your heart and life to receive that special someone. You might run into that person while taking out the garbage . . . or on the subway . . . or at the bank. Look your best from the inside out. Love yourself enough to take good care of yourself. That, in short, is how you turn on the switch for love. Physical, mental, and spiritual health generates the light of your inner being. Let it shine forth.

Making Space in Your Life for Love

Three years after separating from Warren, Susanna's divorce became final. She bought a cake covered with strawberries along with a couple of bottles of champagne and invited her girlfriends over for a new beginnings party.

Susanna's father, a banker, had died when she was ten. When she began to date, she didn't choose guys her own age. She preferred powerful older men. When she met Warren, a San Francisco stockbroker seventeen years her senior, it was love at first sight for Susanna.

Susanna knew Warren loved the social scene and San Francisco night life, but she thought marriage would make him love staying home as much as she did. However, she soon discovered that Warren didn't want to change. He liked being a powerful man in one of the most cosmopolitan cities in the world with money enough to indulge his many passions, including affairs.

Somewhere, oh, My Beloved One, the house is standing,
Waiting for thee and me; for our first caresses.
It may be a river-boat, or a wave-washed landing,
The shade of a tree in the jungle's dim recesses,
Some far-off mountain tent, ill-pitched and lonely.
Or the naked vault of the purple heavens only.
But the Place is waiting there; till the Hour we shall show it
And our footsteps, following Fate, find it and know it.
—Laurence Hope, *Complete Love Lyrics,* "Written in Cananore"

After gaining fifteen pounds and sinking into a deep depression, Susanna asked for a divorce and entered therapy to understand her issues about abandonment and low self-esteem. She began to practice yoga and meditation, exercised, and ate healthier foods. The excess weight dropped off. She felt more energetic and alert. Her desire to love again was fueled by self-knowledge, courage, and the conviction that she was worth it. She spent some time each day meditating, feeling the joy in life, and focusing on attracting a new love.

On the day of her party, Susanna raced up the steep steps to her apartment with all the refreshments. Tripping on the second step and crashing to her knees on top of the cake box, she cried out in anguish as the champagne fizzed out of the broken bottles and down the sidewalk. Then she felt two strong hands lifting her up. They belonged to Frank, a fourth-year medical student who lived in the Victorian next door. He offered to look at her bleeding knee and stayed for the party. The chemistry between them was palpable, but Susanna didn't accept Frank's marriage proposal until she was sure that he was truly Mr. Right.

Like Susanna, practice the art of loving another with understanding, patience, and insight. When you find someone new who might be the one, take care to love that person as you desire to be loved in return. Take time to listen. Compliment him and be truthful and sincere. Remember to say thank you. Draw more love to you by affirming your love, showing love, speaking of love, and writing love poems or letters to the one you love.

Love as a Weapon Against Hostility

Love can be a powerful healing potion. When a friend or romantic partner is upset and directs anger and hostility toward you, find a way to defuse the anger by attempting to understand what is at the heart of the problem and why you are the target of the anger. Discuss the problem in language that is nonthreatening. Show empathy and recognition of what she might be experiencing. Say, "I can see that you are feeling upset," or "You must feel terrible right now," or "I understand how deeply wounded you are feeling."

The angry individual needs to know that you recognize the truth of her frustration, anger, or pain. Seeing your empathy, she may become calm and better able to coherently discuss the situation. Remind that person that you love her and feel that it is important for the two of you to work through such emotionally potent problems.

Recognizing Passive-Aggressive Behavior

An occasional argument can certainly be shifted through love and assertiveness; however, when the disagreement is with someone showing passive-aggressive behavior (think of Shakespeare's *Hamlet* and his classic passive-aggressive behavior (love becomes a weapon) he uses against you. Prince Hamlet, you may recall, was filled with unexpressed rage against his uncle Claudius, whom he suspected was behind the death of his father. Claudius had not only taken his brother's place as king and robbed Hamlet of his birthright, he had married Gertrude, Hamlet's mother. Hamlet wished his mother no harm but silently obsessed about killing his uncle. The emotional turmoil built inside him until it erupted into a play that explicitly re-enacted the death of Hamlet's father as Hamlet imagined it.

Ultimately, Hamlet, his mother, and Claudius died. Hamlet might have lived had he been able to work through his conflicting feelings, but he couldn't. The passive-aggressive person retreats into silence and won't talk with you. He may never directly address his anger toward you, but you can nevertheless feel his rage. The person uses silence as a weapon to make you feel guilty. He may remain unapproachable and give you the cold shoulder.

Passive-aggressive behavior is not always easy to recognize or understand. The passive-aggressive person will dilly-dally to avoid doing a task, even though he knows it is his responsibility. He will also avoid confrontation over not doing it and will feel picked on when he is directly accused. He will get back at you indirectly and won't let you know why. He may have a pattern of saying something mean to you and then brushing it off like he's just kidding. He's not. He may have a persistent pessimistic pattern of thinking.

When you set forth your desire to attract people into your life for interpersonal relationships, you will ask the universe for emotionally and psychologically healthy individuals. It is possible that if you are not clear about your desire, someone with some of the signs of passive-aggressive behavior might show up. Before declaring your desire, take this list of negatives and turn each into a positive statement for what you do want to attract.

- Blames other people; it's always someone else's fault
- Complains; nothing ever goes right

- Resents recommendations from others for a better way to do something
- Fears many things, including authority figures and dependency on others
- Exhibits stubbornness
- Tells lies
- Makes excuses
- Misplaces and loses things

Finding Help and Insight

If you are already in a committed relationship with someone with anger issues or passive-aggressive behavior, or if you have family members or friends with symptoms, take heart. You have myriad sources available to you to learn about how to deal with such behaviors. Read more at the National Institutes for Health at *www.nlm.nih.gov/medlineplus/ency /article/000943.htm.*

CHAPTER 14

The Law of Attraction and Spirituality

When you bow with folded hands and say "namaste," you are repeating an ancient Sanskrit greeting that means "I bow to you." *Namas* means "bow" and *te* means "to you." Place the palms of your hands together, prayerlike, near your heart, bow toward the other person and speak the greeting. *Namaste* serves as a mantra, mudra (hand placement), and greeting, all in intentional harmonious alignment. Aim for that kind of alignment with the Law of Attraction to enhance your spiritual endeavors for success in all areas of your life.

14

Great Thinkers, Spiritual Giants, and World Leaders

If you try to live by deep spiritual convictions but find it difficult to develop spiritually while juggling a career, family obligations, and other responsibilities, you are not alone. People in America are stressed out, get too little sleep, and have so many responsibilities that finding a way to squeeze out an extra hour now and then for meditation or other spiritual practices seems nearly impossible. But the Law of Attraction will bring you spiritual opportunities, teachers, helpers, and other resources you might need. And you may even see the boundaries blurring between the spiritual and physical worlds.

That is to be called soul which through the power of delusion, does not recognize itself as being really God; God the giver of bondage and of deliverance, the head of all things.—Valmiki, *The Ramayana of Tulsidas*, The Forest, Doha 12

Spirituality and Religion

Whatever your spiritual philosophy, be assured that the Law of Attraction works alongside all belief systems. Whatever is at the top of the spiritual mountain, there are certainly myriad paths upward. Stick to what feels right to you and the law will bring you what you pray for, think about, or deeply desire from your belief system. It does not discriminate—it is drawing to you what your emotions and thoughts focus on. If you change your belief system and desire to align with a different spiritual path, the law is still working in tune with your thoughts. A person can be deeply spiritual and not be aligned with a particular religion and yet the law works with them just the same.

While atheists claim Albert Einstein never believed in a personal God, others say he did and point to his famous statement "God does not play dice" as proof. But Einstein, who was raised a secular Jew, abhorred having his spiritual beliefs misrepresented and stated that he did not believe in a personal God. He said that his was rather an admiration without limits for the "structure of the world" inasmuch as science reveals it. Einstein engaged in original thought. He did not let others do his thinking for him. Perhaps that resonates with your feeling about the universe and creation and spirituality.

FACT

Dharma is a way of living in which the body, mind, and spirit are in perfect alignment. You must have faith that you can achieve your goals and dreams regardless of whether anyone else believes in what you want to do. When your life's work is not different from your spiritual work, you are following your dharma.

Or maybe you think more like Shakespeare, who wrote his masterpieces from a decidedly God-centered perspective using many lessons gleaned from the Bible. If you wish to change the direction of your life, take a page from Shakespeare's story and perhaps let the Bible guide you into some new spiritual highways and byways. While Shakespeare's plays are filled with Biblical lessons, truths, principles, and morals, his own world reflected his dream for a life course that was different from the one he began.

Details about the early life of William Shakespeare are disputed, but according to one story, he was the son of a farmer's daughter and a village butcher who was jailed for nonpayment of debt. By age twenty-four, he was already married with three children. Shakespeare may have felt imprisoned by the life he had created. Surely concerned about money and his ability to provide for his family, he desired to make a major shift. He followed the well-worn path out of Stratford village and the spiritual path in his heart as he headed straight to the London stage and playwriting. His life took a decidedly more prosperous turn, undoubtedly through the workings of the Law of Attraction and his heartfelt desire for a major shift in his life.

Your endeavors on the spiritual plane inform your thoughts and actions in the world and set into motion a creative force to help you achieve success in whatever you do. Wallace Wattles noted that when you desire to do something, the desire alone is the proof that the power you need to do that work is already inside you.

Einstein's passion was mathematics and Shakespeare's was playwriting. Before they could manifest new lives they had to align their minds, hearts, and actions with their inner desire to do what they were meant to do. Only then did their efforts bring them success. This is a vital lesson on putting the law to work in your life to achieve your spiritual goals.

In the play *Hamlet*, Shakespeare put the following words into Polonius's mouth, but perhaps they resonated in Shakespeare's own heart: "This above all: To thine own self be true, And it must follow, as the night the day, Thou canst not then be false to any man."

Heed the Call to Spiritual Adventure

Perhaps you have dreamed about undertaking some fantastic spiritual adventure somewhere in the world, possibly to hike the sacred landscape of Machu Picchu in Peru, pray at the shrine of Mary Magdalene at Vezelay in France, trek the last twenty miles of the road to Santiago di Compostela in Spain, or see the caves of the ancient Anasazi in New Mexico. Don't let self-limiting fears of being too old, being out of shape, or being alone limit your experience.

Abraham's Journey

Remember that Abraham, the Jewish patriarch, was seventy-five years old when he received a divine call to leave Ur to undertake a journey to Canaan, a strange and distant place. When you get the call to do something spiritual, don't let fear and old patterns of doubt and negative self-talk hold you back. Feel jubilant that you know from the depths of your being what you are now supposed to do. You, not someone else, have received the gift, the inspiration. Be grateful and make the most of it. Old Abraham might have wondered if he weren't just hatching some crazy plan in his daydreaming mind. Did he think about possible negative consequences of just pulling up the stakes of the tent and setting off toward that strange land? Nope, he heeded the call and felt blessed to be on his way.

Get thee out of thy country, and from thy kindred, and from thy father's house, unto land that I will show thee: And I will make of thee a great nation, and I will bless thee, and make thy name great; and thou shalt be a blessing. So Abram departed . . . and went forth to go into the land of Canaan.—Genesis 12:1–5

What spiritually great things could you accomplish if you, like Abraham, believed that you were being guided, inspired, and blessed in all your endeavors by the greatest power in the universe and you had only to be quiet to receive direction? Abraham's clear inner vision and outer action were perfectly aligned. "Abram: I am thy shield, and thy exceeding great reward." (Genesis 15:1) What tremendous power those words must have had for Abraham. The everlasting covenant between the God of Abraham and the Jewish people, through the rite of circumcision, endures to this day. In the history of humankind, Abraham stands as a spiritual giant because he did not hesitate to follow the guidance he received.

Some individuals seem to set upon their spiritual path early in life. For others, aimlessness and a vague sense that they are not yet on track with their destiny impels them to seek spiritual meaning. Sometimes they discover that when they pursue their spiritual work, it dovetails into their chosen career path.

Wilberforce's Crusade

When you see something you know is morally wrong, whatever your spiritual traditions and beliefs, do something, say something, and be an advocate for right thinking and action. Hold tight to your convictions, for they set up a pull for the Law of Attraction to draw to you other like-minded people who will help you in the cause. It's not always easy to know what to do when you see the tide of public opinion unopposed to something you feel is spiritually wrong. For the eighteenth-century English parliamentarian William Wilberforce, for example, that's just what happened. Yet, he found an alignment between his thoughts and actions, his spiritual work and his business, and that set the Law of Attraction into motion to draw helpful people to him. Wilberforce regarded the slave trade as inhuman and vowed to do everything possible to suppress and abolish it. Branded as a dangerous radical, Wilberforce persisted, the power of his spiritual stand igniting moral outrage in the hearts of fellow Englishmen against the slave ships. He prevailed and England abolished the slave trade.

Whatever your path, your efforts to deepen your spiritual experience, increase your knowledge, and raise your vibration can be done in all types of environments and conditions. Find your path. You'll know you are on it when you see how easily your thoughts, spiritual desires, and actions align. These things synchronize your soul's call with the Law of Attraction to manifest your spiritual gifts.

Gandhi's Work to End Social Injustice

Do spiritual work with a single-minded focus and you will be following your true nature aligned with the Divine. That is *dharma*. Effort in harmonious alignment with dharma will unify. A good example of a historical figure following his dharma is Mohandas Gandhi. He was simultaneously a spiritual giant and a diminutive man in a loincloth who brought Great Britain to its knees and secured India's independence. His life serves as a spiritual model for social change.

You don't have to hold degrees from the best schools, wear this season's haute couture, speak six languages, or serve in the diplomatic corps to be a spiritual force for social change. Gandhi began to study religion and eat a vegetarian diet while he trained as a lawyer in England. Unable to find work after returning to India, he went to South Africa where he encountered racism and social injustice. There, he successfully spearheaded nonviolent resistance to help Indians fight a law aimed at forcing them to register. Returning to India, he again used civil disobedience in the Quit India campaign to expel the English. He became known as the Father of India. Some called him a saint trying to be a politician, but Gandhi rejected that idea, insisting instead that he was a politician trying to become a saint.

If you think your spiritual work can only be done in private, think again. Abraham, Wilberforce, and Gandhi found their spiritual work in the world, in the milieu of their time. You don't have to go off to an isolated cave in the Himalayas. You don't have to join a Carmelite convent. You don't need to go outside of yourself to find spiritual understanding, insights, and peace.

Synchronicity and the Law of Attraction

Many people have experienced coincidences in their lives, but when such events are multiple and meaningful, synchronicity is surely at work. Some people believe that the more a person evolves, the more synchronicity occurs in her life. Others suggest that synchronous events happen because of excitable emotion and a strong expectation that draws such occurrences into manifestation.

The Artist Gets a Nudge

Anna was a young art teacher with an almost obsessive desire to see the *Book of Kells*. Another teacher had given her a small calendar featuring images of the ornately illustrated pages created by Celtic monks, who lived in roughly A.D. 800. Anna thought about traveling to Ireland. But she lived in a cheap apartment in Berkeley, California, and barely made enough money to pay for rent and basic necessities. The *Book of Kells* was housed in Trinity College's library in Dublin. If she closed out her savings, she might have enough to get cheap airfare, but what about lodging, food, and transportation?

Anna stared at the calendar on her desk and vowed to get to Ireland someday. A few hours later, Anna leafed through a textbook returned by one of her students and was surprised to see an Ireland travel brochure in it. Later that afternoon, a postcard arrived in the mail from the United Kingdom. It announced a special weeklong exchange program for art teachers, sponsored by Trinity College. Food and lodging were included. Anna became convinced that the three occurrences were surely more than mere coincidences. She was right. The law of synchronicity responded to her obsessive desire and worked to give her the push she needed.

More than Coincidence

You may not notice it, but synchronicity is going on all the time. Learn to live your life in a magical yet purposeful way, and you'll begin to see the meaningful—even mystical—occurrences in life that you may be missing because you are distracted or too busy or tired to notice. Synchronicities are those little meaningful coincidences that can point you in new directions or provide you with moments of breakthrough understanding. The more you notice them, the more of them, seemingly, there are to notice.

FACT

Swiss psychologist Carl Jung coined the term *synchronicity*. Jung offered psychological insights into human consciousness as a result of viewing the psyche through the lenses of myth, art, religion, philosophy, and dreams. Jung's interest in Eastern religions and philosophies influenced and informed his ideas about the importance of the unconscious and value of daily spiritual practice.

Synchronicity is one indicator that the Law of Attraction is at work and that something you have asked for is beginning to make its way to you. It bears repeating that it is worthwhile to pay attention to coincidences. Watch for evidence of meaningful occurrences and their connectivity. Notice patterns of flow, when things easily happen or come together. Observe how little signs begin to show up and give notice that the universe has received your request.

Manifest Spiritual Results

Maybe you desire to dive deeper in meditation than you have ever gone. Perhaps you want to replace a bad habit with a good one that better serves your spiritual endeavors. Maybe you seek inspiration for meaningful spiritual work you can do to benefit the world or you seek a teacher or inspiration for the direction to take on your personal spiritual path. You can do all those things and even more by deliberate and intentional work with the Law of Attraction.

In an Abraham Hicks' workshop, the point was made that asking must come from wanting and desire rather than mere words. It is the asking you do from the heart charged by emotion that activates the power of the law around your desire. Perhaps your heart feels empty or deadened. You want your heart not to feel so dry but rather filled with love for the divine, like the spiritual oasis it has been before.

Experiencing Higher Vibration

Here's a little technique to try in order to consciously raise your vibration. It's easy and just takes a few minutes. Try recording this in a soft voice with long pauses between the steps. Play it back once you are sitting comfortably with your eyes closed.

1. Sit comfortably with your eyes closed.
2. Inhale a cleansing breath. Exhale stress and negativity. Do this three times.
3. Turn your closed eyes gently upward to the point between your eyebrows and focus there. Imagine powerful rays of light pouring into your head, filling you with warm, holy light as you feel yourself slightly spinning or rising.
4. Listen for a little buzz, the cosmic vibration of atoms throughout creation, and focus on that.

5. Relax and sink even deeper, especially in the spaces between your breaths. Bask in the peace. Feel love radiating out of your heart's energy center to everyone who needs love.

6. Mentally affirm that you are going to count slowly to five and that when you reach five, your energy vibration will automatically rise. As you count, feel the rays flowing in. They are warmer, but not beyond your comfort level. Hear the buzzing sound more loudly. Feel yourself floating higher. You have just raised your vibration. Do you feel the difference?

The Law of Attraction works whether you nurture the divine within and seek increase for your spiritual life or whether you do things that evoke the law of decrease. When you criticize others, demean a person's choices, devalue someone's work, or spread gossip about someone, you are setting in motion three universal laws: the Law of Decrease, the Law of Karma, and the Law of Attraction. Don't waste your mental currency on such negative activity since it will return to you in kind. Instead, focus on working with the Law of Increase and the Law of Attraction to manifest spiritual results.

Infinite Potentiality

The ego is what creates the sense of your separation from the Divine. In meditation, the ego's hold can lessen as you transcend into higher states of consciousness. In his book *The Seven Spiritual Laws of Success*, Deepak Chopra writes that all things are possible within the realm of pure consciousness, and that pure consciousness is your essential nature. You experience the truth of who you really are—a spark of the eternal One in the energy field of pure potentiality. In that realm of knowing, you can manifest anything.

Members of the Nichiren Daishonin sect of Buddhism, originally established in a.d. 1253 in Japan, recite daily the following mantra: "Nam myoho renge kyo." The mantra means "To the mystical law of the Lotus Sutra, I dedicate my life." That mystical law implies the interconnectedness of all life in its seemingly infinite diversity as well as the eternal cycle of life and death, cause and effect—in other words, karma.

While chanting, you must endeavor to feel tremendous joy in the body. This clearly sets up a positive vibration that draws to you what you think about while chanting. You can change the world around you, experience mystical truth, and awaken to your highest and complete potential.

Knowing that you can create any dream from the field of infinite potentiality, you can let go of attachment to the outcome. For some people, the notion of detachment may be a little more difficult to grasp. It doesn't mean you have to let go of your intention to manifest something. Attachment to the outcome might mean, for example, that you hoped for a new car and you expected a Volkswagen but a Ferrari showed up. Are you going to complain to the Universe that the Ferrari was not acceptable? Are you that attached to having a Volkswagen? Unlikely.

You wanted money to start flowing into your life and expected it to come when you won a promotion but you won the lotto instead. Are you going to be disappointed at how the money came? Let go of trying to micromanage the Universe's work and force a particular outcome, including elaborate details pertaining to timing, place, amount, type, color, means, and so forth. Instead, cultivate a deep abiding conviction in your true self's power to create anything you need, want, or desire and let the outcome of your belief, desire, and endeavor bear fruit.

Get Solutions to Problems

Sometimes when you are on a spiritual path, life issues and problems begin to surface unexpectedly, even frequently. Some yogis assert that this happens because you are consciously making efforts at spiritual unfolding and that speeds up processes that make your karmic debts and gifts show up more quickly.

Regular daily meditation, even if you only do it for ten minutes or so, offers a period of relief from life's constant barrage of stimulation and problems. When you meditate, you temporarily shut off the senses, calm your breathing, and allow your brain to rest and recharge. Then, an amazing thing happens. After a period of inner stillness when you again bring mental focus upon a problem, solutions may pop into your mind. Such options may be ones you never thought of because your hyperfocus on the problem blocked them.

You can also bring about an energy shift by doing something physical. Leave your problem at the house or office and take a walk in nature. The energy vibration of nature can calm you. Not thinking about the problem while you enjoy a stroll around a lake, through the woods, on the beach, around a park, or across a meadow clears and refreshes your mind. The Law of Attraction, as you know, is always at work. When you detach from the problems, knowing with deep conviction that inherent in every problem is the means to solve it, the law can effortlessly deliver a solution.

You can overthink or overanalyze a problem and block ideas for possible options. Your brain is constantly bombarded with information and must work like a processor to deal with it all. Think of meditation as a period of relief for the brain. In a calm, yet alert and focused state, ideas will begin to flow.

Inform and Enhance Your Life

The Law of Attraction responds to emotional shifts up and down. Depression, anger, and sadness are stark contrasts to joy, love, and happiness. Dark feelings function as radar. They signal that your thoughts have turned negative. To return to a positive mood and thus a higher vibration, you have to shift your thoughts until your feelings begin to shift.

Your power to shift emotion up and down by your thoughts means you can live your life from the inside out with the knowledge of how to deliberately attract the good things in life. You'll have greater satisfaction as you work your own thoughts and emotions to directly experience your true self and divine purpose in life. Finally, you will have the knowledge and experience to work with the universal laws to create virtually anything.

Throughout the history of time, all cultures have had their visionaries, thinkers, mystics, and poets to serve as beacons of esoteric mystical truths. They were people who understood the great universal spiritual laws at work in the cosmos. Their insightful teachings continue today to light the way for others embarking upon the journey to discovery.

Ralph Waldo Emerson

In the nineteenth century, Ralph Waldo Emerson, essayist, poet, and founder of the Transcendentalist Movement, expressed the idea that you discover your true spiritual identity—as part of the Eternal Oneness—within. You grasp it through intuition and inward examination rather than through the didactic teachings of organized religion. Through that discovery, you find your greatest treasure. By knowing your true identity, nothing is beyond your reach.

FACT

You shift from being confrontational to feeling joyful by removing yourself from the situation and triggers. Breathe slowly to calm your agitation and help you release the anger. Listen to beautiful music. Forgive. Think of a pleasant memory and allow your mind to move into the positive emotions associated with that experience.

Jelalludin Rumi

Another poet, Jelalludin Rumi, writing in the thirteenth century in what is now Afghanistan, left behind a legacy of beautiful mystical poetry. In the following verses, he seems to be counseling people to wake up and not miss the opportunities to learn the great secrets of life. The vast majority of people "sleep" through life unaware of the powers within them. Capable of attaining spiritual heights, they seem to prefer the great dream of life instead of awakening to the true reality of themselves as a spark of the Divine Light.

Across the Doorsill

The breeze at dawn has secrets to tell you.
Don't go back to sleep!
You must ask for what you really want.
Don't go back to sleep!
People are going back and forth across the doorsill
where the two worlds touch. The door is round and open.
Don't go back to sleep!

— *Rumi, Spring Giddiness*

The goal of spiritual evolution, according to many New Age spiritual seekers, is to arrive at the following realization: That which you seek, you already are. As a child of the Divine, all of creation is your playground. You can do and have whatever you desire. In tune with the wisdom of your heart, be ever conscious that you are a spark of the Great Light. Let love flow unimpeded from your heart. Remember the counsel of Rumi: "Let the beauty we love be what we do."

CHAPTER 15

Manifesting Success in Your Career

Your career might be in liftoff by now if only you could find more funding, a personal assistant, a bigger office, a larger client base, and more workers. You are certain that those factors are why you have not achieved your goals. However, the problem may not be the lack of those things but rather your thoughts about such lack. You will begin to witness a shift once you energize the Law of Attraction to manifest success. The other factors will take care of themselves.

15

Chart a Course for Success

Your success in business happens in alignment with your core values and your business beliefs and practices. Business is about relationships. In Chapter 13, you assessed your core values as they pertain to relationships. It would be wise to also know your values and beliefs as they pertain to your relationships in the business world.

There are many reasons why you may not be manifesting success on your chosen career track, with your job, your small business, or other areas pertaining to work. One possibility could be a conflict between your core values and those of the company that employs you or other companies with whom you must conduct business. Perhaps you are expected to do something that conflicts with your ethics.

Since your beliefs lead to your thoughts about things, consider that you may first need to examine your beliefs since many of them were taught to you as a child. Take, for example, "You can't trust someone with shifty eyes." What if that person wears contacts and they are particularly irritating the day you meet him? Re-examining such beliefs may reveal untruths and distortions that are now thwarting your efforts to attain success.

The following are core values and/or guiding principles that business leaders working for some of America's most successful companies have embraced:

- Celebration of diversity
- Customer satisfaction
- Efficiency
- Giving back to communities
- Honesty
- Innovation
- Integrity
- Leadership
- Passion
- Quality
- Social responsibility

- Teamwork
- Transparency
- Winning spirit

Many business professionals also understand that a dynamic work environment that nurtures the creative spirit plays an important role in the success of workers and the company. Companies usually state their core values in their mission statements. Disney has perhaps the shortest mission statement ever. It succinctly states that its goal is to make people happy.

QUESTION?

What information does a mission statement include?
A mission statement tells your customers, community, workers, suppliers, and funding people what your business is about. It briefly states the enterprise's purpose, intention, and guiding principles and core values. A mission statement is sometimes combined with a vision statement focusing on future goals. See *www.businessplans.org/mission.html*.

Some Law of Attraction teachers suggest in their wealth or business coaching programs that participants create their own mission statements. Start with your intent to fill a need, something like: "My purpose/desire/ intent is to create/develop/foster/provide/nurture/build _____ _____."

Add to the end of that sentence what your action verb is going to accomplish—for example, "to create a web-based travel agency for physically challenged people," or "to establish a wellness clinic for expectant Native American mothers," or "to build a computer and technology center for teens and seniors."

Once you have established your company's purpose, explain how you intend to fill the need you have identified. Next add your core values to the statement. They are important because they reveal what is of paramount importance to you and your community, clients, backers, and workers.

Creating the Ideal Job

If you are employed with a company in a job that does not feel right but you need the paycheck and have no good options for moving, consider working with the Law of Attraction to inspire and guide you to a new position in your current company. Until you can locate another potential place of employment, you have to think of what to do from where you currently are. It may mean staying in the dead-end job until exit is possible. Don't be disheartened. Plant the seeds of desire and intent today so that the universe can rearrange itself to give you that new job.

Why You Have to Know Where You Are Going

Remember the words of the Cheshire Cat in Lewis Carroll's Alice in Wonderland: If you don't know where you are going, "then it doesn't matter which way you go." When you know what you desire and where you intend to head and for what purpose, the paradigm shifts and sets into motion a new reality for you.

Be on the lookout for great new ideas. You don't have to be first at something, but endeavor to be the best. If you are the person in charge of your company, hire excellent workers who are quick at executing orders. Create incentives to inspire employees to be innovative, organized, efficient, and forward-thinking. Motivate your employees to do impeccable work, maintain quality, and stick to deadlines.

FACT

Mihaly Csikszentmihalyi researched the lives of ninety highly creative individuals, including author Madeleine L'Engle and Dr. Jonas Salk. He discovered that some creative people created jobs or invented a career for themselves. Those findings are published in his book *Creativity: Flow and the Psychology of Discovery and Invention*.

Create Your Ideal Job

Begin thinking about your dream job and how passionate you feel doing it. If that job doesn't exist, don't give up. Create that ideal job by impressing your thoughts and your dreams upon what Wallace Wattles calls the "formless substance." Simply see it in your mind. In the energy field of the all-pervasive spirit, all things are related through interconnectedness. When you change, the universe changes, too. Some of the most creative people in the world have imagined totally new jobs and careers that didn't exist.

Develop Specificity in Your Vision

Envision everything associated with your ideal job. Tailor your desires. Be specific. Refine. Just the thought of being able to achieve your goals increases clarity and determination. What type of work is it? What tasks are you required to do? What does the office building look like? Who are the other workers (for example, are they highly skilled international workers or highly diverse college-age whiz kids)? What are the work hours/schedule? How much money do you make? What is your title? Can you see yourself owning the company?

Through wisdom is a house builded; and by understanding it is established: And by knowledge shall the chambers be filled with all precious and pleasant riches. A wise man is strong; yea, a man of knowledge increaseth strength.—Proverbs 24:3-5

Cultivate Strong, Persistent Desire

If you want success and financial prosperity in the business area of your life, you must hang on tenaciously to your dream and deeply focus your intention on having it. Know that you are not living in a zero-sum universe. When abundance comes to you, that does not mean it leaves someone else. See your work as increasing the good in the lives of your coworkers and customers. Believe that your business transactions enrich the lives of others and never subtract.

Use Intuition as a Powerful Tool

Regardless of what you call it—intuition, sixth sense, instinct—to some degree, everyone has the ability to sense things. By practicing relaxation and calming of the mind, you clear out the mental clutter and quiet the chattering to allow your intuition to bring forth innovative ideas, solutions, and concepts to help you meet professional business goals and get results.

Understand the Value of Gratitude

The creative force of the universe responds to expressions of gratitude. When you feel and express your appreciation for the good things that have manifested in your life, an attraction is established with infinite potential to bring more goodness. When you inform your friends of your desire to find a new job, for example, and they start bringing you notices of employment opportunities, praise their efforts. After your interviews with prospective employers, say thank you and send a follow-up card expressing your appreciation.

FACT

Donald Trump relies on his instincts in business and is also guided by a few principles: discipline, honesty, hard work, responsiveness to others, flexibility, and reliance on and trust in a core group of talented, smart people.

Think of Others

Consider how your business decisions positively impact others in your business environment and your community. The recent scare over lead paint in toys imported from China is an example of how a business and its leaders impact others, in that case, the end users—children and their families. Another example is paying lower than cost-of-living wages to unskilled workers. Aim for the moral high ground. There is nothing wrong with always trying to do the right thing.

When you have a business problem, try to solve it so that all involved parties benefit from the solution. Get involved in outreach programs on behalf of your business to help others. Become a socially responsible citizen. As you seek the highest good for all concerned, increased goodness returns to you in myriad ways.

Career Advancement Techniques

Perhaps you have carefully orchestrated your climb to the top and have taken on more and more responsibility along the way. In the final analysis, you—and every other worker—are always going to be judged on the quality of the work done. If your organization is one in which the structure emphasizes a team approach rather than dazzling solo acts, you will want to be a team player. The quality of the team's work will be more important than any individual's.

How does the Law of Attraction work when the competitive spirit of others creates an environment in which you have to go head to head? Teachers of the Law of Attraction suggest that you, possibly with others, have created the reality in which competition drives the outcome of winner and loser. You must then work under the rules created. If your single-minded attention had been to achieve that specific goal, you'd have done it . . . but your intention was to compete for that goal.

You, perhaps with coworkers or others, created a reality that dictated a winner and loser. You may have the intention to win, but the rules you created make it possible for you to lose. Change the rules and you set up a different environment for the outcome; that is, maybe you don't win at the top, but you win in some way on some level. Here's an example of the same idea using others in the company. Instead of celebrating the achievement of only your top salesperson, establish several levels of winners. In that way, one person's gain (in this case, the top seller) won't dictate that everyone else necessarily loses. High achievers are rewarded, others are acknowledged for their hard work, and no one gets left out.

Manifest a Raise, Promotion, or Dream Job

The secret to working with the Law of Attraction to manifest the perfect job, raise, or promotion is to create a powerful, compelling mental video that excites you every time you play it forward in your mind. To get the raise you want, see yourself meeting with the person empowered to grant the raise. Think, act, and speak during the meeting as if the raise has already been approved. Feel the elation of knowing that your next paycheck will include that money. Imagine how you will use it.

Use the same process for manifesting a promotion. See yourself in your mental video receiving the news that your promotion has come through. See yourself at a company meeting where your promotion is announced. Now play the video forward to hear the high praises your boss shares about you and your work with others attending your celebration party. Feel all the positive emotions associated with being in your new elevated position.

For the mental video of your dream job, see yourself already in that job. Take a look at the business card you are holding with your name on it. Feel the pleasure of seeing your name and position. Hand your card to someone influential in the sphere of your chosen field of work. See yourself easily discussing your mission statement with that person. Talk, act, and conduct business with the conviction that you are already doing that work and are associating with industry leaders in that field of endeavor.

Use affirmations, visualizations, journal writing, and poster-making projects to intentionally reprogram your thoughts to accept that you have been given the raise. See this as your business plan for getting what you desire from your career.

Molly's Story

Molly was out of work when she spotted an opening in retail at a local department store. It would be the perfect job since she planned to pursue her studies in fashion merchandising in the spring. She told the store owner that she would love to work in the women's dress section. The owner, however, explained that he did not need help in that area. So Molly resigned herself to working in the stockroom, occasionally delivering some item to the floor. But while she worked in the basement, she dreamed she was up on the main floor, draping mannequins with the latest fashions, helping customers select dresses, and figuring out the best ways to merchandise the garments.

One day, Molly was summoned by Nadine, the store manager, to help set up a display in the store's main window facing a busy intersection. Nadine couldn't finish the holiday window because she was late for an appointment off-site with the store owner and some new vendors. She gave Molly all the display items and instructions. Molly enthusiastically went to work.

Her display dazzled holiday shoppers and the traffic into the store increased sharply. Sales went up. The store owner offered to let Molly do the future window displays and also transferred her out of the stockroom to the children's department. Molly knew she would do her best working with children's clothing, but she was already seeing herself working in the women's dress section.

FACT

It is possible to unconsciously make the Law of Attraction work for you. Everyone possesses the instincts and passion needed to harness the Law of Attraction, but making a concerted effort makes you more effective and focused in your journey.

Without realizing it, Molly was working with the Law of Attraction. Molly believed in her dream, persistently held onto it, did the best job she could do where she was placed, and remained optimistic that her dream job would open at some point. By all of her thoughts and actions, Molly made her own good fortune. She created success in small increments, first doing a good job in the stock room, then with the window display, and finally in the children's department.

Affirm Your Way to Greater Prospects

Try the following affirmation for finding the perfect new job. "I am elated to know that the Law of Attraction is in the process of guiding me to a new job where I can best express my skills and talents and where my salary increases and my coworkers and bosses appreciate my contributions." Now you write your own affirmation by filling in the blanks. "I feel _____ (name a positive emotion) to know that the job of _____ (name the job) is in the process of manifesting in my life right now."

Grow Your Business

Perhaps you are self-employed and love your work but would like to see the company grow and become more profitable. You can hasten the arrival of that desire by raising your vibration with optimism and hope and opening your heart to allow for the dream to manifest. Let go of self-limiting beliefs and doubts. You need to create and hold in your mind a clear new vision for your company. When you are passionate about your endeavors and do the best you are capable of, the fruit of the labor—increased business, profits, expanded contacts, more clients and customers—naturally unfolds according to the law.

When formulating an intentional desire for your company, consider all aspects of your business, including productivity, profitability, environment, workers, morale, and scope of projects. Determine the number of hours you desire to work, the best size for your customer base, the amount of money needed to capitalize new growth, and the size of profits to be generated, among other things. Envision success in every area.

Create the Master Plan in Your Imagination

Write your vision as a declaration of desire or a mission statement. Turn the vision into images you put on a poster. Find a symbol that represents everything you want the company to become. Use that symbol as a touchstone throughout the day to remember to visualize, affirm, feel the emotion of succeeding, and know that everything you have created in your vision is in the processes of manifesting. Napoleon Hill counseled that to receive that which you desire to manifest, you first have to believe it is possible that you can acquire it.

Cultivate Wisdom

Work from joy. Feel gratitude for the blessings of your current work and the abundance of the business that is soon to be. Be smart about the work you do and be open to inspiring ideas. Be alert to intuitive promptings. Ask for divine guidance to shed light on a work situation or on ways to shift the paradigm. In this way, you become wiser about all possibilities and options.

Treat Others Well

In the world of business, people have different styles of working together or managing and leading others. Some are confrontational; others are consensus builders. Treat everyone—from the lowest-level position in the company to managers to your millionaire investor—with the same respect and appreciation for their contributions to your business. Negative emotion does not place you in harmonious alignment with the Law of Attraction, but positive, respectful, and visionary energy does. See everyone as deserving of riches, success, prosperity, and recognition of achievements.

Strategies for Rapid Advancement

You believe that you are ready for fast-track advancement to the top of your company or career. Remember that what you focus on, you attract. Make a list of all the things you want in terms of advancement. For example, your list could include task-related items such as more and varied responsibilities, opportunities for the most challenging assignments, a senior-level management position, and greater autonomy to do your job. You could also include rewards and perks such as performance bonuses, increased industry recognition, a company car, and international travel.

Stop worrying about how things will happen. Aim your mental laser beam on what you want. You will find that your intuition or instincts begin to guide you to opportunities for rapid advancement. Most importantly, the movement will occur effortlessly and easily.

If you want to create something, like shifting a negative attitude to a positive one, it can happen instantly because your consciousness is timeless, or eternal. The negative thought "I resent how my boss works with me under pressure because that frenetic energy causes me to feel stressful" can instantly become "I am grateful for how my boss mentors me because learning from her helps me to advance rapidly within the company." It's always a good idea to de-emphasize the negative and focus on the positive.

Success manifests from the inside out. To be successful in the world, you have to feel successful. There are plenty of people who seem to have everything—money, family, friends, beautiful children, an affluent life-style, a great job—and yet satisfaction with life eludes them. They may have addiction problems because of the excesses of their lifestyles or legal problems or tax issues. Trouble follows them like a dog nipping at their heels no matter where they go and what they do. They chase success and never find it.

FACT

Thought, mood, or attitude changes can manifest instantly because they occur in the mind; however, when you work to manifest something in the framework of the physical world, in which time and space are elements, you need to establish a time frame for your intention. For example, "I desire to become director of new products of XYZ Company by the end of this year."

Cultivate your belief in yourself as a successful person. What does your success look like? Wealth, health, great relationships, fabulous job—whatever it is, play the mental video of it over and over again. Think and feel successful. Don't let anything or anyone dim that vision.

Know When You Are On Track

Aristotle noted roughly 2,300 years ago that humans seek happiness more than anything else. When you feel happy and fulfilled, you know you are on track. Focusing on that happiness expands it. Conversely, when you feel dissatisfied and unhappy, you are off track. The following tips may help you get on the right track and stay there.

Aligned with the Law of Attraction, you will find actualizing a business dream to be easier than perhaps you believed possible. When you are on your path in life, doing work you feel passionate about, the law, like wind in the sail of a boat, pushes powerfully forward and causes impediments to float away. Here are some tips to try:

- Take stock of what every aspect of your dream looks like. Journaling works wonders for fleshing out your ideas.
- Believe in your dream, follow your passion, and don't let anyone talk you out of it.
- Notice the obstacles, especially family, friends, and associates who are naysayers. Remove the obstacles and find a way to navigate around these people.
- If you can't do the endeavor alone, surround yourself with the best people you can find, especially if they are smarter or have more experience than you.
- Be prepared to make your own rules if you have to. Sometimes there are no other good options.
- Establish a timeline and stick to it.
- Celebrate the milestones. They will encourage your continued forward momentum.

Believe that you deserve the best. Enjoy getting it. When you are on track in your job, business, or career, you exude happiness. Joy fills every fiber of your being when you are engaged in doing what you love. Though you may do it repeatedly, you still look forward to that activity.

Absorbed in doing work for its own the sake, you lose your sense of time while the creative force of the cosmos flows through you. The late Madeleine L'Engle, author of numerous books including *Walking on Water: Reflections on Faith and Art*, explained that when you are in that flow state, the ego slips away and time becomes *kairos* (holy or God-given) rather than *kronos* (chronological).

Mihaly Csikszentmihalyi, professor and former chairman of the University of Chicago's Department of Psychology, has been called the world's leading researcher in positive psychology. He noted that when you are in the flow, each of your thoughts, actions, and movements proceeds in continuity from the previous one; you are completely absorbed the way a musician loses himself playing jazz or a painter becomes merged with the process of painting. See *www.brainchannels.com/thinker/mihaly.html* for more information.

If you are starting a new business or other kind of venture, the following ideas are offered to help you succeed:

- Don't lose control of the balance in your life: family, work, play, spiritual activities.
- Stay current with your knowledge of your particular industry.
- Develop and stick to your financial plan; do accounting twice monthly so you don't lose control of the money in your start-up phase.
- Predict expenses, income, and monthly cash flow.
- Seek out a mentor or board of advisors.
- Network with diverse industry groups to expose your company and products and learn better ways to market your idea/product from other professional people.
- Maintain discipline.
- Stay motivated.

Whatever type of work you are involved in, do it well. Earn as much money as you honorably can and, as you are able, give some to others. Strive for excellence and live by noble principles and values. Stay positive and optimistic and know the Law of Attraction is working with you. Remember the old adage that nothing succeeds like success.

CHAPTER 16

Art and Music

You can use music to help you draw closer to the Divine, plunge deeper into meditation, or attain a more elevated vision for your life in and away from the world through an expansion of your consciousness. Whether you listen to someone else's music or play your own, use music as a point of departure to turn within.

Stay Aligned with the Law of Attraction

Use music and art to redirect patterns of negative thought into positive channels to shift your consciousness. Not only does music help raise your mood and thus your vibration, the right choice of music can establish a conducive atmosphere for prayers or a meditation and relaxation session. It can also diffuse undesirable energies of others around you.

Listen to quiet, uplifting music when reciting mantras or prayers on your japa mala or rosary. Strive to stay in harmonious alignment with the Law of Attraction to effect change in your life and for the greater good. Use music to dive more deeply into everything you do.

Apollo was the Greek god of music and insight. His son Asclepius was considered by the Greeks to be the demigod of the healing elements of medicine. Apollo also kept an entourage that included the muses of music, dance, dreams, and poetry. As you connect with music, you might say you are also connecting with the muses and healing and insight associated with Apollo.

Music plays an integral role in gratitude. As you have learned, expression of gratitude is a major key to living an abundant life. Listening to a beautiful piece of music such as Mozart's "Laudate Dominum" from *Vesperae Solennes de Confessore* or Handel's *Messiah* inspires reverence and appreciation for the gifts of the Divine and the grandeur and wonder of life.

Chakra Vibrational Makeup

Chakras, the force centers of the ethereal body, respond to sound vibrations. Some musicians and yogis say that chakra tuning and healings can be brought about through the use of sound. According to some metaphysical schools of thought, your chakras have an energetic vibration associated with psychological well-being. The right music can help you function at optimum levels.

To reach the deepest levels of spiritual consciousness and superior wisdom is akin to peeling away layers of ignorance like the skin of an onion until you reach the heart. Music can take you down into deeper layers. One way to penetrate those layers is to use music you like to elevate your mood. When you are feeling positive, you are most likely to feel gratitude for your spiritual gifts, especially on days when they seem to be burdens, not gifts.

Louise, a middle-aged woman who strives to meet the challenges of caring for six dogs, two dementia-stricken relatives, and a two-acre ranch, often plays a CD of Latin dance music when she feels she can't cope with the latest crisis. Salsa, cha-cha, and tango music never fail to lift her spirits. Often before she realizes it, she is dancing around the room and feeling gratitude for the lessons she is being taught by those living with her. When you spend time reflecting on the gratitude, the Law of Attraction responds to that powerful vibration.

FACT

Most people don't realize they are the prize of their own lives. Harvard psychologist Daniel Gilbert asserted that Americans think they want to be rich and thin. Gilbert noted that beyond earning enough for the basic necessities in life, extra money doesn't add much to the pursuit of happiness. Many people don't know what truly makes them happy; worse, they don't know that they don't know.

Receive Healing

Art and music are often combined in therapy sessions aimed at helping you work through psychological pain and emotional trauma. In a safe environment provided by a therapist or health professional, you may be encouraged to listen to the soothing cross-species sounds of nature, perhaps set to strains of classical music such as Pachelbel's "Canon in D major" or Barber's "Adagio for Strings."

If you are feeling stuck or emotionally pulled in different directions, express your innermost feelings by playing music or creating art. Working through grief, illness, abuse, or deep psychological wounds enables you to finally release the energy associated with holding on to that pain. Breakthroughs of insight or understanding are also possible. With release, damaging stress levels dissipate and healing is facilitated. The goal is to restore emotional well-being and positive feelings.

Merge with the Mother of All Sounds

Adept sadhaks—those who faithfully practice daily regimens of sadhana (spiritual practices) and who have advanced along the spiritual path—may tune in to celestial strains heard in deep meditation. Shabda or Nada is the yoga of sound. Follow the sound current of Om (the cosmic vibration of atoms in creation) inward and your absorption into that Nada or Mother of All Sounds can take you to a state of samadhi, or at-oneness with the Divine. The most powerful place in meditation is the space between thoughts. For however long you can experience the absence of thought, dive deeply inward, toward the Source of your being.

In Shabda practice, you concentrate on not only sound but also meaning and vibration. Of the three, the sages say that vibration is the most important because when you tune in to the vibration of Om, in which all sound is contained, you are aligning with those holy ones from ages past who have spiritually worked with the sound. Om is an expression of the Divine.

Music has been hailed as a powerful tool in healing. Some say it works at the cellular level. The key to gaining the maximum benefit from music is to listen attentively and then mentally check in to see how you feel. If it makes you feel good, use it often to raise your vibration to be in harmonious alignment with the Law of Attraction.

The Role of Art and Music

Ever wonder why you can put a jigsaw puzzle together more quickly if you do it while listening to music? The reason has to do with the way music enables the brain to more easily accomplish tasks associated with spatial thinking. Listening to music prepares your brain to do spatial tasks, but the effect is short-lived because the improvement in your ability to solve spatial problems lasts only a short time after the music ends. The opening of the neural pathways may respond best to strains of classical music, which is more complex than other types of music. If your most burning desire is to create a masterful piece of art or composition, try listening to music to begin the Law of Attraction's pulling power. With focus and intent and a heightened sense of expectation, your masterpiece will emerge from within you.

FACT

By listening to complex music compositions, your brain becomes primed to open pathways for solving spatial problems, forge connections that may make learning new subjects easier, and enhance positive mood. Such "improvement" in brain functioning enables clarification of intention and raises your vibration for working with the Law of Attraction.

Stimulating Young Brains

Babies have billions of brain cells. Exposing them to classical music such as Mozart or Bach can foster a lifelong love of music and facilitate the work of their brains to forge connections between patterns, language, and rhythms. As your children grow, offer them a course of musical training and allow them to learn to play a musical instrument to encourage a deep and abiding attraction for music in their lives.

Studies have shown that learning to play music can stimulate the brain in positive ways. People who can play music learn more quickly and can more easily solve spatial tasks (for example, solve or put together puzzles). A love of music can help young adults begin to realize their dreams of being better students and problem solvers.

Feel Music's Vibrations and Frequencies

Music can evoke strong emotions and brain activity in the listener. In 1993, scientists at the University of California at Irvine published in the journal *Nature* their findings that memory immediately improves from listening to classical music. The effect has been dubbed the Mozart Effect. In 2007, Stanford scientists studying music and its effect on brain activity found that music moves the brain to focus and maintain attention. The point is that humans are hard-wired to appreciate music.

Music is said to be the mechanism that causes new neural pathways to link the left and right hemispheres of the brain, enabling what scientists call whole-brain functioning. Music is the language of the soul. Individuals seeking to enter higher states of consciousness for healing, decision-making, and creative endeavors might respond best to repetitive musical notes and words as found in the chanting of a mantra such as *Deva Premal Sings the Moola Mantra* (*www.whiteswanrecords.com*). Others might prefer the hot licks and backbeats of rhythm and blues or rock music.

Consider How Music Helps Infertility

Modern infertile couples of the Jain religion sing lullabies to demonstrate a faith in the unseen Divine power to bring them children. During Paryushana, the festival of fasting and forgiveness that commemorates the birthday of the Jain god Mahavira, couples sing lullabies and rock a cradle to demonstrate their desire to manifest conception and childbirth. Many children are said to have been born as a result of such practices.

Musical instruments were used in the ancient world, in particular in Sumeria and Egypt, where reed flutes were played as long as 5,000 years ago. More recently, a flute crafted from a cave bear bone and dubbed the Neanderthal Flute was found by musical expert Ivan Turk in Slovenia. Scholars date it to 50,000 B.C.

Music to Heal Social Ills

As expressions of the human spirit, music and art hold the potential for healing the social ills of the planet. Dr. Jean Houston, a Human Potential Movement founder who helped Hillary Clinton write *It Takes a Village*, has asserted that humans in partnership with Creation now must become spiritual leaders to bring about the "restoration of the biosphere, the regenesis of society, and . . . a new type of culture: the culture of Kindness."

The work of the social architects' bold vision is made easier with the harmonious alignment with the Law of Attraction and other spiritual laws of success. Through her books, seminars, conferences, and guest speaking engagements, Houston has established a far-reaching global network of visionaries and social reformers to imagine new solutions to the complex social problems that plague humankind. Find out more about her ideas of social change and her journey of mythic proportions at *www .jeanhouston.org*.

Learning the Secret Alchemical Formula of Music

Law of Attraction experts assert that humans are vibratory beings and thus respond to the language of music. Music touches something ancient inside us. The alchemical formula for using music to manifest your dreams is the repetition of agreeable, harmonious, and inspiring words and sounds and positive and uplifting lyrics. The human voice, according to the beliefs of the ancient Egyptians, represented the most powerful instrument for praying. Thus, their priests studied singing.

Are you a lover of world music with a special appreciation for Gregorian chant? Or do you love Indian bhajans or the Shona Mbira music of the people of Zimbabwe? Heed the call to devotion by listening to the music you love most. The best place to begin your deliberate work of manifesting is from an emotional place of gratitude and happiness.

The Centrality of Music

Steve directed music events at San Jose State University while he attended school there. Although he loved traditional rock 'n' roll, he also enjoyed progressive music and jazz. For Steve, music seemed more vital than blood. After graduating from college, he started *Collage*, a successful music and art magazine for the San Francisco Bay Area. In his early forties, he was told he had to have a heart transplant. Steve held his wife and cried. He told her that if he didn't make it, he'd come back as a rock 'n' roll musician. Would she still marry him? The two of them made their respective lists of what to do next. Steve informed her that since he wanted to manifest healing he was going to make a dozen CDs of his favorite music and that she should bring them to the ICU where he would be taken after his surgery. He intended to rock his way through recovery.

Steve was forty-five when he underwent the transplant. Two weeks later, he was listening to the Beatles, Rod Stewart, Peter Gabriel, and the Who and asking repeatedly when he could go home. He had nicknamed his new heart Boomer because its beat was as strong as the booming backbeats of Phil Collins's drums. Steve's birthday rolled around two months later. He had two cakes: one for his chronological birthday and the second to mark the first year of his life with a new heart. His positive outlook on healing, helped along by his love of music, no doubt contributed to his recovery following the transplant.

Create a Dream-Fulfilling Collage or Painting

Let music give pleasure to your heart and the words of great beings inspire your thoughts as you get to work manifesting. Use touchstones such as fetishes, symbols or icons, and words with special meaning to prepare you for your undertaking. The Taoist sage Lao Tzu asserted that "when you realize that there is nothing lacking, the whole world belongs to you." He also pointed out that "to the mind that is still, the entire universe surrenders."

Putting Your Dream on Paper

In the stillness of peace, declare your intention to seek something from the universe or to give your own gifts to the world. Maybe you want to create a CD of spiritual music, a piece of visionary art, a self-help book, a Law of Attraction program that you can teach all over the country for income, an orphanage for children whose parents have succumbed to HIV/AIDS, a water treatment plant for a Third-World community, a documentary about autism. Whatever your dream is, create a collage or painting that depicts it.

Maybe your desire has not yet come into clear focus. Be patient and continue thinking about it. Lao Tzu also said that "at the center of your being, you have the answer; you know who you are and what you want." Let your subconscious guide you to powerful images. Clip them from magazines to use on a collage. As you listen to the strains of your favorite music, remember that in the ancient world, music was integrated into society in almost every conceivable way, from stick-banging in fields to frighten away birds (later accompanied by song) to the prayers offering religious sacrifices to the celebration of battle victories. Let music lead you to the art that represents the new life or good world you are creating.

FACT

A collage is a work of multimedia art that might include such things as clippings of magazine pictures, photographs, string, beads, seeds, paints, sand, wax, cloth, stamps, travel maps, passport images, feathers, quotes, declarations, words, and any other items with meaning for you. A collage becomes a powerful tool for helping you see your goals and manifestation desires.

Use of Conscious and Unconscious Images

When you flip through a magazine, your brain processes a staggering amount of information in rapid-as-lightning calculations in response to the visual cues. More than 200 million light receptors are found in the eyes, according to the National Academy of Sciences. Gazing upon a picture triggers a brain response that can include rational, emotional, associative, and subconscious thought and stored memories. Visual images can powerfully reinforce your intention to manifest your desires, whether they are conscious or subconscious.

Healers from a wide variety of cultural traditions understand that the brain needs both reason and feeling. The brain and heart must harmonize to best serve a healthy wholeness. Modern science, too, now embraces that paradigm.

Some Processes for Tapping the Subconscious

The following list includes ways that New Age practitioners and Law of Attraction teachers may help people tap into their subconscious minds to manifest results or make good choices to create the life desired.

- Affirmation: the process of making a declaration of truth or statement of judgment
- Autosuggestion: the process in which the suggestion for a belief, opinion, or course of action arises from within the self rather than from an external source
- Emotion Freedom Techniques: the process by which disturbances in a person's energy field are healed through tapping on the body's energy meridians as the person thinks negative thoughts, thus dispersing the negativity and restoring harmony and balance
- Eye Movement Desensitization and Reprocessing (EMDR): the integrative therapy technique developed by Dr. Francine Shapiro to help a person's brain reprocess the memory of a highly distressing event
- Hypnosis: the process of engaging a person in the spirit of cooperation, acceptance, and abeyance of critical judgment to allow her to enter a state of heightened suggestibility in which she accepts a statement to be factual; often used to change self-limiting belief
- Subliminal messages: the process in which a person accepts messages or suggestions aimed at the subconscious without the awareness of the conscious mind

When you cut out images from a magazine for your collage, your conscious mind may choose many of the pictures or words, but something else may be taking place. You might be strongly attracted to a particular image without any idea why. The reason you are drawn to it is found in your subconscious mind. It just might represent a long-suppressed desire that you would have manifested long ago if your life had gone differently. Pay attention to the things that capture your attention. What are they telling you about unfulfilled dreams or self-worth?

Austrian neurologist and psychiatrist Sigmund Freud (1856–1939) theorized that the subconscious communicates with the conscious mind through dreams. His protégé Carl Jung asserted that each human's developmental task is to discover the unique truth of who he or she is by integrating unconsciousness into consciousness. Dreams, Jung believed, represented the most important means by which that process took place.

The Need to Offer Gratitude

Let sound bring you peace, exhilaration, contentment, and happiness. Use sound to draw you into a prayerful mood and guide your thoughts and feelings to create declarations of gratitude throughout your day. Listen to an inspirational vocal, a responsorial song, the chanting of hymns, a devotional bhajan, a symphony, or popular music intended to create a sense of peace or invoke the sacred. Make music part of a daily devotional walk or recite a hymn or chant as you prepare a meal for your family or friends that you want to infuse with love.

As you make known to the universe your desire to have increased confidence, heightened self-esteem, increased weight loss, a profitable new business, the perfect mate, a baby, or any of a thousand other things, remember to be thankful for the things you currently have and also use your feelings and thoughts to express your gratitude.

Some experts on the Law of Attraction say gratitude is the most powerful tool at your disposal to aid in manifesting your goals, dreams, and desires. You can certainly use music, art, affirmations, visualizations, journaling, dream incubations, and other modalities to establish an attraction for the things you want in your life, but you hasten the work of the law when your thoughts, feelings, and actions harmoniously align in an attitude of gratitude. Music can lift your spirits to lofty heights and make you feel gratitude for the priceless treasures already in your life (such as family, your spiritual traditions, a belief in God, and so forth). Art can deepen your understanding and appreciation for the past, emphasize your compassion and awe for the highs and lows of the human condition, and trigger feelings of gratitude for the aesthetic gifts in nature that are all around you.

FACT

The Secret author Rhonda Byrnes and the speakers who contributed to her mega-bestseller stressed the importance of gratitude in working with the Law of Attraction. In 2007, Byrnes wrote a follow-up book to *The Secret* titled simply *The Gratitude Book* in which she included affirmations and tools to transform your life.

Unlock and Open Yourself

Use music and art to gain greater understanding of the human condition and perhaps do something about the plight of others who are less fortunate than you. View art that represents the best of human endeavors and accomplishments or art that suggests or asserts a hope in the power of a greater force helping humanity. Let the emotions that viewing art stirs inside you inspire you to action. Kindred spirits who believe that human civilization has evolved to a place of potential destruction share a common desire for social transformation and are using music, writing, discourse, and art to shift old paradigms.

Consider using what you've learned in the journey of life and your deliberate work with the Law of Attraction to make the world a better place. Your effort doesn't have to be grandiose. It might be something quite simple, such as a small contribution to a school in South Africa or purchasing your birthday and holiday gifts from artists living in remote regions of the Andes. By opening your heart to help them, you are making a channel for the Law of Attraction to bring good things and the love of others to you.

Love, some say, is itself a vibration. Left unimpeded, love can flow easily between humans. But when love meets resistance in the form of deep-seated selfishness, fear, angst, and a need to control, its flow becomes as impeded or erratic as surely as when a stream hits a narrow gorge or tumbles onto a craggy beach filled with boulders. When you block giving or receiving love, you thwart your opportunity to be nourished as intended by the heart of the Divine. Music can soften the hard edges of your own life experience and open you to the plight of others. Music can inspire lofty ideas of an interconnectedness of each person as part of a greater whole.

Visualization, Aromatherapy, and Music Exercise

Consider the following exercise as a way to shift consciousness. Let's say that you have always wanted to own a small villa in Italy. Crush some fresh rosemary, citrus leaves, lavender, or other herb whose scent inspires thoughts of Italy. If you enjoy wine, have a sip of your favorite. Put on a romantic Andrea Bocelli CD. Sit back, relax, and give your mind time to become calm. Guide your thoughts to the Italian countryside. See your house in your mind's eye. What does its exterior look like? Observe the shape, color, texture, and material from which it's made.

What about the villa's surroundings? Do you see a sweeping vista of vineyards across a valley? Citrus trees in giant clay pots? Olive groves bathed in a late afternoon's golden rays of light? A cool, leafy courtyard enclosed in stone with a fountain? Let your mind wrap around every detail. Enjoy the experience.

Open the door and enter your villa. Notice the details of every room and how they make you feel. The scent of rosemary is there. The music is there. The taste of Italian bread, pastry, pasta, or drink is on your tongue. You are there and vibrantly experiencing it in sensory detail. Feel the joy. It's yours. Take ownership. Express your gratitude.

Summon Kindred Spirits

An art show or musical event can bring people together for a common cause. Just as people band together to effect social change and work for political goals, they can be attracted into your life through cultural venues featuring art or music to help you achieve success. Such individuals include teachers, community leaders, clergy, business advisors, financial planners, feng shui experts, personal coaches, psychologists, musicians, artists, or those belonging to a support network.

Value Your Intuition

Do you place more value on your rational thinking than your intuitive thoughts? Perhaps you should rethink that. As Einstein famously said, "I never came upon any of my discoveries through the process of rational thinking." Noting that the gift of an intuitive mind was the only thing of true value, Einstein also believed that the spirit manifested in the harmonies of the universe best represented the God in whom he deeply believed.

Draw upon music to induce a relaxed state in which you rely less upon rational thinking and more upon intuition and inner guidance. Clear your mental clutter. Open yourself to information that is accessible from realms other than that of the material/physical and be willing to doubt the current thinking about something in order to entertain new ideas about it.

Some people believe strongly that angels and nature spirits are around each person and available for help as you travel on the journey through your life. Generally, you seek such help through intuition. You may also benefit from learning to bring forth intuitive thoughts through automatic writing, pendulum dowsing, and deciphering information from tarot cards, the *I Ching*, and scrying (interpreting images or messages revealed in a bowl of water or a crystal ball). The latter involves your ability to connect the images you see to deep insights, much like you would examine a work of art to gain an understanding of the cultural or historical milieu in which the artist lived or symbols to uncover hidden meaning in a painting or illustrated manuscript.

CHAPTER 17

The Law of Attraction in Your Home

If the Law of Attraction isn't working as well as you'd like, try empowering your attracting factors through feng shui. The heart and soul of feng shui, the ancient Chinese art of placement and arrangement, is the energy called chi, qi, or prana that permeates everything in the universe. A feng shui belief states that all of creation is made up of that energy vibrating at various frequencies and the flow of that energy impedes or enhances attracting power. Some assert that feng shui doubles the power of the Law of Attraction.

Stagnant Versus Flowing Energy

You influence the flow of the life-affirming chi throughout your surroundings by the way you incorporate physical objects and plants in interior spaces as well as by your color choices, furniture and art placement, interior lighting, art objects, and symbolic items representing nature.

Take stock of your home to ascertain whether clutter blocks easy navigation through the entry and all areas of the house. Is the home painted and furnished in a way that creates a warm welcome? Has your collection taken over one or more areas of the house? Has your love of furniture over-filled rooms so that they feel crowded and cramped?

FACT

In houses staged for sale, furniture is positioned in such a way as to allow potential buyers to see 70 percent of walls and floors because people who are in the market for a house want to see walls, ceilings, floors, and windows—not the items in the home. Likewise, in feng shui, floors and walls should be somewhat open to allow the free flowing of life-affirming chi.

When rooms are stuffed, the flow of energy is blocked and can become stagnant. Your goal is to ensure that there are open pathways through your home to allow the energy passage. When the energy can freely swirl around your environment (and by feng shui association, every area of your life), your good fortune or luck changes along with your power to intentionally attract what you desire.

Choose Furniture and Lighting

Furniture needs to not only support you but also give you enough of a feeling of safety and the security to express yourself. It shouldn't be too large or too small but rather be of a proper scale for the space. In group seating in living rooms, for example, furniture should offer options for differently sized people. The space should appear welcoming to all—an invitation to come, sit, and enjoy one another's company.

Living spaces need adequate illumination through the use of ambient lighting, spot lights, overhead lights, torchière lights, sconces, and candles. The most important source of illumination, however, is natural light. Even on dark, wintry days, throw open the curtains to let natural light into the rooms of your home. The light's positive energy brings with it the healing chi of nature.

Strengthening Walls and Using Mirrors

Walls are the support system for the building. They introduce earth energy into a living space. Walls can make you feel more secure if they appear strong. Painting and texturing walls can suggest further strength and safety. The addition of columns can contribute to a stronger support for the structure of your house and, metaphorically, the support structure for your life.

Use a mirror positioned toward a window to reflect nature into a room and also make a room seem larger. For example, a room in the sixth-floor condo of a beachfront complex might not provide a direct ocean view until a floor-to-ceiling wall-length mirror is positioned on the wall adjacent to the sliding glass doors. Suddenly, the ocean and sky are reflected in the mirror. You had to look at an angle through the glass doors to see magnificent sunsets and starry nights, but now you can enjoy them comfortably.

When you add candles, books, art pieces, and chairs in groups of three, you keep the energy expansive. Stagnant or blocked energy is created when you leave a solitary dead plant in the room, random boxes or piles of stuff that you haven't gotten around to organizing, or dark corners you have failed to illuminate.

Establish Better Energy Flow

There are several ways to improve energy flow and establish a balance of masculine and feminine elements (yin/yang). For example, you could add some healthy plants, a judicious splash of contrast color, objects to represent nature, and some good illumination to let the chi flow easily. You will know that the chi is moving through that space because you will feel happy, harmonious, healthy, calm, peaceful, and relaxed. Those positive feelings associated with flowing chi are exactly the positive feelings that aid the work of the Law of Attraction in bestowing abundance in your life.

The point of feng shui is to create an energetically balanced space that supports you and your life choices, that invites you and your friends, and family members into a sense of community. The interior space in which feng shui is properly utilized fosters the flow of energy that is correct for the function of that space. In a bedroom, the energy will be grounded and safe, harmonious, and peaceful. A living room, on the other hand, might have more lively energy flowing through it. The energy in that space encourages acceptance, love, safety, and grounding, but with a smidgen of risk as represented by the use of a splash of vibrant color, a precariously placed object, or a piece of visual art depicting something wildly imaginative in bold line and color.

The Nine Quadrants of the Basic Bagua

A simplified version of the *bagua* or map used to determine the relationship of a house or room to the directions of north, east, south, and west is laid out like a tic-tac-toe grid with nine squares. To correctly position the bagua over your house layout, hold the bagua with both your thumbs on the square denoting "career," with the grid row containing "wealth," "fame," and "love" farthest out from your body and the row with "knowledge" closest to you.

1. Bottom row left—wealth
2. Bottom row center—fame
3. Bottom row right—love
4. Middle row left—family
5. Middle row center—health
6. Middle row right—children and creativity
7. Top row left—knowledge
8. Top row center—career
9. Top row right—helpful people

When preparing your home to receive the things you desire to attract into your life, pay special attention to the center of the bagua or center of the house. This is a gathering place where the energies collect and then proceed to flow in various directions. Although the area should be aesthetically appealing, warm, and welcoming, avoid clutter, pay attention to proper lighting (glass and crystal, for example), and add a round floor rug instead of a square or rectangular floor covering.

Necessity for Eliminating Clutter

Clutter suppresses and even obstructs energy flow. Stagnant or blocked energy or chi makes your life difficult. Sapped of energy, your health suffers. Stagnant energy also blocks the flow of money. It impedes the manifestation of healthy relationships. It obstructs advancement in your chosen career path. It can bring on depression and negative patterns of thought.

Organize a particular room or area of your home or office. Once that area is completed, tackle the next room and the next until the whole house is re-energized. Baskets (symbolizing the reeds and grasses of nature) with lids are great for organizing objects in a room that were carried in and forgotten. Left to pile up, they begin to slow down or block the natural flow of energizing chi.

FACT

In *Feng Shui Living*, Sharon Stasney noted that accumulation and letting go is actually part of an ancient yin/yang cycle. The yin part of the cycle is the accumulation of items while the yang portion is the letting go of those things. In the Law of Attraction, this is akin to making space in your life for something to manifest.

Your health and well-being section of the bagua is the point at which the horizontal and vertical axes of the entire map meet. It is the center. If you want vibrant health, give some attention to where that position of the bagua lies when the map is superimposed over a scale drawing of your house. If the bagua's center square is positioned over the center of your home, pay special attention to what that area of your house looks like.

Have piles of books been there so long that you had forgotten about them and don't even see them when you enter the room? Are there piles of books, dead or dying plants, or a couch, chair, or table with loose screws or broken legs? Since these things represent bad feng shui, there's a pretty good chance your health is being affected. Have you noticed feeling fatigued, drained, stressed, or unhappy? Such symptoms indicate an imbalance in the energy of your home.

To fix that room, remove any broken or damaged items. Take away or organize and store objects of clutter. Bring in fresh flowers, aesthetically pleasing pictures, and objects of art in the healing colors of nature. Add an accent in the colors green (earth) and gold (sun), two powerful elements of nature that are both necessary for a healthy life-giving energy.

Principles of Feng Shui

Use your knowledge of feng shui to aid the work of the Law of Attraction to bring you robust health, increased stamina, enthusiastic energy, emotional and mental acuity, and exceptional dexterity and flexibility. Learn to balance the accumulation and release, the ancient yin/yang energies. Incorporate elements of nature and add feng shui cures to problem areas. Transform your life through the use of those principles and you will be establishing excellent feng shui. Your life will begin to change according to your new, more harmonious alignment with the Law of Attraction.

Understanding Yin/Yang Energies

Yin and yang energy together make up chi. Yin and yang forms of energy are opposites of each other, just as the earth is opposite the sky, heads is the opposite of tails, and matter is opposite energy. Each needs the other to be complete, yet too much or too little of either creates imbalance. Think of yin as inert, matter, earth, quiet, reflective, dark, female, shadow, cold, valleys, moon, and grounded while yang is active, energetic, sky, boisterous, creative, light, male, sunbeams, hot, mountains, and upward moving.

Working with the Earth Element

The art of feng shui in home environments relies on incorporating five key elements found in nature—earth, metal, water, wood, and fire. Although it seems obvious, earth energy is that which is close to the ground. In a home, earth energy is represented by floor cushions, a low coffee table, an Indian charpoy bed on short legs, and pinecones in a basket or a pottery bowl on the fireplace hearth.

Discovering Metal and Water Elements

Metal energy is found in rooms with minimalist furniture, white or monochromatic color schemes, lots of space, and order everywhere. Metal is symbolized by the color silver or gray. Water is found in fountains (great for the wealth sector of your home, since the energy of money needs to circulate), plants like ivy or baby's tears that cascade, and circular or organic shapes in furniture and art objects.

Lillian Too, author of *168 Feng Shui Ways to Declutter Your Home*, has stated that old yang energy (such as too much old clothing no longer used but still in your closet) eventually turns into yin energy. This creates imbalance. Prune out the clothing and thereby create new yang energy. In so doing, you are inviting in new invigorating chi.

Using Wood and Fire Energy

An object's elemental character is often determined by the material it is made of as well as its shape and color. For example, you will find wood energy in bamboo poles or wood columns, candlesticks, and objects that have vertical height. Fire energy is represented by the color red, candles, fireplaces, and wood-burning stoves. Fire symbols also include diamond shapes.

Detecting a Feng Shui Problem

You may need to do a little detective work to locate the feng shui problems or blockages in your home. You may not immediately know you have a problem or you may observe some signs and symptoms that an imbalance exists but you don't know where. For example, are you too tired to make love to your spouse? Check out your bedroom for chipped, broken, or otherwise damaged furniture or problematic mattress and box springs. These things, if broken or damaged, need to be fixed pronto to prevent your marital relationship from undergoing stresses that might cause it to completely break down.

A bedroom needs to be suitable for sleeping—no piles of clothes on the side of the bed or file folders of office work on the bedside table. There must be no clutter since it represents emotional junk, something you definitely don't want in the bedroom. Think of your bedroom as the most sacred of all the spaces in your home environment. The energy there must never be thoughtless, negative, hostile, burdensome, or stagnant.

FACT

To attract a sizzling hot romance, place a length of red silk ribbon horizontally across the foot of your bed under your mattress or staple it from one side of your bed's undercarriage to the other. Place two ceramic lovebirds on your bedside table with objects such as rose quartz (magnifies love), gold-colored rings that symbolize commitment, and fresh sweetly scented red or pink roses (true love).

Surround yourself with colors and bed linens that are serene and peaceful. Avoid wild and jazzy patterns. Ensure that the outside light flows easily through clean, washed windows and opened curtains. Make certain that art is tasteful and serene—even holy since your bedroom is the place where you leave behind the daily cares and worries to cross the threshold of the dreaming mind into the subconscious.

Making the Foyer into an Energy Passageway

A foyer is a place where people often place a desk or a parson's table for keys, purses, receipts, and extra change. But a cluttered foyer creates hostile or negative energy. The foyer should represent the conduit for positive energy coming into and flowing throughout your house. Make it a place of interest and beauty and ensure that it is welcoming and warm so your family and friends will want to enter your home.

Effect Emotional Shifts

Your thoughts and emotional state can be affected by the chi in your home, which, in turn, affects the working of the Law of Attraction. Negative energy can be counteracted and replaced by new, positive chi. One way to do that is tear down old structures and replace them with new ones. Remodeling a kitchen is an example of shifting the old patterns or ways of living in a space to accommodate a new thinking/feeling approach.

Changing Things to Re-Energize the Space

If you no longer have an attachment for a room or anything in it, it may be time to totally change things around to replenish or create new pathways for the flow of chi. If you just want a little lift of the energy, bring in a table-top fountain, build a comfortable window seat with a view outside, or install a new kitchen island with space to hold cookbooks and a counter where you can sit and sip tea while staring outside into nature. Incorporate the five elements of nature in some way in that room to either soften or reinvigorate it.

Deflecting a Neighbor's Bad Energy

In your garden near your neighbor's fence, install a wide-mouth urn of still water in close proximity to the neighbor's property. If he has demonstrated hostility toward you, his negative energy will be neutralized by the water. Do a mental check-in to make certain that you did not give him a reason to feel so angry toward you. If you did, face it, fix it, release, and replace it.

Hanging Wind Chimes for Increased Energy

In a room where the energy seems weak, bring in sound in the form of music with more high notes than low. A wind chime with high-pitched bells or cylinders will give you more energy than ones with low sounds. Tibetan bells are the best of all because they are often harmonically tuned. Your mood will become more positive with every breeze that moves the bells. Another way to shift energy for a more positive mood is to put on a CD of feng shui music and do some yoga or breath work.

Music is a moral law. It gives soul to the universe, wings to the mind, flight to the imagination, and charm and gaiety to life and to everything. It is the essence of order, and leads to all that is good, just, and beautiful, of which it is the invisible, but nevertheless dazzling, passionate, and eternal form.—Plato

A New Language of Expression

The world of feng shui is permeated with symbols. Since symbols are the language of the mind, symbolic images can readily magnify your thoughts and intensify focus on a desire that you intend to manifest. You can literally shift the energy of any place or space in your home by invoking symbols.

In the ancient practice of feng shui, spiritual symbols were used to change the quality, strength, and flow of energy. Many symbols were associated with the elements of fire, earth, water, metal, and wood and expressed both yin and yang qualities. Today, such symbols might be used as a new language of expression when working with the Law of Attraction. Symbols can be used as points of departure into deliberate intention. For example, if you seek a healing, you might begin a daily meditation with a period of time focusing on a circle to symbolize wholeness and completion.

Feng Shui Cures

Experts in feng shui capture bad energies in a room or house through the use of special consecrated mirrors. However, you can use mirrors as cures for problems like a bed or desk positioned in such a way as to prevent you from seeing someone enter the room. If the mirror reflects a cluttered portion of your living space, remove the items that make up the pile of junk. Alternatively, cover the mirror. Not covering it means you allow the mirror to double the effect of the negative things it reflects.

FACT

The dragon is an ancient Chinese symbol of good fortune. It means new beginnings, prosperity, and continued success. The dragon and tiger (symbol of courage and dignity) together represent the primordial yin and yang energy. Other symbols include the pearl (wisdom), clouds (associated with heaven and the gods), a pair of mandarin ducks (bliss, harmony), and Chinese coins with square-holed centers (wealth).

Using Crystals

Some cures include hanging a beautiful, multifaceted crystal on a piece of clear fishing line or red silk ribbon so that sunlight will hit it. Use this cure in a room where the energy has become weak. The result of the sun against the crystal will project a rainbow over the ceiling or walls of your space. Rainbows invigorate the energy of a space and make you feel happy. Quartz crystal energy can be amplified through your emotions, thoughts, and intent and can be particularly effective if you use it to help you work with the Law of Attraction.

Utilizing Affirmations

Just as you used affirmations in working with the Law of Attraction, you can also use affirmations in feng shui to release the past and embrace the future. It is not enough to clear the clutter from the various spaces in your house. Of paramount importance is clearing clutter from your mind and emotions. Release feelings of fear and replace them with feelings of safety and grounding. Whatever it is that makes you fearful and powerless must be discarded.

Visualize White Light or Beams of Sunlight

Light is cleansing, invigorating, and empowering. Whatever makes you feel empowered and strong must be embraced. You replenish chi when you clear out the mental clutter and negative chatter, let go of psychological dead weight, and open the way for new energy to come in. By visualizing brilliant white light or sunbeams bathing every room of your home, your life, and your family, your mental/emotional energy shifts. Experience that light as restorative and curative, its energy as love permeating everything in the cosmos.

Use a three-legged toad (wealth talisman) near your cash register as a reminder of your prosperity goal. A pair of mandarin ducks in your bedroom heralds a blissful marriage. Metal and gemstone jewelry fashioned into a meaningful symbol for you, the wearer, can symbolize your goal or a desire for good fortune. Use these with your affirmations, visualizations, action goals, and expressions of gratitude.

Dissipating Yin Energy with Red Color

If you live near a hospital or cemetery, you may be vulnerable to yin chi. One way to dissipate that energy associated with illness, dying, and death is to paint the wall facing the cemetery or hospital a bright red color (such as you might see on a Chinese lacquer box or festive holiday ribbon). Make certain to have plenty of lighting around your home. Use your newfound understanding of feng shui's life-affirming energies to create the life you desire for yourself and your loved ones.

Find ways to ground yourself using earth energy, renew yourself using the psychic current of water energy, invigorate your passions through fire energy, deal with hectic schedules and dozens of tasks using wood energy, and connect to the source of all that exists through metal energy. Find meaningful symbols to remind you of those things you intend to manifest. Work with the Law of Attraction with intent that is focused, balanced, magnetized, and energized through the ancient Chinese art of feng shui.

CHAPTER 18

Pendulum Dowsing to Know If You Are On Track

Pendulum dowsing has been around for thousands of years. Recently it has gained acceptance as a divining tool in conjunction with the Law of Attraction. It helps determine if a person is on the right track for drawing in the things he wants. The pendulum can give yes or no answers. One of the earliest dowsing images dates to circa 6000 B.C. Found in the Tassilin-Ajjer Mountains of eastern Algeria, it shows a human figure holding a forked stick. Ancient Egyptian and Chinese images of dowsing have also been discovered on papyruses and shards of pottery.

Use the Pendulum to Turn Inward

To use the pendulum for dowsing or divining answers, you must enter a state of calm alertness. If you do not know how to calm yourself and become relaxed while entering a state of clear focus, try the following. First, take a warm bath, perhaps with some aromatherapy oil. The point is to let go of the stresses of the day and to become grounded, centered, and focused.

Dress in comfortable clothes and sit in a softly lit area where there are fresh flowers, a glass of water, and peaceful instrumental music. Breathe deeply to release any remaining tension in the body. Once you are fully relaxed, offer a prayer to the Divine. Clap your hands three times or ring a sacred bell to summon your guardian angel or guide(s) who are bearers of light and knowledge. Tell them that you have questions for them, that you seek only truth, and that you appreciate their help. Offer heartfelt thanks every time you engage in pendulum dowsing. You may then drink the water or pour it onto a living plant such as lucky bamboo or a money plant, as it becomes magnetized by your spiritual vibrations.

FACT

Today, oval-shaped quartz crystals are favored for working with earth energies, while amethyst or rose quartz crystals might be preferable if you have questions about relationships or life issues. The more emotionally charged your question, the more likely that your pendulum will be accurate in providing the answer.

Choosing or Making a Pendulum

Through history, pendulums have been used to find water, precious metals, gems, oil, and gas as well as lost people, lost objects, ghosts, and negative earth energies. While a common type of pendulum is a forked stick, other types are made of a piece of string, cord, or chain with some kind of weight hanging from one end. The object with weight can be made of almost anything that is not magnetized—a key, wooden bead, paperclip, ring, metal fishing weight, quartz crystal, or glass ball, or even a Chinese coin with a square hole often used in feng shui—that can freely swing from a lightweight cord or chain. Cord length ranges from around nine to fifteen inches; use whatever is most comfortable for you.

Suspending Your Pendulum

To work with the pendulum, suspend the cord with its weighted object by looping a bit of excess cord or chain over your index finger. An alternative technique is to use a bead at one end of the chain and a heavier object, such as a crystal, at the other end. Place the bead between your index and middle finger of your dominant hand, allowing the string or chain with the crystal to dangle vertically to about an inch from the open palm of your other hand.

The pendulum and chain should feel so natural that it is like part of you, your arm, and your hand. The pendulum will swing back and forth, in circles, or side to side, hovering just above the open palm of your bottom hand. Picture your open palms facing each other and you will have the correct position.

Determining Dates and Time

The pendulum works through the force of your intuition or sixth sense. Some people use the pendulum to find out the hour or date something will happen. For such questions, it is helpful to cut from paper a circular clock with the increments marked or use a calendar with the dates and days in squares over which you can swing the pendulum. For example, you might ask which date in August would be best to start your summer vacation. Swing the pendulum over the days you are considering and see if it gives you a sign (downward pull or wildly swinging over one of the dates).

You can get simple yes or no answers if you phrase the questions carefully. Consider asking questions like "Would the beginning of August be better than the end?" "Would the first week be better than the second?" "Would a weekday be better than a weekend?"

The Downward Pull

In The *Art of the Pendulum*, Cassandra Eason recommends another way to work with your pendulum. That method focuses upon a single movement—a downward pull. Ask your angel or guide to cause the pendulum to pull downward to indicate a correct choice—for example, the correct herb in a garden that would best treat your ailment.

The downward pull indicator could also be used to divine the correct piece of paper out of several on which you've written various options for a career move, job transition, or amount to ask for in a raise. The pendulum can thus be used for clarification of information about your business ventures.

Access Your Higher Self

In the process of working with the Law of Attraction, you may seek a clear and immediate response to a question. Pendulums are believed to operate as transmitters of psychic energy. They represent intuitive information expressed by your higher self or God-self through the channel of intuition. Veteran pendulum dowsers swear that the more you use the pendulum (thus relying on your intuitive powers), the more your psychic powers will develop. Your pendulum should be considered a personal sacred object or tool. You should not let others handle it and you should keep it in a velvet or silk bag when you are not using it.

In order to get the answers you seek about your life, you first must understand how to interpret the way your pendulum responds to your questions. There are a variety of ways of working with the pendulum, but the following method takes the guesswork out of what the basic yes/no pattern might look like.

When you are ready to start working with the pendulum, establish your ground rules. Tell your higher self or your angels or guides that a clockwise circle indicates a yes answer and counterclockwise indicates a no. Show them by deliberately swinging the pendulum in each of those directions. Ask them to show you when they are ready by demonstrating a yes response. Watch the pendulum start to swing in a clockwise circular pattern. When it does, thank them for demonstrating that they are present and ready. Ask your first question.

Many pendulum users also ask to be shown what a maybe response looks like. It may be a forty-five degree movement, side to side, or some other pattern distinctively different from the circular yes and no patterns.

To test the accuracy of your pendulum, intermittently ask questions for which you already know the answer, such as "Is my name Mergatroid?" You know the answer is no and the pendulum should swing in a counter-clockwise circular pattern, according to the rules you've established.

Eliminate Self-Limiting Thoughts

Don't doubt or second-guess or rationalize the answers you may receive when you work with the pendulum. Doing so impedes or blocks the energy from your higher self just as surely as clutter blocks the vital energy swirling through an environment.

Working with the Law of Attraction, you know that the self-limiting thoughts and the criticisms and self-doubt will limit your effectiveness. When you work with the pendulum, let go of doubt. Trust the truth of the information you receive.

One way to validate the information you receive through pendulum dowsing is to keep a journal of the questions you ask and the responses you get when you pendulum-dowse for answers to help you with decisions. Later on, you can read how many answers were correctly given. This will also inspire you to seek answers about your life that will keep you moving forward in a positive direction.

Use Pendulum Dowsing for Information about Your Life

You want to know if the man you have fallen madly in love with is "the one," or whether or not to take that job in Denver, or if the time is right to launch your new business venture. You'll notice that the above are all yes or no questions that can be followed up by additional, in-depth questions. Try using dowsing to get the information you need for important decisions. Some examples include the following areas:

- Health—to determine the underlying cause of the illness; assess whether or not to pursue a particular course of treatment or analyze whether the treatment is working
- Love and relationships—to discover the truth about issues pertaining to specific aspects of your romantic liaisons and other relationships
- Career—to aid in decision-making about career moves and helpful people versus problematic ones
- Family—to discover ways to shift the family paradigm so that it serves everyone better; problem-solving for family issues
- Prosperity—to make vital decisions about creating income streams, building wealth, growing a business, and getting answers to help you move toward financial freedom

And about the ninth hour Jesus cried with a loud voice, saying, Eli, Eli, lama sabachthani?—that is to say, My God, my God, why hast thou forsaken me? . . . Jesus, when he had cried again with a loud voice, yielded up the ghost.—Matthew 27:46–50

You learned in Chapter 17 that in feng shui, the nine-square grid, or bagua, is used as a tool to determine which sector of your life correlates to a specific area of your home. In pendulum dowsing, there is also a role for the magical nine-square grid. Cassandra Eason refers to it as the Sacred Grid of Nine and explains how the downward movement of the pendulum can be used over that type of grid to help you discover answers about areas of your life. You could use the same squares as those of the feng shui bagua.

The number nine has special relevance in many magic, esoteric, and spiritual traditions. In tarot, the ninth card of the Major Arcana is the Hermit. The image is an old man or woman who provides wisdom, guidance, training, and direction. These are beneficial when you are working with the Law of Attraction to manifest growth, happiness, and abundance as well as before undertaking new endeavors or to know when a karmic cycle is complete.

Pay attention when the number nine shows up in your life. It can signify that you may need to take a retreat or enter a period of isolation for your growth and renewal. It might indicate that your work in a particular area or relationship is finished. In the Bible, the number nine represents Divine completion. Jesus completed his work on the cross in the ninth hour.

Find Blocked Chakras

You have a physical body and a subtle or spiritual body. The latter has energy pathways (nadis) and a channel (sushumna, the central corridor up the spine from the tailbone to the head) along which lie seven major wheels or vortices of energy (chakras). Together they make up the esoteric anatomy of the subtle body. An energy imbalance or blockage in one or more of the chakras can adversely influence your spiritual work and your health and well-being. A blocked chakra or a wide-open chakra can result in mental and physical illnesses, according to some holistic practitioners, teachers of Tantra yoga, and energy workers, such as Reiki masters.

Chakra Contemplation for Empowerment

Focusing on a particular chakra as part of your regular spiritual work yields empowerment as the chosen chakra becomes more energized. For example, the Ajna or third-eye chakra opens your psychic vision, strengthens your intuition, and helps you see more clearly the meaning of life. The proper functioning of this chakra enables you to recall dreams and to see into realms that are not accessible to ordinary human vision.

Chakra Healing

When chakra energy becomes imbalanced and is too strong or diminished, illnesses in the physical body can develop. When you feel as if your vibration no longer rises into higher (or deeper) realms of consciousness, you may need a little chakra tune-up. To obtain optimum results in your work with the Law of Attraction, you want your mind, body, and spirit to be in harmonious alignment and the chakras to function as intended. For those times when they aren't, there are many excellent ways to heal chakra issues—Reiki or touch therapy, crystals and gem work, and aura cleansing, to name a few.

The Seven Main Chakras

Yogis say that you have a physical body and also an ethereal body. Along the ethereal body's central channel, corresponding to the spinal cord of the physical body, are the energy centers—the chakras. Through the process of spiritually unfolding, the latent powers of your chakras become activated. Swami Vivekananda noted in his book Raja Yoga that through rhythmic breathing, molecules in the body all begin to move in the same direction. That, in turn, can bring about a single-pointedness of your mind.

The seven main chakras are:

1. Muladhara, located at the base of the spine
2. Swadhisthana, located in the area of the navel
3. Manipura, located in the area of the solar plexus
4. Anahata, located at the heart center
5. Vishuddha, throat center
6. Ajna, located at the midpoint between the eyebrows (psychic third eye)
7. Sahasrara, shaped like a thousand-petaled lotus at the crown of the head

The Muladhara, or root chakra, represents the site of your spiritual potential. Swadhisthana is the center of unconscious desire, while Manipura is associated with your spiritual forcefulness or dynamism. Love emanates from the Anahata chakra. The Vishuddha represents the site of wisdom and the ability to discern between truth and ignorance. The Ajna chakra is associated with sacred prayer, and Sahasrara is the center of higher consciousness.

Each of the seven powerful chakras is associated with certain colors, sacred symbols, sounds, and relationships to specific body and esoteric powers such as clairaudience, clairvoyance, and the ability to travel astrally and to receive deep spiritual truths and insights. Meditation and all types of spiritual work can energize any or all of the chakras to further your evolution along the spiritual path.

Rise of the Kundalini

One of the most important goals of yogis is to bring about the awakening of the dormant divine energy, the kundalini, so that the energy rushes upward from the Muladhara to the Sahasrara or crown chakra at the top of the head, which is the seat of consciousness. Such an event bestows a state of samadhi or unity of mortal consciousness with Divine Mind.

The ancient Vedic text *The Chandogya Upanishad* (number nine of the 108 Upanishads of the Muktika Canon) noted that when a yogi entered the all-important energy pathway leading up through the head, he became immortal.

Modern yogis say that enlightenment is possible when kundalini, the sacred energy also referred to as the goddess Shakti, moves up the center channel of the sushumna through the crown chakra to unite with Shiva, the masculine aspect of the Divine that destroys ignorance. The energies yin/yang, female/male are completely balanced in that state, where you lose all consciousness of separateness, of duality. Instead, you rest in supreme bliss, in union with the Divine. You become godlike.

You can create a chakra chart by drawing a large circle on paper with seven circles ringing the internal perimeter. Allow the pendulum to swing over each of the seven circles symbolizing the chakras, and ask your yes/no questions about chakra blockages, spiritually based physical illness, and appropriate healing methodologies.

Answer Life's Dilemmas and Lessons

Everyone struggles with issues in her life. You can probably remember a time when you felt like you were in the trough of a great transition and could not see the end or even know exactly how things might turn out. Those moments of crisis or upheaval potentially represented a period of accelerated growth in your life.

Such transitional periods are often accompanied by feelings of uncertainty, apprehension, and a vague sense of disconcertedness that nothing will ever be the same. Your fears during such periods don't have to overwhelm you. Use your pendulum to get answers and information about the most pressing issues or insight into what life lesson you are learning.

Patterns of thinking can radically shift when you are in any of the big transitions of life, such as having a baby, grieving over the loss of a loved one, moving away from your support network and family, suffering a major illness, making a major purchase, or renovating a house when you literally experience the breaking down of old structures. Thought patterns can become fearful, anxious, and doubtful, dragging down your emotional energy. Those times would be good periods to work with the pendulum to re-energize your vision, intent, and goal.

Strengthen Self-Care and Eliminate Self-Sabotage

One of the most vital aspects of working with the Law of Attraction requires that you take care of yourself. Self-care begins with self-nourishment and self-acceptance. Only when you have these things will you find meaning in all the other things you desire to attract. A million dollars won't mean much if you are too ill to spend it. The love of your life can show up, but if you aren't emotionally healthy enough to receive him, the relationship won't satisfy you for long.

Turn Love upon Yourself

Love yourself as though you were showing love to your spouse or lover. If you've just broken up with someone, turn all the love that you were turning toward the other person back upon yourself. When you are in love, you have energy to spare. You are happy, perhaps obsessively so, as you consider doing special things for that special someone. Do those things for yourself.

Find relief in nature. According to feng shui and geomancy theories, trees, bodies of water, and living plants are all natural sources for healing energy or pranic energy. *Prana* is the Sanskrit word for life-sustaining or vital energy. When you feel restless, consider that you won't find relief and meaning in the world but rather from within the self.

Notice Apathy

You can use the pendulum-dowsing techniques you've learned in this chapter to help you understand how to treat yourself better. You may not feel energetic enough to pick it up and start, but give yourself the opportunity to begin moving in the right direction again. If you don't move your body, it simply won't work as well. The muscles begin to shrink. Flexibility lessens along with your range of motion. You start to gain weight.

That won't make you feel good about yourself. Life becomes dull. It seems to take a lot of effort to just get motivated to go through your day. It's a snowball effect; things go from bad to worse. Until you shift the energy and start down a different path to becoming fully alive and engaged in your life, the Law of Attraction will continue bringing you the same old stuff.

Healing with Nature's Energies

Seek out a special tree, rose garden, clump of bushes, or gurgling stream. Draw close to such energy sources and stay near while you ponder what ails you. Then suspend your pendulum from your fingers. Sit near the water or circumambulate a boulder, mountain, tree, or bed of flowers. Attune yourself to the feelings of energy in the pendulum.

When you begin to feel tingling sensations in your fingers and arms, tiny buglike movements across your back, warm or cool energy moving along your spine, or a current coursing through your pendulum hand and arm, you can be assured that you are drawing energy from nature. Direct that energy to your heart if it's been broken, or to whatever area in your body most needs it. Allow healing to take place. Perhaps you are grieving and would like to ask the universe or that loved one who has crossed over a yes or no question. Use the pendulum. When you are finished, express your gratitude to the life-giving, fecund Goddess or divine Creator.

Pendulum dowsing can be used to help you clarify a big dream for your life. Perhaps it's been a daydream for a long time and you have decided to work with the Law of Attraction to make it a reality. Do a mind map of your dream. Draw a big circle on a piece of paper and write your dream in the center of the circle. As the energy of your mind flows around the thought of your dream, began drawing spokes originating from the large circle and ending in smaller ones containing all your ideas about making your dream a reality.

Use your pendulum and yes or no questions to clarify details and to help you prepare to-do lists, timelines, and goals. Benjamin Franklin once said that God helps those who help themselves. Update that quote by adding the words "through the Law of Attraction and the many self-help tools available to people today."

CHAPTER 19

Share the Knowledge

When you began to put the Law of Attraction to work in your life, did you begin to keep a journal noting the dates and times when the law gave you exactly what you asked for and when it manifested? Such documentation can serve not only as validation but also as future inspiration as you continue working with the law. You have learned the secret power of cocreation in harmony and gratitude with the Divine. Now it's your turn to share your knowledge, experience, insights, and enthusiasm with others.

Create Better Lives by Teaching Others

You know people who are always complaining that they can't get ahead in life no matter what they do. They are the walking wounded. They may have lost jobs, be in pain, or be at risk of losing their homes. They may wonder if they are living under some kind of curse. At church, they find comfort in hearing that God loves them, watches over them, and can help them, but they don't know how to help themselves. These are people you can teach to avail themselves of financial prosperity, joy, and success in every area of life.

FACT

Leaders, whether in organizations or businesses, motivate people. But no two leaders are exactly alike in their style and approach. Some leaders use negative motivational tools such as intimidation, fear, and ridicule and, consequently, find that these hurtful tactics usually work in the short-term and can backfire. Positive motivation not only helps people help themselves, but it can also function as self-motivation for leaders.

You can also learn from them. Questions and comments posed by others inevitably provide different lenses for examining a subject. Sharing knowledge is often a two-way flow. Teaching someone else something is a sure-fire method for learning more about it yourself.

The Taoist Lao Tzu once propounded that if you give a man a fish, he eats for a day. But if you teach the man to fish, he can eat for the rest of his life. The point is not to promote another person's reliance upon you to keep providing the fish, but to empower that individual to find the sustenance from life on his own. When he understands how to manifest his heart's many desires and his body's assorted needs in alliance with the Law of Attraction, he will be able to sustain himself without your intervention. That is not to say you can't emotionally and psychologically support him and others.

Enough for Everyone

A common question that pops up in conversations about the Law of Attraction is that if everyone gets to have as much abundance in their lives as they want, will it take something away from others? The answer is no. The world of formless energy and substance out of which all of creation takes shape is boundless and limitless. It's not a scale that tips when weight is added or rises when something is removed. Perceiving the truth that an abundant life is available for all may require a new way of thinking for some people.

Mary Baker Eddy, founder of the Christian Scientists, asserted that the simple declaration that in God you are perfect will unleash God's infinite health-generating power into the body. According to the Law of Attraction, such a dynamic thought sets in motion the attraction to draw perfection to you. For more information about Eddy, see *www.marybakereddylibrary.org*.

Seeing Beyond Duality

Enlightened beings from ancient times to the present day have said that the creation of the universe (or multiverse for those who believe that there could be infinite universes) occurred first in the Divine Mind where ideas of less and lack and their opposites do not exist. The infinite Divine Mind perceives everything in perfection and completeness, beyond duality, ever present and without the limitations of time, space, and dimensions.

Even if everyone on earth understood how to manifest a pink Cadillac and everyone received a car, the infinite storehouse of the universe could still provide a car for everyone who wanted two or three or more. You can have as many as you want. It simply requires you thinking consecutive thoughts that are sustained over time.

Seeing Beyond Error

Appearances of things (for example, disease) can produce an idea in the mind and it will manifest in the body. But if you know the truth—for example, that health, not disease, is the true reality—then you can let go of the appearance and embrace the truth. This is an important concept for those who want financial prosperity but see the absence of wealth and consider poverty to be the truth. The fear of disease can cause it to manifest, but a focus on health can bestow vitality. Fear of poverty can impede finding wealth, but a focus on abundance can draw prosperity.

Christian Scientists—not to be confused with Scientologists or material or physical scientists—are guided by the principle that the spiritual reality is the only real truth and all else is spiritual error. That is why they believe they can heal through the power of prayer. When a person's faith is strong enough to see the body's illness as no more than an illusion or a spiritual error in the mind, that faith restores perfection and wholeness. This is another important truth to be shared with others who desire to work with the Law of Attraction to attract optimum health.

Empower Others

Every person comes up against limits throughout life. Assuming that each person has a God-given mind for reasoning, a heart for feeling, and a healthy and whole body for getting through life, what makes one person able to push past limitations to become a magnet for the things they desire while the other person fails? Someone who struggles with lack most likely experiences one or more of the following limiting habits: inability to focus, lack of imagination, tendency to procrastinate, doubt, judgmental and critical self-talk, fear, and self-limiting beliefs.

Find the Good

Empower others everywhere you go. Do as the late Alex Haley, the author of *Roots*, advocated: "Find the good and praise it." Celebrate life and let your enthusiasm for doing good and seeing good be a lightning rod for others so that they will desire to live in that kind of happiness. Remind yourself and others that in every moment is the power to change the course of your day or your life. The miracles that go on around us— miracles we often don't even notice—are manifestations of the law at work in the world. Now that's a reassurance to celebrate!

Moving Beyond Self-Limitations

You can encourage others to recognize the negativity in their thoughts and behaviors. Since they alone own them, they must be the ones who shift the paradigm. By choosing to break the destructive cycles of negative thoughts, words, and actions and to move into alignment with positive and happy thinking, feeling, doing, and speaking, they become empowered to move beyond the appearances of limitations.

Energy, Enthusiasm, and Expectation

Not surprisingly, many people working with deliberate intention and the Law of Attraction have sought and found support among others who share their ideas about how to achieve the good things in life. The group energy and enthusiasm is often infectious and spurs individuals in the group to believe in the value of their dreams and let go of doubt and the negatives of the past that may weigh upon them.

Canst thou not minister to a mind diseased; pluck from the memory of a rooted sorrow; Raze out the written troubles of the brain; And, with some sweet oblivious antidote, Cleanse the stuffed bosom of that perilous stuff Which weighs upon the heart?—William Shakespeare, *Macbeth*, Act 5, Scene 3

Sometimes members of a Law of Attraction networking group will help you clarify and establish goals or work toward new ones. You, in turn, help them stay on track. The group can help you identify behaviors that may create luck in bringing success or factors that may be chasing it away. You reinforce each other's pursuit of goodness, not just the acquisition of material wealth but in the expectation that your sacred dreams, your goals of working service groups, and your humanitarian efforts will come to fruition.

Challenging the Status Quo

People who are successful in creating their exciting dream life are always on the move. They don't sit still and wait for life to come to them. They won't write one book in a year, they'll write two, four, or five. They won't start just one business in a lifetime. They will build one until it becomes mega-successful, and then they'll begin again with something new. They sail into life each day with zeal and gusto, ever on the lookout for a new idea, a more fun way to do something, or a new enterprise, ever challenging the status quo. By demonstrating that passionate way of being, you are demonstrating how to best work with the law. You may be motivating yourself as well.

FACT

Scholar David Ellerman, author of *Helping People Help Themselves: From the World Bank to an Alternative Philosophy of Development Assistance*, has taken a humanist approach to how to best help humanity and nations. The success of any economic development aid works, he asserted, when people and countries become empowered to help themselves. Doers must see their own problems to discover workable solutions.

Learning Metaphysical and Esoteric Teachings

Some Law of Attraction practitioners join support groups to share metaphysical or esoteric teachings behind the Law of Attraction. Others are attracted to the open and honest ways that members engage in self-disclosure and friendship. They no longer feel isolated in the pursuit of a new and better life. Still others find that it helps to work with fellow Buddhists or survivors of some life-threatening disease who support one another through several layers of common interest, such as a desire for compassionate living or a sense of shared common ground.

Showing Others How to Create a New Life

Some Law of Attraction teachers talk about how to get everything you want from positive thinking. They expound on various points that they believe are key to becoming an attraction magnet for abundance of every kind. Many people will remain skeptical and won't believe it is possible to create such a life until they see someone else do it. Show them how to create a good life, centered in thanksgiving and gratitude. Inspire others to become self-reliant and independent.

Key Points

When sharing information that is critical to working with the law, it is helpful to emphasize that the most successful individuals refuse to settle for mediocrity in life. They see change as exciting and necessary. In fact, they create it when they form intention for their new life of prosperity and joy. They don't just desire something; they go after it with a passion. They let go of old paradigms and patterns that did not bring successful results.

QUESTION?

What exactly is a naysayer?
A naysayer is someone who has an aggressively negative attitude and who tends to criticize instead of praise, degrade instead of build up an idea or relationship. A naysayer often feels vulnerable or threatened when faced with change or new ideas that push her outside her comfort zone. Consequently, she postures defensively instead of opening herself to possibility.

Another key point to emphasize is the importance of persistence, not only in formulating the belief that a goal is worthwhile but in continuing to believe that the goal can be reached. Further, it is critical that an individual who is starting to work with the law firmly believes that he is worthy of the goals and desires he sets forth to achieve. He must have the persistence of Henry Ford, whose engineers at first did not believe it was possible to create a six-cylinder motor, and hold on to his vision passionately despite the naysayers.

Taking the Law Where It Is Most Needed

Some critics have suggested that those who have most passionately rallied behind the Law of Attraction are members of America's middle class. But the people who really need the hope promised by the law are poor people, the hungry, those living in shelters and on the streets, and the disenfranchised. The teachings of Jesus found resonance with just such groups because their society 2,000 years ago failed them.

Help a Younger Generation

Young people today face many of the same challenges of growing up as those of previous generations but, in addition, must find ways to deal with media messages that glorify negative patterns of thinking and living. Gangsta rap and some hip-hop lyrics glorify gang life and romanticize infidelity, promiscuity, abuse, hatred, and drug use. America's prisons are full of young people who associated with the wrong peer group and ended up dead or behind prison walls.

Why not put together a proposal for a workshop on the Law of Attraction through an adult education program sponsored by your local park and recreation center? If you can't write a book, record your ideas in booklet form. Offer to sell it for $1.00 as part of your seminar or presentation. You will share the information and create a small income stream.

Who are the positive role models for today's youth? Celebrities like Paris Hilton, Britney Spears, Lindsay Lohan, and other gals and guys in the film and music industries get a lot of media attention, but rarely for sterling behavior. More often, the tabloids and TV shows run stories of such individuals entering or leaving rehab, partying endlessly, or showing off a destructive lifestyle with an emphasis on sensual indulgence and disregard for the rule of law.

Teachers, youth counselors, parents, and peers could do more to help the younger generation relate to better role models, to celebrate their success as if it were their own, to promote their interests as if they were self-serving interests. It's a radical concept to teach young people, but if they can conceive that all of humanity is interconnected on some level and that one act of goodness affects everyone, perhaps they would be inspired to live noble lives.

FACT

In Irish folklore, a crock of gold sits at the point where the rainbow touches the earth. Other societies view the rainbow as a benevolent serpent whose energy flows in a half-circle between earth and heaven. In the Tantra of Hindus and Buddhists, the rainbow symbolizes the dissolving of the physical body into the spectrums of light in the highest realms.

Counseling Young Adults

Surely it could greatly benefit young people to learn about how they can create a positive and meaningful life for themselves. A self-centered, decadent lifestyle that leaves one burned out by the age of thirty does not benefit the individual, the family, the community, or society at large. Begin to reach out to young people, at first your own, to give them the tools to go after their dreams. Remind them that it is possible to change the world one person at a time and that making the world a better place for everyone, including future generations, is an admirable goal.

Many teens, as they push up against the boundaries of their world as part of their biological task to individuate away from the family, tune out adult guidance. But they listen to each other. One of the best ways to get across a message of hope is to let the teens spread it among themselves. Just imagine how such teaching might help someone scared and confused and ready to give up completely on her life.

Offer to participate in career day at your local high school. Use that venue to discuss how the Law of Attraction helped you find the right job, get promoted, start your own company, or further your career. Show genuine passion and enthusiasm for your work and your life to inspire your young audience. Use concrete examples from your life.

The Answers Are Out There

When Crystal and her husband Don walked hand-in-hand along the beach on Maui to celebrate the renewal of their vows after twenty years of marriage, Crystal never dreamed that one year later she would face widowhood and possible foreclosure on the house she and Don had shared. Lonely and scared, she struggled to pay the bills and keep her home, but her substitute teaching job was threatened by district-wide cuts. Crystal began to take in some freelance editing work for a couple of local companies. For five years, she kept juggling work and creating new income through odd jobs, but she finally realized she couldn't keep up with the high mortgage payments. She vowed to sell the house.

Crystal watered her yard and cried. She called Vera, a new friend she had met in a grief support group who talked about how you could change your life working with the universal laws, including the Law of Attraction. With Vera's support, Crystal released her fears. She sold the house and bought a condo. Soon there was money for things like dance lessons. During a ballroom dance class for the tango, she met a businessman who needed her editing skills for his start-up company, which dealt with Brazilian eco-tourism. Her new job involved occasional travel to remote places with her boss. Crystal discovered that she not only loved her new job but also the attentions of her new boss. Money was no longer an issue. She felt intensely alive and passionate about such meaningful work.

Creating High Quality Golden Years

Senior citizens represent a sector of the population who could use knowledge of the Law of Attraction. They are often vulnerable, sometimes suffering more than others from a lack of money, health care coverage, affordable medications, and sometimes even food and housing. Sharing techniques and strategies for intentionally working with the Law of Attraction might help members of the aging population create not only longer and healthier lives but a better quality of life. While they may not have the energy or the same dreams they had in their youth, some may still hope to find a pot of gold at the end of the rainbow and likely would share it with others.

Through the sharing of your experience of intentionally working with the Law of Attraction, remember to include a discussion of the roles of faith and gratitude. Teaching others about the law so that they might have better lives, greater happiness, and a more prosperous future has resonance in the Buddhist idea of humanity's interconnectedness and the necessity of each person to have a sense of responsibility toward the welfare of others. In Buddhism, the highest ideal is the path of the bodhisattva. The bodhisattva finds the source of all fulfillment—that is, the Ultimate Truth—but he denies himself enlightenment in order to bring all other fellow beings to that same holy Source.

CHAPTER 20

What's Next?

You can now draw to yourself a brighter future, vibrant health, transformational thinking, financial prosperity, abundance of every kind, and deeper and more profound spiritual connections. You have risen above the fetters that have been holding you back through self-limiting thought to discover the world anew. You have allowed your newfound sense of wonder to inspire feelings of gratitude. But what if, after you have attracted to you everything you ever dreamed of, emotion still tugs at your heart? Perhaps it's your sense of altruism asking you to give as generously as you've received.

A Brighter Future

Consider how you might envision ways of attracting to you the means to help others build a better and brighter future. Consider how you could use your powerful and magnetized thoughts to bring about change in your community, country, and the world. Some say the Berlin Wall came down through the prayers of the world and the inspiration of then President Ronald Reagan telling the Russian president, "Mr. Gorbachev, tear down this wall."

Who Else Would You Help?

As you previously learned, you can't change another human being, but you can choose to behave differently around that person, and that is enough to shift the dynamics of a relationship with her. If you are in a bad relationship, dissatisfied with your employer, or have reached the end of your patience with a disgruntled client, you can choose to sever the connection and go in a different direction in your life. Bless those individuals as you move forward. But why not also see them bathed in holy light in your mind and silently bless them so that they may have the highest good that can come to them? Ask yourself, "Who else might benefit from my knowledge of how to work with the Law of Attraction?"

QUESTION?

What is the Gaia philosophy?
Gaia is a name used within the green community and in certain scientific circles to explain the concept that all the living organisms of a host planet cooperate with their environment to function as a single self-regulating system. In Greek mythology, Gaia was the goddess of the earth.

Work Toward Open Doors

Perhaps one of the most important things the late mythologist Joseph Campbell said was to follow your bliss. What if you were at a crossroads in your life, feeling like you didn't know which way to turn? Maybe a door has closed on your marriage or career. Perhaps now the time is right to visit Italy or France, set up your software business in Ireland, start your import store on eBay, or establish an orphanage in India. If those ideas seem too grand, consider doing some volunteer work at home or abroad. Use the Law of Attraction to draw in those doors that Campbell said will open as you follow your bliss. As they do swing open, confidently walk through them. Just as the law has drawn a door closed, it will open others and help you across the threshold.

Find Your Joy

Are you someone who laughs easily at the craziness of life? You have already learned how important emotion is in magnetizing thought. Find your inner child and laugh often with his childhood delight as you move into your new life of working with the Law of Attraction. You'll find that humor helps defuse tense situations, adds levity to the most serious moments, and ensures that you never take yourself (or anyone else, for that matter) too seriously.

Material or Spiritual Gain?

The Law of Attraction is available to all. But some people practice working with it more than others. You might choose to make an in-depth study of its working in your life and the lives of others. Consider disseminating your knowledge and experience in working with the law. Teach seminars, write a newsletter, direct a conference, produce a video or CD, or establish a website devoted to the Law of Attraction. From your work and special expertise and insights, you could charge fees that could become an income stream, perhaps the means of helping yourself get out of debt or begin to build wealth. Doing such work with a sense of high-minded purpose, not greed, makes it noble. However, you might also decide that you want to help others who are less fortunate and pursue Law of Attraction work as a purely spiritual endeavor. When you are motivated by selflessness to do good for others, your activities generate spiritual dividends.

Collective Envisioning for Global Change

Consider how you join in with others working with the Law of Attraction to build a better world. With them, you would need to be unified in purpose, hold the same collective vision and intentions, and make a deep emotional commitment to imagine a world without war, leaders coming up with solutions to global social ills, and corporations becoming good citizens and responsible stewards of the planet. Perhaps you and your group could focus on the eradication of hunger, cures for HIV/AIDS and cancer, abolition of racism and bigotry, or other issues.

Positive Thinking for the Planet

Think of yourself as one member of a global family who works with the Law of Attraction to envision the well-being of planet Earth. Many people, not just those who embrace the Gaia philosophy, are persuaded that much has to be done to reduce the human footprint, not only on earth but in the heavens.

Transformational Thinking That Goes Beyond Personal Dreams and Goals

As you begin to manifest helpful people, wonderful relationships, and the things you've always wanted, begin to think outside the box in radical new ways. Try envisioning new life goals, determining a new purpose or career path, or projecting new plans for a business or organization. That's exactly what a couple of young college law students decided to do. One thought he wanted to be a criminal defense attorney but changed his mind after a discussion with his roommate, who was studying economics.

The two young men shared a philosophy that one person could bring about change through a grassroots movement. They began a brainstorming session in which they entertained myriad ideas about what they could do with their educations and their lives. The two hit upon the concept of establishing a think tank for social reform. They envisioned a new way of living on the planet because they believed that through viral marketing on the web, they could reach millions of Americans who could make their votes count to effect policy changes for social reform. Without their evening of transformational thinking outside the box, both young men would have undoubtedly continued down the conventional paths they were on.

Use the Law in Your Place of Worship

Use the Law of Attraction in your place of worship to achieve fund-raising goals, restore the building, buy new materials, expand outreach programs, envision a return to health for the sick, and in myriad other ways. Share ideas about positive thinking and how to work with the Law of Attraction with fellow parishioners.

Learn more about how to work with the Law of Attraction from experts who hold Law of Attraction seminars to help people achieve transformational thinking. With a focus on peak mental performance and superior cognitive functioning, students are taught a variety of skills to enhance their leadership abilities and to achieve lofty goals.

Use the Law to Bring about Ecological and Environmental Changes

You can join with others to dream a grand dream of ecological and environmental change. Develop affirmations for group recitation. Prepare and implement to-do or action lists that might include calling upon government representatives to ensure environmentally friendly products, good alternatives to fossil fuels, safer food supplies through reduction of harmful pesticides and hormone injections of animals, responsible e-waste recycling, preservation of the rain forests, and safer water supplies.

Mind and Body Control for Perfect Health

By using the Law of Attraction, you can manifest perfect mental and physical health. Using the power of your mind you can bring about healthy changes in your body, even overcome the kinds of diseases that can shorten your life. Life extension is certainly possible through an understanding of dietary rules, exercising, stress reduction, smoking cessation, moderate consumption of coffee and alcohol, and deliberate work to manifest perfect health in harmony with the Law of Attraction.

FACT

You can learn to increase your vitality by becoming like a yogi, yoking your will to the energy you already have and using the Law of Attraction to draw more energy in from the Cosmic Source. Avoid declaring that you are tired; doing so makes you feel instantly depleted. Instead, affirm that all the energy you need is flowing into your body now.

Some Indian yogis have been able to slow their heartbeat and breathing in order to demonstrate mental power over their bodies. Stories that defy human logic and understanding have circulated. People have even been buried alive, slept on pallets of pointed nails, or pulled a heavy object using hooks in the skin of their backs. Still others were able to know things about total strangers or the nature and composition of a certain object. Sathya Sai Baba, a controversial Hindu holy man born in the Indian village of Puttaparthi, can manifest things out of the air by the power of his thought. He has done hundreds of demonstrations throughout his lifetime and is considered by millions to be an avatar or incarnation of God. When he materializes things such as gems and sacred ash, he is said to chant "It is coming now." That phrase, spoken with resolve and faith, is an excellent one to use when working with the Law of Attraction.

Think of other examples of what you could manifest in your life. For example, you might manifest approval, love, higher ethical standards, understanding, insight, acceptance, hopefulness, peace, agility, strength, purpose, tenderness, fearlessness, veracity, confidence, a winning spirit, deep spiritual insights, and exceptional competence.

When the mind is free from distraction, it is possible for all the mental processes to be involved in the object of enquiry. As one remains in this state, gradually one becomes totally immersed in the object. The mind, then, like a flawless diamond, reflects only the features of the object and nothing else.—*Yoga Sutras of Patanjali*, Sutra 41

Altered States of Consciousness

You may not have yet reached such transcendental states of consciousness as to be able to know your past and future, but perhaps you can use the Law of Attraction to draw that ability, know how to use it, and experience fantastic results. Some esoteric teachers say it is the destiny of each person to evolve spiritually. If you need a teacher to guide you, you can attract her and anything else you need into your life. Whatever you can think of with feeling again and again, you can make so.

Saints of various cultures have been able to know, see, or do things that seem beyond human ability. The Sufi mystics known as dervishes dance themselves into altered states of consciousness. Shamans of certain cultures also perform sacred dances to bring about trances. They have shown transcendence over the body that defies a logical and rational understanding of how the human organism functions. Undoubtedly, they have been able to tap into something far greater and more powerful than simple human intellect and emotion. They have set up an attraction for spiritual awakening, and the transcendental states of consciousness become the doorway between ordinary consciousness and the transcendent mind.

Shamans enter states of consciousness, often self-induced, that can produce long-term radical shifts in their perception of themselves, others, and the world. Mystics share with shamans a state of consciousness commonly referred to as trance and often refer to the universe and all within it as coming from God in an outward flow rather than through immersion.

Awakening Powerful Energy Centers

Your body contains two extremely powerful energy centers, the heart and the crown chakras. Your destiny, and that of everyone, some say, is to be transformed into spiritually evolved beings. That happens through the awakening and ascent of the kundalini energy up through the spinal channel known as the sushumna. Kundalini is the divine transformational energy that can bestow knowledge of the past and future, the mysteries of the universe, and the secrets of all creation when it is activated or awakened.

Getting Started

The Law of Attraction will bring you what you deeply desire and need. If you need a teacher to help you on your spiritual path, you have only to ask for him. There's an old adage that states that when the student is ready, the teacher appears.

Your greatest benefit of an awakened kundalini is the culmination of the process of spiritual maturation. Kundalini arousal can bring about self-realization or the recognition of the atman, knowledge of the true self. Some say it confers immortality.

Triggering Awakening of the Latent Divine Energy

Some yogis and yoginis say that you can attract the conditions for the awakening of the kundalini through mantra, mudra, breath work, meditation, and other spiritual practices. The kundalini awakening can occur spontaneously or through shaktipat, the transference of energy from a teacher to her student for the purpose of initiation and awakening of the kundalini. Such awakening confers powers from all the energy centers of the body and brings about superconsciousness.

You may feel pressure, especially at the base of the spine, a column of heat from the tailbone to the top of the head, sounds such as tinkling bells or thunder, the sensation of ants crawling along the spine, the sound of the cosmic vibration of atoms heard as Om, and cool and hot energy flowing along the spinal column. These are just some of the signs and symptoms. Others have heard bees buzzing and seen (through the third-eye chakra) streams of light. In India, some practitioners of yoga have found themselves spontaneously doing certain yoga poses or mudras (hand positions).

FACT

The Sanskrit meaning of *kundalini* is "coiled up." Yogis believe that at the base of the spine a latent divine energy awaits awakening. Usually depicted in religious or spiritual literature and imagery as a coiled serpent, it is wrapped around itself three and one-half times.

Living Your Life Inside Out

Kundalini Shakti is perceived as a manifestation of the energetic feminine form of the Divine. When you decide to seek a higher spiritual life and begin to attract wisdom and spiritual understanding instead of "stuff," she will begin to open and empower the energy centers of the body, according to the teachings of Kundalini Maha yoga. You will become transformed. Instead of living in a material world and having your body senses dictating how you live your life, you can choose to live out your days in a different way—from the inside out.

Eternal Now

When your heart is open and your mind is beyond duality thinking, you can truly live in the present moment with consciousness of all moments—past, present, and future—contained in one time/space continuum. Yogis say that for such holy beings, there is nothing that can't be known or done.

The purpose of life, some believe, is self-development and the unfolding of the divine latent powers within. In *The Seven Spiritual Laws of Success*, Dr. Deepak Chopra references the Law of Pure Potentiality, also known as the Law of Unity (because underlying infinite diversity is the unity of the One). These are universal laws, just like the Law of Attraction. As you dream this dream of your life, you tap into the realm of infinite possibility. It isn't to be found outside of you but rather within.

Infinite Possibilities

The Law of Karma will bring experiences into your life as you consciously and unconsciously send out your thoughts, but you get to decide how to handle what comes. Imagine the possibilities of always knowing the right thing to do and the right moment in which to do it. Consider being able to block illness from ever coming into your body or to attract unfathomable wealth. Imagine being able to traverse the cosmos by imagery and thought. Think about how you might use infinite power and wisdom for peace and high and noble purposes. You have the power to transform yourself into a self-realized or enlightened being. In fact, an Indian sage named Patanjali wrote a book to explain how.

The Yoga Aphorisms of Patanjali, also commonly called *The Yoga Sutras of Patanjali*, is a collection of terse verses, pregnant with meaning, albeit sometimes obscure or hidden, taken from Vedic Hinduism. The text dates to roughly 200 B.C. but has gained popularity in recent times because of the burgeoning interest in yoga as a means of health and harmonic mind/body alignment.

When you desire enlightenment, the power switch is flipped on, and light dispels darkness or ignorance. Your usual state of being becomes one of peace and joy or bliss. Enlightened, you possess the kingdom of God, for in the state of self-realization, you become godlike. According to some yogis, god-realized individuals know all that is knowable, and even if the sacred texts from all religious paths were destroyed, a god-realized being could re-create them. People won't recognize you by all the "stuff" you have attracted and manifested but rather by your expression of love, wisdom, and power. Find the secret hidden deep inside your heart. As Rumi, the Sufi mystic might say, someone is calling you; maybe it's your own soul asking you to open the door.

Glossary of Terms

~ **affirmations**

Positive statements that are repeated to impress and reinforce a particular belief.

~ **aphorism**

A succinct saying that embodies a truth—for example, the *Aphorisms of Patanjali.*

~ **Ayurveda**

The ancient Hindu art of medicine that emphasizes the vital energies of the body as well as knowledge of prolonging life.

~ **covenant**

The promises made by God to humans that are found in the Scriptures.

~ **Creator**

One of many monikers for God; others include Divine Intelligence, Holy One, Divine Mind, Powers that Be, the Universe, and the Nameless Formless One; the aspect of the omnipotent, omniscient, and omnipresent God that brought and brings all things into being.

~ **Damasio, Antonio**

Author of *Descartes' Error* and *Looking for Spinoza*, Damasio is a neurologist and neuroscientist notable for his research into the mind/body interrelatedness to emotion and feelings.

~ **dharma**

A way of living in which a person strives to have in perfect alignment his or her body, mind, and spirit.

~ **dowsing**

The method by which a pendulum or forked stick is used to detect energies from the earth or environment as a means of finding water or divining information.

~ **Eddy, Mary Baker**

Spiritualist who established the Christian Scientist organization.

~ *Emerald Tablet*

A tablet discovered by archeologists with verses attributed to the Egyptian Hermes.

~ **emotion**

The mood created by positive or negative feelings in the body in response to internal or external stimulus.

~ **feng shui**

The ancient Chinese art of placement and energy flow.

~ **Hermes**

An Egyptian sage believed to have lived circa 800 B.C. The verses of the *Emerald Tablet* are attributed to him.

~ Job

The biblical man who successfully passed God's many tests. Job's story is found in the Old Testament's Book of Job.

~ Kabbalah (also Cabala, Qabalah)

The practices and texts of Jewish mystical teachings that were developed by rabbis from the seventh to the eighteenth centuries. Initiates interpreted sacred Scripture through insights that allowed them to foretell the future. Kabbalah reached its zenith, perhaps, in the medieval period to the Renaissance.

~ Kahlo, Frida

Mexican artist and wife of muralist Diego Rivera.

~ kami

In the animist Shinto religion, kami represents a divine force or being that may be found in rock formations or along rivers and in mountains.

~ karma

The Hindu philosophy of retribution in the current life of an individual attributed to his or her past thoughts, words, or actions.

~ Kundalini Shakti

The latent divine energy in the subtle (spiritual) body that, according to ancient Vedic philosophy, awakens spontaneously or through initiation by a teacher to move up the pathway along the spine to the top of the head to union with Divine consciousness.

~ mudra

Movement of the hands in yoga positions, meditation, or classical Indian dance, the latter as a way of expressing feeling.

~ Om (also Aum)

In Hinduism, regarded as the sound that is a complete expression of the Divine in that it encompasses Brahma (the Creator), Vishnu (Preserver), and Shiva (the Destroyer); also the primordial sound of vibratory creation.

~ Patanjali

A sage in the tradition of Vedic Hinduism who collected verses known as sutras or aphorisms that expounded the philosophy of the raja yoga path to enlightenment.

~ Pearce, Joseph Chilton

The author of *The Death of Religion and the Rebirth of the Spirit*, *The Biology of Transcendence*, *The Crack in the Cosmic Egg*, *The Magical Child*, and *Evolution's End*. For more than three decades he has lectured at the university level as well as at seminars and conferences focusing on such eclectic fields of study as human potential, child development, biology and spirituality, and education.

~ pendulum

A device, such as a forked stick or a crystal suspended from a chain and bead, used to detect energy (often water) sources or to divine information.

~ prana

In yoga, one of five vital breaths.

~ psychic energy

A mental energy that can be detected and utilized in certain psychological activities.

~ raja yoga

Raja or "royal" yoga is one of six schools of orthodox Hinduism. It emphasizes the control of the mind as a necessary process on the path to attaining enlightenment.

~ *Ramayana of Tulsidas*

An ancient poem composed by Valmiki that represented the force of good over evil as revealed in the exploits of Lord Rama that became a legendary Indian epic. It has been translated from the original Sanskrit into Hindi and many other languages.

~ sadhana

Spiritual practices aimed at helping a soul advance toward enlightenment.

~ Shabda Brahma

The manifestation of the Divine as the cosmic sound of creation, that is, Om.

~ Solomon

Son of David; considered perhaps the wisest of all the ancient Hebrew kings named in the Bible's Old Testament.

~ Steiner, Rudolf

Steiner (1861–1925) was an Austrian philosopher, educator, esotericist, advocate of ethical individualism, and founder of Anthroposophy and Waldorf education.

~ sushumna

The channel of the subtle body that in Vedic philosophy connects the chakra, or energy center, at the base of the spine with the crown chakra on the top of the head and through which the sacred kundalini rises.

~ **tarot**

Cards used for divination; fortune-telling cards that originated during medieval times.

~ **transformational thinking**

Radical new ways of thinking that create a shift in consciousness.

~ **universal laws**

Various forces at work in the universe that conform to given behaviors under specific circumstances but not, however, necessarily recognized by orthodox science as provable.

~ **visualization**

The act of intentionally creating images in the mind through use of the imagination.

APPENDIX B

Print and Web Resources

The following books may prove to be excellent resources for rounding out your knowledge of various disciplines that tie into a fuller understanding of deliberately working with the Law of Attraction.

Barrett, Jayme. *Feng Shui Your Life*. New York: Sterling Publications, 2003.

Byrne, Rhonda. *The Secret*. New York: Atria Books, 2006.

Chopra, Deepak. *The Seven Spiritual Laws of Success*. Novato, CA: Amber-Allen/New World, 1994.

Csikszentmihalyi, Mihaly. *Flow: The Psychology of Optimal Experience*. New York: Harper Perennial, 1991.

Eason, Cassandra. *The Art of the Pendulum*. Boston: Weiser Books, 2005.

Ellerman, David. *Helping People Help Themselves, From the World Bank to an Alternative Philosophy of Development Assistance*. Ann Arbor: University of Michigan Press, 2005.

Fontana, David. *The Secret Language of Symbols: A Visual Key to Symbols and Their Meanings*. San Francisco: Chronicle Books, 2003.

Foster, Carolyn J. *The Family Patterns Workbook, Breaking Free from Your Past and Creating a Life of Your Own*. Los Angeles: J. P. Tarcher, 1993.

Fox, Matthew. *Illuminations of Hildegard of Bingen*. Rochester, VT: Bear & Company, 2002.

Gimbutas, Marija. *The Language of the Goddess*. New York: Harper & Row, 1989.

Goldwell, Bruce and Tammy Lynch. *Mastery of Abundant Living: The Key to Mastering the Law of Attraction*. Calgary: Saga Books, 2007.

Grouse, F. S., translator. *The Ramayana of Tulsi Das, Valmiki*. Allahabad: Ram Narain Lal, Publisher and Bookseller, no copyright date.

Hicks, Esther and Jerry. *The Law of Attraction, The Basics of the Teachings of Abraham*. Carlsbad: Hay House, 2006.

Hill, Napoleon. *Think and Grow Rich*. New York: Tarcher, 2005.

L'Engle, Madeleine. *Walking on Water: Reflections on Faith and Art*. Colorado Springs, CO: Shaw Books, 2001.

Losier, Michael J. *The Law of Attraction, The Science of Attracting More of What You Want and Less of What You Don't*. New York: Wellness Central, 2007.

Peale, Norman Vincent. *The Power of Positive Thinking*. New York: Fireside, 2003.

Ray, James Arthur. *The Science of Success: How to Attract Prosperity and Create Harmonic Wealth Through Proven Principles*. Carlsbad, CA: Sun Ark Press, 1999.

Stasney, Sharon. *Feng Shui Living*. New York: Sterling Publications, 2003.

Too, Lillian. *168 Feng Shui Ways to Declutter Your Home*. New York: Sterling Publications, 2003.

Walker, Barbara. *Women's Dictionary of Symbols and Sacred Objects*. San Francisco: Harper & Row, 1983.

Wattles, Wallace D. *The Science of Getting Rich: Financial Success Through Creative Thought.* New York: Barnes & Noble, 2007.

Weil, Andrew. *8 Weeks to Optimum Health, Revised Edition: A Proven Program for Taking Full Advantage of Your Body's Natural Healing Power.* New York: Time Warner Paperbacks (New Ed.), 2005.

Weil, Andrew. *Spontaneous Healing: How to Discover and Embrace Your Body's Natural Ability to Maintain and Heal Itself.* New York: Ballantine, 1995.

Web Sources

About.com
> *http://altreligion.about.com/library/glossary/blsymbols.htm*

Center for Consciousness Studies
> *www.consciousness.Arizona.edu/mission.htm*

Self-Improvement-e-Books.com
> *http://phineasquimby.wwwhubs.com*

New Thought Library
> *http://newthoughtlibrary.com/mulfordPrentice/thoughtAreThings/title.htm*

Christian Science
> *www.christianscience.com*

New Advent
> *www.newadvent.org*

Project Mind Foundation
> *www.projectmind.org*

Life Enthusiast Co-op
www.life-enthusiast.com

Dr.Weil.com
www.drweil.com

Meetup.com
www.meetup.com

Project Gutenberg.org
www.gutenberg.org

The Franklin & Eleanor Roosevelt Institute
www.feri.org

Hinduism Today
www.hinduismtoday.com

Pulse of the Planet
www.pulseplanet.com

White Swan Records
www.whiteswanrecords.com

Jean Houston
www.jeanhouston.org

The Mary Baker Eddy Library
www.marybakereddylibrary.org

APPENDIX C

Assorted Worksheets

Worksheet 1: Nine Tips for Setting Intentions

This exercise is designed to help you clarify your desire to manifest an object. You know what you want, but if you were asked to describe that item in detail, could you do it? The universe will bring you exactly what you ask for, so it is important that you be specific. When you see something you want, you will perhaps remember only the general shape, maybe the color, and perhaps a detail or two. Use this exercise to establish a clear statement of your intention for manifesting a particular object with as many details as possible.

1. Name the category of the material thing you most desire to manifest (for example, car, house, boat, jewelry, furniture, art, musical instrument, dishware, clothing, or electronic item).
2. Name the specific item make or style (for example, a car might be a Mercedes S-500; a musical instrument might be a Gibson folk guitar or a Stradivarius violin; an electronic item might be a Toshiba Satellite Pro laptop or seventy-five-inch plasma screen television).
3. What is its color?
4. What size and shape does it have? If you don't know, find a picture of the object you desire on the Internet or in a magazine and cut it out. Knowing what it looks like will be important for your visualization exercises.
5. What does it taste like? Of course, this may not be relevant to the object you desire to manifest, but if it happens to be a 100-year-old bottle of Scotch, being able to imagine the taste will be important.
6. Does it have a scent? If so, write down your thoughts about what it smells like (new clothes or wooden instruments may have subtle scents, for example, while a piece of china probably will not have a scent).

7. What does it sound like? Sound may not have relevance for some objects but for cars, musical instruments, computers, or electronic equipment, the sound it makes is an important detail.

8. Mentally run your fingers over the object of your desire. How does it feel? What is its texture?

9. Now that you have employed your senses of sight, taste, touch, smell, and hearing in order to better imagine the object you intend to manifest, write a simple declaration of your intention. Here's an example to get you started.

I am elated to know that the Law of Attraction is in the process of bringing into my life the _____ that I deeply desire. I can see it clearly in my mind now (mentally imagine it) and am grateful (feel the gratitude) that it already exists in the realm of pure potentiality. I deserve this, am ready to receive it, and know that it is on its way to me and in the right moment it will manifest in my life.

Worksheet 2: Three Ways to Clarify and Refine a Vision

The Law of Attraction has no bias and does not differentiate between your positive and negative thoughts. It continually responds to your vibration. Words in a positive affirmation make you feel happy, excited, and anticipatory. When you affirm and visualize your desire for something in positive language and images, your feeling creates a magnetic vibration that draws the desired object into your experience. Use the following three techniques to clarify and refine your vision:

1. **Correct your declaration language.** Use breath work or meditation to move into a quiet, centered place in your mind where you can name and visualize the object, experience, or relationship that you desire to manifest. Tell the universe what it is you want. Notice whether you used any negative words in your statement—for example, "I don't want any more bills." Check in with your feelings. How does the word *bills* make

you feel? Most likely, it makes you feel negative. Rephrase your statement to include positive terms and get rid of words like *don't*, *won't*, and *can't*. Replace the negative statement with a positive one such as "I desire financial prosperity and the means to easily meet my financial responsibilities." Now how do you feel? Notice the difference.

2. **Fix visualization problems.** The mind/body connection ensures that you will experience feelings in response to your mental visualization. Let's say you need to attract powerful and influential people into your career path. Consider the imagery you are using to depict them in your mind. If you see powerful people as stern, harsh, and demanding and bringing into your life more misery, stress, and unreasonable deadlines and responsibilities, you most likely will feel apprehension and dread. Instead, reimagine them as warm, friendly, helpful, generous, and wise associates, perhaps even mentors with a vested interest in helping you advance in your chosen field of endeavor.

3. **Eliminate any image that muddies or confuses your vision.** Perhaps you dream of having a trim, flexible, and muscular body, but you can't get rid of the extra pounds you gained during a pregnancy. You started a walking program with neighborhood friends and are now eating a healthy, balanced diet and still the weight clings. In your mind, you see yourself in the bikini you wore at eighteen and you are doing affirmations. Why isn't it working?

   The problem is that deep down on a subconscious level, you know you can never be eighteen with that same body again. Try taking a picture of yourself as you look today. Adjust your body size using scissors or a computer tool such as Photoshop. You want to create an image that your mind believes is possible to achieve. Psychological experts say that any time there is a struggle between the conscious and unconscious mind, the unconscious wins. You must convince yourself that a flexible and leaner body is possible for the person you are now. Start with a photo image and make it plausible. Paste that image on your refrigerator, bathroom mirror, and scale. Feel gratitude for each pound or inch lost and find positive ways to reward yourself as the Law of Attraction works with you to create a beautiful, strong, healthy, and leaner body.

Worksheet 3: Six Steps to Clear Blockages

Do you have a fear of success? Are you going through the steps of deliberately manifesting and yet not seeing results? Perhaps you are subconsciously blocking the outcome you seek. Try these six steps to clear blockages:

1. **Cultivate positive feelings.** Imagine you have just received whatever it was that you hoped to manifest. Using that moment as a point of departure in a journal entry, write about how you feel at having that object, situation, or relationship now manifested in your life. Remember that the Law of Attraction responds to feelings around specific thoughts rather than the thoughts themselves.

2. **Feel worthy.** Redirect negative self-talk into positive statements. What are some of the reasons why other people (for example, your mother, father, spouse, lover, and children) love you? Make a list of all the lovable qualities and traits you have and why you are worthy to receive the gifts you seek from the universe. Love yourself and others the way you want to be loved and cultivate feelings of self-worth.

3. **Make every day the best day of your life.** If something goes wrong in your day, shift the energy of that moment as soon as possible. Don't go through an entire day with a negative attitude after breaking the handle off a china cup because you awoke late for an important early morning meeting. Listen to beautiful music, get physical and take a walk, lie down for a quick power nap, rejuvenate and refresh by doing some yoga or breath work, listen to a Law of Attraction CD, or offer a prayer of thanks to the Divine. You have phenomenal power in every moment of your life to change that moment, to shift the negative into neutral or positive energy, and to regain forward impetus.

4. **Focus on what you want rather than what you don't have.** Perhaps you can easily recount all the reasons why you don't own your own home, but you deeply desire to own a house. Make a list of all the positive reasons why you deserve it, and how living there will change your life and the lives of your spouse, children, and pets. As a point of departure for writing about your hopes and dreams and feelings of love and gratitude, imagine a celebratory meal with relatives, a holiday gathering, or a quiet peaceful moment in your own home. Take a mental snapshot of how

you feel after that writing exercise. Remember those positive feelings every time you move into feelings of lack.

5. **Fine-tune the direction and intention of your desires.** Be decisive when working with the law. Remember that it is always at work to bring you the things you mentally focus on, both positive and negative. Think of your mind as a canoe floating along the river of life, buffeted and buoyed by forces of energy (wind and currents) that you can't see. For certain, that canoe is going somewhere, perhaps places you like or don't. Instead of going with the flow, remember that you have the power to navigate the direction you desire to go in through the paddles of your feelings and thoughts.

6. **Create space in your life for what you desire to manifest.** Consider that the new love of your life might not come in until your current relationship has ended. If there is a lot of negative emotional baggage associated with the relationship you are in, you have to clear out those patterns of thought and replace them with positive feelings of anticipatory excitement, hope, and expectation that your clear and determined focus is attracting to you the new love you desire and deserve.

Worksheet 4: Four Ways to Create a Vacuum for Manifesting

Release what isn't working in your life and open your heart and mind to allow in new energy, relationships, and surprises that the universe may be ready to give you. Sometimes when the things you desire don't readily appear, you have to make space for them. For example, if a relationship has soured and counseling or other avenues for repairing it have not helped, it may be time to move on. If your life seems stalled because your career has hit an impasse, your job doesn't inspire you, or everywhere you look things are broken, outdated, or not used, bless and release them. Here are four ways to start the process:

1. **Shift the status quo when the passion dies.** If you hate your job and want to find a new one or even start your own business, tender your resignation. Bless and release the old work and get started manifesting your

dream vocation. Feel the excitement of embarking upon a new path to a new dream. Brainstorm, write a business plan, figure out marketing, find funding, and set your dream into forward motion. When you do, you'll see how the universe puts the wind into the sail of your ship and pushes you quickly onto your chosen course.

2. **Clear the clutter from your life.** Energy flow is impeded when you are surrounded by clutter. Get that energy moving again by removing things that you no longer use, don't work properly, or are broken. Also put away pictures and the myriad things throughout your house that remind you of the demise of relatives and friends. Establish a special designated area in your home to honor them (for placement, read books about feng shui). Nourish relationships with helpful people and you'll open yourself to the inflow of healing, vibrant, and beneficial energy.

3. **Reprogram your thoughts.** Your outer life is a manifestation of your inner thoughts and feelings. When you release old patterns of negative thinking and replace them with powerful positive thoughts and expectations that make you feel hopeful and happy, you set into forward motion vibrations that can then attract an abundance of good things to you. Do you desire love with a man who is trustworthy, capable, and emotionally healthy? Examine your thoughts to see why he is not already in your life. Maybe the pain and drama associated with a previous relationship caused you to fear a future one. But if you can't imagine the possibility of a wonderful new love, how will it ever come to you?

4. **Learn to rely on your emotional guidance system of intuition or sixth sense to know when to let go.** If something is not right in your life, you may be overriding the signals from your emotional guidance system that warn you to steer clear or break away. The more you rely on your inner guidance, the more you will trust it when it warns you to shift direction. Sometimes just a little shift is all that is needed to create a vacuum for financial prosperity and the abundance that you may seek.

Worksheet 5: Eight Visualization Exercises

Law of Attraction experts advocate using visualization when you are deliberately working with the law because your body responds to the feelings created by positive mental images and thoughts. Choose one of the following topics and focus on, fantasize, and visualize as though you had already achieved phenomenal success in that area.

As you visualize (no negative feelings or thoughts allowed), focus on how you feel as you place yourself in your chosen scenario. Allow any/all details to unfold in your mind's eye. It's a little like daydreaming your way to success. Write down any insights or ideas for goals, timelines, and specific action steps to ramp up for quicker attainment of your desire.

1. Financial prosperity/wealth
2. Romantic love or partner
3. Birth of a child or pet project
4. Robust health
5. Peaceful life or exciting life of travel and new experiences
6. Career advancement or establishing/running your own successful business
7. Meaningful and passionate work/journey in life
8. Spiritual advancement

Feel free to add your own special desire to the list. Reinforce your visualization work by doing one or more of the following:

- Write a desire/intention declaration or vision statement.
- Create a manifestation poster (using images, words, symbols, and statements clipped from magazines and glued to the poster) for what you want to create or manifest.
- Record in your journal all the positive feelings you experience whenever you visualize your desire actualized in your life.

Worksheet 6: Three Techniques for Dream Incubation

Dream work can inspire, enlighten, and amuse you, even if you have never done it before. The most important thing besides remembering your dreams is to know how to incubate a dream for understanding, insight, and guidance. When you are working with the Law of Attraction in an intentional way, you may find it helpful to incubate a dream to clarify whether you are on your path or are obstructing the manifestation of something you deeply desire or guidance on how to turbo-charge your intention to get what you want.

- Place a pad of paper and a pencil next to your bed. Even better, purchase and use a dream journal (any blank book will do).
- Upon awakening, remain in that sleepy state and notice how you feel from having that dream. Try to recall all the images you can about your dream.
- Without judging or analyzing your dream, write everything you can remember about the dream, especially your feeling and mood as you awakened.
- After you have recorded your dream, consult a good dream dictionary to choose meanings for the symbols that make sense to you.
- Once you have interpreted all the symbols, actions, messages, themes, and any particularly potent images, rewrite the dream to expose its relevance and meaning. Meaning can be revealed in the layers of the dream or even over a period of time during which you dream the same dream again, so consult books about dream work to learn how to extract as much meaning as possible.

Incubating a dream requires a little preparation. Before going to sleep, do some breath work. As you breathe out, visualize dark negative energy that you've acquired during the day flowing out through the soles of your feet beyond the horizon line. As you breathe in, visualize white light or positive energy flowing in through your heart or head and filling your body.

Ask for the dream you desire. Be clearly focused and specific—for example, "I open my heart and mind to receiving a dream about _____."
Here are three techniques for dream incubation:

1. **Prepare and pray for the dream.** Ask your dreaming mind for exactly what you want. Don't try to incubate a dream after consuming heavy food or drink. Likewise, avoid incubating a dream when you are extremely tired or grumpy or overstimulated by work or conversations with friends. Take a hot shower or bath to wind down from your day. Make certain your bedroom is clean with fresh linen on the bed. You should feel peaceful and ready to sleep. Ensure that you have placed the necessary tools for recording your dream close by.

2. **Fantasize and explore every aspect of your dream topic until you can write out a short one-sentence dream question or goal.** During a meditation or quiet period, think about every aspect of the type of information you require or desire to receive from the dream. Clarity of what you seek and how you feel about what you seek to discover is essential.

3. **Open your heart and mind to any and all possibilities for information your dream (or dreams) may bring you about the topic in question.** Understand that sometimes your dreaming mind may offer the dream in different ways on different nights. In essence, your dreaming mind brings you the information you desire sequentially, as if it were a flower slowly unfolding and yielding its secrets.

Index

Abraham, 180–81, 183
Alchemy, 61–62, 83, 85–86, 211
Anusthans, 34, 74–75
Art and music
  centrality of music, 211–12
  chakra vibrational makeup and, 206–7
  creating dream-fulfilling artwork, 212–13
  feeling vibrations/frequencies of music, 209–10
  gratitude and, 206, 207, 215–16
  healing with, 207–8, 210–11, 213–14
  helping infertility, 210
  intuition and, 218
  Mother of All Sounds and, 208
  music and magnification, 95–96
  raising mood and vibration, 206
  roles of, 208–12
  secret alchemical formula of music, 211
  stimulating young brains, 209
  summoning kindred spirits, 217–18
  unlocking/opening yourself with, 216–18
  using conscious/unconscious images, 213–15
  visualization/aromatherapy and, 217
Augustine of Hippo, 71–72
Ayurveda, 137, 138, 146
Aztecs, 60

Babylonians, 52–54
Behavior modification, 130–31
Blockages, 11–12, 124–25

in chakras, 239–41
removing, 33, 125–26, 223–24, 237–39, 282–83
sabotaging manifesting efforts, 114
seeing, 11–12
stagnant vs. flowing energy, 220–23
Breathing exercises, 33, 136, 139, 143, 144, 147–48, 184–85, 189
Buddha (Siddhartha Gautama), 35, 75, 76
Buddhism, 75–76, 137–38, 139

Campbell, Joseph, 47, 48, 258
Career, 191–204
  advancement techniques, 197
  affirmation for perfect new job, 199–200
  charting course for success, 192–93
  creating ideal job, 194–95, 198–99
  cultivating wisdom, 201
  growing business, 200
  imagining master plan, 200
  knowing when on track, 202–4
  manifesting raise, promotion, dream job, 197–99
  mission statements, 192
  rapid-advancement strategies, 201–2
  treating others well, 201
Catholic mystics, 68–72
Chakras
  awakening, 264–65
  blocked, finding, 239–41
  contemplation on, 239

delineated, 240–41
healing, 240
Kundalini rising, 241
vibrational makeup of, 206–7
Chopra, Dr. Deepak, 145–46, 186, 266
Christianity, 64–72
Consciousness, expanding, 33, 263–64. *See also* Spirituality
Critical comments on Law of Attraction, 39–49

Dating/relationship programs, 95
Desire
  clarifying, 100–102, 105–6
  reinforcing, 126–27
  Desperate people, 43–44
  Divine Power, 34–35. *See also* Source
Dream incubation, 53, 84, 116, 216, 286–87

Ecological/environmental changes, 261
Egyptians, 56–57
Einstein, Albert, 29, 47, 178–79, 180, 218
Emerson, Ralph Waldo, 189
Emotions
  distorting decision-making, 111–12
  expectation, anticipation and, 113–16
  healthy expression of, 112–13
  managing, 111–13
  negative vs. positive, 128–30
  role of, 110–11

THE EVERYTHING SERIES!

BUSINESS & PERSONAL FINANCE

Everything® Accounting Book
Everything® Budgeting Book, 2nd Ed.
Everything® Business Planning Book
Everything® Coaching and Mentoring Book, 2nd Ed.
Everything® Fundraising Book
Everything® Get Out of Debt Book
Everything® Grant Writing Book, 2nd Ed.
Everything® Guide to Buying Foreclosures
Everything® Guide to Fundraising, $15.95
Everything® Guide to Mortgages
Everything® Guide to Personal Finance for Single Mothers
Everything® Home-Based Business Book, 2nd Ed.
Everything® Homebuying Book, 3rd Ed., $15.95
Everything® Homeselling Book, 2nd Ed.
Everything® Human Resource Management Book
Everything® Improve Your Credit Book
Everything® Investing Book, 2nd Ed.
Everything® Landlording Book
Everything® Leadership Book, 2nd Ed.
Everything® Managing People Book, 2nd Ed.
Everything® Negotiating Book
Everything® Online Auctions Book
Everything® Online Business Book
Everything® Personal Finance Book
Everything® Personal Finance in Your 20s & 30s Book, 2nd Ed.
Everything® Personal Finance in Your 40s & 50s Book, $15.95
Everything® Project Management Book, 2nd Ed.
Everything® Real Estate Investing Book
Everything® Retirement Planning Book
Everything® Robert's Rules Book, $7.95
Everything® Selling Book
Everything® Start Your Own Business Book, 2nd Ed.
Everything® Wills & Estate Planning Book

COOKING

Everything® Barbecue Cookbook
Everything® Bartender's Book, 2nd Ed., $9.95
Everything® Calorie Counting Cookbook
Everything® Cheese Book
Everything® Chinese Cookbook
Everything® Classic Recipes Book
Everything® Cocktail Parties & Drinks Book
Everything® College Cookbook
Everything® Cooking for Baby and Toddler Book
Everything® Diabetes Cookbook
Everything® Easy Gourmet Cookbook
Everything® Fondue Cookbook
Everything® Food Allergy Cookbook, $15.95
Everything® Fondue Party Book
Everything® Gluten-Free Cookbook
Everything® Glycemic Index Cookbook
Everything® Grilling Cookbook
Everything® Healthy Cooking for Parties Book, $15.95
Everything® Holiday Cookbook
Everything® Indian Cookbook
Everything® Lactose-Free Cookbook
Everything® Low-Cholesterol Cookbook

Everything® Low-Fat High-Flavor Cookbook, 2nd Ed., $15.95
Everything® Low-Salt Cookbook
Everything® Meals for a Month Cookbook
Everything® Meals on a Budget Cookbook
Everything® Mediterranean Cookbook
Everything® Mexican Cookbook
Everything® No Trans Fat Cookbook
Everything® One-Pot Cookbook, 2nd Ed., $15.95
Everything® Organic Cooking for Baby & Toddler Book, $15.95
Everything® Pizza Cookbook
Everything® Quick Meals Cookbook, 2nd Ed., $15.95
Everything® Slow Cooker Cookbook
Everything® Slow Cooking for a Crowd Cookbook
Everything® Soup Cookbook
Everything® Stir-Fry Cookbook
Everything® Sugar-Free Cookbook
Everything® Tapas and Small Plates Cookbook
Everything® Tex-Mex Cookbook
Everything® Thai Cookbook
Everything® Vegetarian Cookbook
Everything® Whole-Grain, High-Fiber Cookbook
Everything® Wild Game Cookbook
Everything® Wine Book, 2nd Ed.

GAMES

Everything® 15-Minute Sudoku Book, $9.95
Everything® 30-Minute Sudoku Book, $9.95
Everything® Bible Crosswords Book, $9.95
Everything® Blackjack Strategy Book
Everything® Brain Strain Book, $9.95
Everything® Bridge Book
Everything® Card Games Book
Everything® Card Tricks Book, $9.95
Everything® Casino Gambling Book, 2nd Ed.
Everything® Chess Basics Book
Everything® Christmas Crosswords Book, $9.95
Everything® Craps Strategy Book
Everything® Crossword and Puzzle Book
Everything® Crosswords and Puzzles for Quote Lovers Book, $9.95
Everything® Crossword Challenge Book
Everything® Crosswords for the Beach Book, $9.95
Everything® Cryptic Crosswords Book, $9.95
Everything® Cryptograms Book, $9.95
Everything® Easy Crosswords Book
Everything® Easy Kakuro Book, $9.95
Everything® Easy Large-Print Crosswords Book
Everything® Games Book, 2nd Ed.
Everything® Giant Book of Crosswords
Everything® Giant Sudoku Book, $9.95
Everything® Giant Word Search Book
Everything® Kakuro Challenge Book, $9.95
Everything® Large-Print Crossword Challenge Book
Everything® Large-Print Crosswords Book
Everything® Large-Print Travel Crosswords Book
Everything® Lateral Thinking Puzzles Book, $9.95
Everything® Literary Crosswords Book, $9.95
Everything® Mazes Book
Everything® Memory Booster Puzzles Book, $9.95

Everything® Movie Crosswords Book, $9.95
Everything® Music Crosswords Book, $9.95
Everything® Online Poker Book
Everything® Pencil Puzzles Book, $9.95
Everything® Poker Strategy Book
Everything® Pool & Billiards Book
Everything® Puzzles for Commuters Book, $9.95
Everything® Puzzles for Dog Lovers Book, $9.95
Everything® Sports Crosswords Book, $9.95
Everything® Test Your IQ Book, $9.95
Everything® Texas Hold 'Em Book, $9.95
Everything® Travel Crosswords Book, $9.95
Everything® Travel Mazes Book, $9.95
Everything® Travel Word Search Book, $9.95
Everything® TV Crosswords Book, $9.95
Everything® Word Games Challenge Book
Everything® Word Scramble Book
Everything® Word Search Book

HEALTH

Everything® Alzheimer's Book
Everything® Diabetes Book
Everything® First Aid Book, $9.95
Everything® Green Living Book
Everything® Health Guide to Addiction and Recovery
Everything® Health Guide to Adult Bipolar Disorder
Everything® Health Guide to Arthritis
Everything® Health Guide to Controlling Anxiety
Everything® Health Guide to Depression
Everything® Health Guide to Diabetes, 2nd Ed.
Everything® Health Guide to Fibromyalgia
Everything® Health Guide to Menopause, 2nd Ed.
Everything® Health Guide to Migraines
Everything® Health Guide to Multiple Sclerosis
Everything® Health Guide to OCD
Everything® Health Guide to PMS
Everything® Health Guide to Postpartum Care
Everything® Health Guide to Thyroid Disease
Everything® Hypnosis Book
Everything® Low Cholesterol Book
Everything® Menopause Book
Everything® Nutrition Book
Everything® Reflexology Book
Everything® Stress Management Book
Everything® Superfoods Book, $15.95

HISTORY

Everything® American Government Book
Everything® American History Book, 2nd Ed.
Everything® American Revolution Book, $15.95
Everything® Civil War Book
Everything® Freemasons Book
Everything® Irish History & Heritage Book
Everything® World War II Book, 2nd Ed.

HOBBIES

Everything® Candlemaking Book
Everything® Cartooning Book
Everything® Coin Collecting Book
Everything® Digital Photography Book, 2nd Ed.

Everything® Drawing Book
Everything® Family Tree Book, 2nd Ed.
Everything® Guide to Online Genealogy, $15.95
Everything® Knitting Book
Everything® Knots Book
Everything® Photography Book
Everything® Quilting Book
Everything® Sewing Book
Everything® Soapmaking Book, 2nd Ed.
Everything® Woodworking Book

HOME IMPROVEMENT

Everything® Feng Shui Book
Everything® Feng Shui Decluttering Book, $9.95
Everything® Fix-It Book
Everything® Green Living Book
Everything® Home Decorating Book
Everything® Home Storage Solutions Book
Everything® Homebuilding Book
Everything® Organize Your Home Book, 2nd Ed.

KIDS' BOOKS

All titles are $7.95
Everything® Fairy Tales Book, $14.95
Everything® Kids' Animal Puzzle & Activity Book
Everything® Kids' Astronomy Book
Everything® Kids' Baseball Book, 5th Ed.
Everything® Kids' Bible Trivia Book
Everything® Kids' Bugs Book
Everything® Kids' Cars and Trucks Puzzle and Activity Book
Everything® Kids' Christmas Puzzle & Activity Book
Everything® Kids' Connect the Dots
            Puzzle and Activity Book
Everything® Kids' Cookbook, 2nd Ed.
Everything® Kids' Crazy Puzzles Book
Everything® Kids' Dinosaurs Book
Everything® Kids' Dragons Puzzle and Activity Book
Everything® Kids' Environment Book $7.95
Everything® Kids' Fairies Puzzle and Activity Book
Everything® Kids' First Spanish Puzzle and Activity Book
Everything® Kids' Football Book
Everything® Kids' Geography Book
Everything® Kids' Gross Cookbook
Everything® Kids' Gross Hidden Pictures Book
Everything® Kids' Gross Jokes Book
Everything® Kids' Gross Mazes Book
Everything® Kids' Gross Puzzle & Activity Book
Everything® Kids' Halloween Puzzle & Activity Book
Everything® Kids' Hanukkah Puzzle and Activity Book
Everything® Kids' Hidden Pictures Book
Everything® Kids' Horses Book
Everything® Kids' Joke Book
Everything® Kids' Knock Knock Book
Everything® Kids' Learning French Book
Everything® Kids' Learning Spanish Book
Everything® Kids' Magical Science Experiments Book
Everything® Kids' Math Puzzles Book
Everything® Kids' Mazes Book
Everything® Kids' Money Book, 2nd Ed.
Everything® Kids' Mummies, Pharaoh's, and Pyramids
            Puzzle and Activity Book
Everything® Kids' Nature Book
Everything® Kids' Pirates Puzzle and Activity Book
Everything® Kids' Presidents Book
Everything® Kids' Princess Puzzle and Activity Book
Everything® Kids' Puzzle Book

Everything® Kids' Racecars Puzzle and Activity Book
Everything® Kids' Riddles & Brain Teasers Book
Everything® Kids' Science Experiments Book
Everything® Kids' Sharks Book
Everything® Kids' Soccer Book
Everything® Kids' Spelling Book
Everything® Kids' Spies Puzzle and Activity Book
Everything® Kids' States Book
Everything® Kids' Travel Activity Book
Everything® Kids' Word Search Puzzle and Activity Book

LANGUAGE

Everything® Conversational Japanese Book with CD, $19.95
Everything® French Grammar Book
Everything® French Phrase Book, $9.95
Everything® French Verb Book, $9.95
Everything® German Phrase Book, $9.95
Everything® German Practice Book with CD, $19.95
Everything® Inglés Book
Everything® Intermediate Spanish Book with CD, $19.95
Everything® Italian Phrase Book, $9.95
Everything® Italian Practice Book with CD, $19.95
Everything® Learning Brazilian Portuguese Book with CD, $19.95
Everything® Learning French Book with CD, 2nd Ed., $19.95
Everything® Learning German Book
Everything® Learning Italian Book
Everything® Learning Latin Book
Everything® Learning Russian Book with CD, $19.95
Everything® Learning Spanish Book
Everything® Learning Spanish Book with CD, 2nd Ed., $19.95
Everything® Russian Practice Book with CD, $19.95
Everything® Sign Language Book, $15.95
Everything® Spanish Grammar Book
Everything® Spanish Phrase Book, $9.95
Everything® Spanish Practice Book with CD, $19.95
Everything® Spanish Verb Book, $9.95
Everything® Speaking Mandarin Chinese Book with CD, $19.95

MUSIC

Everything® Bass Guitar Book with CD, $19.95
Everything® Drums Book with CD, $19.95
Everything® Guitar Book with CD, 2nd Ed., $19.95
Everything® Guitar Chords Book with CD, $19.95
Everything® Guitar Scales Book with CD, $19.95
Everything® Harmonica Book with CD, $15.95
Everything® Home Recording Book
Everything® Music Theory Book with CD, $19.95
Everything® Reading Music Book with CD, $19.95
Everything® Rock & Blues Guitar Book with CD, $19.95
Everything® Rock & Blues Piano Book with CD, $19.95
Everything® Rock Drums Book with CD, $19.95
Everything® Singing Book with CD, $19.95
Everything® Songwriting Book

NEW AGE

Everything® Astrology Book, 2nd Ed.
Everything® Birthday Personology Book
Everything® Celtic Wisdom Book, $15.95
Everything® Dreams Book, 2nd Ed.
Everything® Law of Attraction Book, $15.95
Everything® Love Signs Book, $9.95
Everything® Love Spells Book, $9.95
Everything® Palmistry Book
Everything® Psychic Book
Everything® Reiki Book

Everything® Sex Signs Book, $9.95
Everything® Spells & Charms Book, 2nd Ed.
Everything® Tarot Book, 2nd Ed.
Everything® Toltec Wisdom Book
Everything® Wicca & Witchcraft Book, 2nd Ed.

PARENTING

Everything® Baby Names Book, 2nd Ed.
Everything® Baby Shower Book, 2nd Ed.
Everything® Baby Sign Language Book with DVD
Everything® Baby's First Year Book
Everything® Birthing Book
Everything® Breastfeeding Book
Everything® Father-to-Be Book
Everything® Father's First Year Book
Everything® Get Ready for Baby Book, 2nd Ed.
Everything® Get Your Baby to Sleep Book, $9.95
Everything® Getting Pregnant Book
Everything® Guide to Pregnancy Over 35
Everything® Guide to Raising a One-Year-Old
Everything® Guide to Raising a Two-Year-Old
Everything® Guide to Raising Adolescent Boys
Everything® Guide to Raising Adolescent Girls
Everything® Mother's First Year Book
Everything® Parent's Guide to Childhood Illnesses
Everything® Parent's Guide to Children and Divorce
Everything® Parent's Guide to Children with ADD/ADHD
Everything® Parent's Guide to Children with Asperger's
            Syndrome
Everything® Parent's Guide to Children with Anxiety
Everything® Parent's Guide to Children with Asthma
Everything® Parent's Guide to Children with Autism
Everything® Parent's Guide to Children with Bipolar Disorder
Everything® Parent's Guide to Children with Depression
Everything® Parent's Guide to Children with Dyslexia
Everything® Parent's Guide to Children with Juvenile Diabetes
Everything® Parent's Guide to Children with OCD
Everything® Parent's Guide to Positive Discipline
Everything® Parent's Guide to Raising Boys
Everything® Parent's Guide to Raising Girls
Everything® Parent's Guide to Raising Siblings
Everything® Parent's Guide to Raising Your
            Adopted Child
Everything® Parent's Guide to Sensory Integration Disorder
Everything® Parent's Guide to Tantrums
Everything® Parent's Guide to the Strong-Willed Child
Everything® Parenting a Teenager Book
Everything® Potty Training Book, $9.95
Everything® Pregnancy Book, 3rd Ed.
Everything® Pregnancy Fitness Book
Everything® Pregnancy Nutrition Book
Everything® Pregnancy Organizer, 2nd Ed., $16.95
Everything® Toddler Activities Book
Everything® Toddler Book
Everything® Tween Book
Everything® Twins, Triplets, and More Book

PETS

Everything® Aquarium Book
Everything® Boxer Book
Everything® Cat Book, 2nd Ed.
Everything® Chihuahua Book
Everything® Cooking for Dogs Book
Everything® Dachshund Book
Everything® Dog Book, 2nd Ed.
Everything® Dog Grooming Book

Everything® Dog Obedience Book
Everything® Dog Owner's Organizer, $16.95
Everything® Dog Training and Tricks Book
Everything® German Shepherd Book
Everything® Golden Retriever Book
Everything® Horse Book, 2nd Ed., $15.95
Everything® Horse Care Book
Everything® Horseback Riding Book
Everything® Labrador Retriever Book
Everything® Poodle Book
Everything® Pug Book
Everything® Puppy Book
Everything® Small Dogs Book
Everything® Tropical Fish Book
Everything® Yorkshire Terrier Book

REFERENCE

Everything® American Presidents Book
Everything® Blogging Book
Everything® Build Your Vocabulary Book, $9.95
Everything® Car Care Book
Everything® Classical Mythology Book
Everything® Da Vinci Book
Everything® Einstein Book
Everything® Enneagram Book
Everything® Etiquette Book, 2nd Ed.
Everything® Family Christmas Book, $15.95
Everything® Guide to C. S. Lewis & Narnia
Everything® Guide to Divorce, 2nd Ed., $15.95
Everything® Guide to Edgar Allan Poe
Everything® Guide to Understanding Philosophy
Everything® Inventions and Patents Book
Everything® Jacqueline Kennedy Onassis Book
Everything® John F. Kennedy Book
Everything® Mafia Book
Everything® Martin Luther King Jr. Book
Everything® Pirates Book
Everything® Private Investigation Book
Everything® Psychology Book
Everything® Public Speaking Book, $9.95
Everything® Shakespeare Book, 2nd Ed.

RELIGION

Everything® Angels Book
Everything® Bible Book
Everything® Bible Study Book with CD, $19.95
Everything® Buddhism Book
Everything® Catholicism Book
Everything® Christianity Book
Everything® Gnostic Gospels Book
Everything® Hinduism Book, $15.95
Everything® History of the Bible Book
Everything® Jesus Book
Everything® Jewish History & Heritage Book
Everything® Judaism Book
Everything® Kabbalah Book
Everything® Koran Book
Everything® Mary Book
Everything® Mary Magdalene Book
Everything® Prayer Book

Everything® Saints Book, 2nd Ed.
Everything® Torah Book
Everything® Understanding Islam Book
Everything® Women of the Bible Book
Everything® World's Religions Book

SCHOOL & CAREERS

Everything® Career Tests Book
Everything® College Major Test Book
Everything® College Survival Book, 2nd Ed.
Everything® Cover Letter Book, 2nd Ed.
Everything® Filmmaking Book
Everything® Get-a-Job Book, 2nd Ed.
Everything® Guide to Being a Paralegal
Everything® Guide to Being a Personal Trainer
Everything® Guide to Being a Real Estate Agent
Everything® Guide to Being a Sales Rep
Everything® Guide to Being an Event Planner
Everything® Guide to Careers in Health Care
Everything® Guide to Careers in Law Enforcement
Everything® Guide to Government Jobs
Everything® Guide to Starting and Running a Catering Business
Everything® Guide to Starting and Running a Restaurant
Everything® Guide to Starting and Running a Retail Store
Everything® Job Interview Book, 2nd Ed.
Everything® New Nurse Book
Everything® New Teacher Book
Everything® Paying for College Book
Everything® Practice Interview Book
Everything® Resume Book, 3rd Ed.
Everything® Study Book

SELF-HELP

Everything® Body Language Book
Everything® Dating Book, 2nd Ed.
Everything® Great Sex Book
Everything® Guide to Caring for Aging Parents, $15.95
Everything® Self-Esteem Book
Everything® Self-Hypnosis Book, $9.95
Everything® Tantric Sex Book

SPORTS & FITNESS

Everything® Easy Fitness Book
Everything® Fishing Book
Everything® Guide to Weight Training, $15.95
Everything® Krav Maga for Fitness Book
Everything® Running Book, 2nd Ed.
Everything® Triathlon Training Book, $15.95

TRAVEL

Everything® Family Guide to Coastal Florida
Everything® Family Guide to Cruise Vacations
Everything® Family Guide to Hawaii
Everything® Family Guide to Las Vegas, 2nd Ed.
Everything® Family Guide to Mexico
Everything® Family Guide to New England, 2nd Ed.

Everything® Family Guide to New York City, 3rd Ed.
Everything® Family Guide to Northern California and Lake Tahoe
Everything® Family Guide to RV Travel & Campgrounds
Everything® Family Guide to the Caribbean
Everything® Family Guide to the Disneyland® Resort, California Adventure®, Universal Studios®, and the Anaheim Area, 2nd Ed.
Everything® Family Guide to the Walt Disney World Resort®, Universal Studios®, and Greater Orlando, 5th Ed.
Everything® Family Guide to Timeshares
Everything® Family Guide to Washington D.C., 2nd Ed.

WEDDINGS

Everything® Bachelorette Party Book, $9.95
Everything® Bridesmaid Book, $9.95
Everything® Destination Wedding Book
Everything® Father of the Bride Book, $9.95
Everything® Green Wedding Book, $15.95
Everything® Groom Book, $9.95
Everything® Jewish Wedding Book, 2nd Ed., $15.95
Everything® Mother of the Bride Book, $9.95
Everything® Outdoor Wedding Book
Everything® Wedding Book, 3rd Ed.
Everything® Wedding Checklist, $9.95
Everything® Wedding Etiquette Book, $9.95
Everything® Wedding Organizer, 2nd Ed., $16.95
Everything® Wedding Shower Book, $9.95
Everything® Wedding Vows Book, 3rd Ed., $9.95
Everything® Wedding Workout Book
Everything® Weddings on a Budget Book, 2nd Ed., $9.95

WRITING

Everything® Creative Writing Book
Everything® Get Published Book, 2nd Ed.
Everything® Grammar and Style Book, 2nd Ed.
Everything® Guide to Magazine Writing
Everything® Guide to Writing a Book Proposal
Everything® Guide to Writing a Novel
Everything® Guide to Writing Children's Books
Everything® Guide to Writing Copy
Everything® Guide to Writing Graphic Novels
Everything® Guide to Writing Research Papers
Everything® Guide to Writing a Romance Novel, $15.95
Everything® Improve Your Writing Book, 2nd Ed.
Everything® Writing Poetry Book